Inside the
Dark Tower Series

Inside the
Dark Tower Series

*Art, Evil and Intertextuality
in the Stephen King Novels*

PATRICK MCALEER

McFarland & Company, Inc., Publishers
Jefferson, North Carolina, and London

LIBRARY OF CONGRESS CATALOGUING-IN-PUBLICATION DATA

McAleer, Patrick, 1980–
    Inside the Dark tower series : art, evil, and intertextuality
in the Stephen King novels / Patrick McAleer.
      p.   cm.
    Includes bibliographical references and index.

    ISBN 978-0-7864-3977-5
    softcover : 50# alkaline paper ∞

    1. King, Stephen, 1947– — Criticism and interpretation.
    2. Fantasy fiction, American — History and criticism.   I. Title.
PS3561.I483Z783   2009
813'.54 — dc22   2008052460

British Library cataloguing data are available

Cover photographs ©2009 Shutterstock

Manufactured in the United States of America

McFarland & Company, Inc., Publishers
  Box 611, Jefferson, North Carolina 28640
   www.mcfarlandpub.com

This book is dedicated to my folks, Lee and Denise.

Thanks for opening the door(s) for me.

Acknowledgments

THE BOOK CONTAINED HEREIN could not have been accomplished alone. And although there will certainly be many names I forget to include in the following list of individuals to whom I owe a debt of gratitude, I do extend a heart-felt thanks to everyone named hereafter (and those not named who undoubtedly have been of help and inspiration). First, I would like to thank Mary Findley who encouraged me to write this text and connected me with the editors at McFarland. Mary, your influence, guidance and friendship are treasured and valued more than you know. Next, I thank my parents Lee and Denise, to whom this book is dedicated, as they introduced me to the world of Stephen King as a child. I also extend my appreciation to my friends Matt Campbell and Kim Socha, whose support (and editing) has been invaluable. I would also like to thank Tony Magistrale, who has been an excellent source of information and scholarship on Stephen King as well as a very helpful colleague. Thanks to my extended family, namely Candace Dunlop, Jennifer McAleer, and Art Novosel, as well as my friends Joel McKinney and Sandy Krenkel, is also given. Next, I would like to acknowledge all the students who I have taught over the last several years as they not only were subjected to, from time to time, my musings on King, but also provided insights and suggestions to me along the way. And I thank the many friends, family members, and teachers who not only have been there for me and have nurtured my interest in King in their own ways, but who also have been a pleasure to know — while your names are too many to list, I am sure that you know who you are.

Table of Contents

Preface

As STEPHEN KING IS CONSTANTLY typecast as a horror writer, *The Dark Tower* series seems to be a drastic departure for King's Constant Reader as well as those who have seen King's films and have been swept up in the horror label attributed to him. The discrepancy between King's better-known fiction and *The Dark Tower* instigates several questions, including those which ask why King decided to write outside of his designated genre. The resulting initial reluctance from readers to approach *The Dark Tower*, along with the harsh criticisms from book reviewers and scholars, suggests that these texts hardly reflect King's best writing. And although King himself says, "I know — none better, alas — that it [*The Dark Tower*] has not been entirely successful," the perceived faults of the series should not be seen as motive to either condemn the books or avoid reading them (*The Dark Tower* 845). To the contrary, even though *The Dark Tower* may not be King's most representative work or wholly indicative of the skill and craft observed in his other novels, it is the cornerstone work for an oeuvre that consists of over forty novels and hundreds of short stories. It is with this in mind that this book has been written — not only does *The Dark Tower* call for attention and study as the center of King's fictional universe, but also with no purely scholarly-oriented texts available on Stephen King's *Dark Tower* series, the need for a book like this is evident.

I became immersed in the world of *The Dark Tower* in the mid 1990s just before *Wizard and Glass* was published. While I am by no means a fanatic of fantasy tales, I do consider myself a fan of *story*, and King's *Dark Tower* books certainly provide an abundance of story. Like J.R.R. Tolkien's *The Lord of the Rings* and Ursula LeGuin's *A Wizard of Earthsea* books, *The Dark Tower* immerses readers with a taste for the expansive and even the epic, tales which focus on the imaginative and

1

the speculative of which academics tend to be skeptical. Still, scholarship on King's fiction is hardly unheard of, and research on King's other books and stories that will be discussed in this book was not hard to come by. Indeed, commentary and criticism on King's other works extends almost seamlessly into discussion on *The Dark Tower*. However, scholarship either entirely devoted to *The Dark Tower* or that even mentions this series is more difficult to find. As the range of scholarship on King's *Dark Tower* series remains sporadic or even inadequate, this text seeks to not only discuss and integrate what little previous scholarship on *The Dark Tower* is available, but to also provide an examination on this series that is long overdue.

With early research on *The Dark Tower* providing commentary and analysis on the first four books in the series, those composed by King before his 1999 accident, these articles are faced with the problem of *context*. Criticism and scholarship on *The Dark Tower* without the complete series at hand is research that has gaps that can only be filled with the entire series at one's disposal. And now that the series has been completed, the primary purpose for composing a book-length volume dedicated to the study and examination of Stephen King's *Dark Tower* series stems from a true need for such a work. As King's seven-book series has now been completed for four years, there has been very little critical and scholarly work offered for these stories. While there have been conference presentations, master's theses and even doctoral dissertations that focus on or at least work with *The Dark Tower* series, many scholars still tend to work with King's earlier works such as *The Shining, Carrie*, and *Pet Sematary*. This is not to say that *The Dark Tower* has gone completely unnoticed by academics; however, detailed and extensive analyses, along with those that maintain a consistent academic focus and voice, are lacking when compared to research on the rest of King's canon.

With the immense popularity Stephen King has garnered during his career, many volumes which have been published on King and his fiction typically steer towards the casual reader leaving the academic searching for works that are more aligned with study, interpretation, and critique, as is the case with *The Dark Tower*. Still, selections of academic scholarship have been available on *The Dark Tower* since 1987, with James Egan's "*The Dark Tower*: Stephen King's Gothic Western," opening the way for additional attention given to this cycle of stories, a door through which Heidi Strengell stepped, albeit not entirely. Strengell's 2005 text *Dissecting Stephen King* does provide some rather exceptional insights into particular elements of *The Dark Tower*, especially when considering that any scholarship on *The Dark Tower* prior to 2004 is incomplete as the series had not been finished, but the gunslinger's story is not the focus of her book. Also, Robin Furth's *The Dark Tower: A Concordance* provides detailed references for those wishing to locate specific information on characters, places, and the like, which is certainly helpful, but this text does not include any lengthy or constant scholarship and commentary on the *Dark Tower* series itself. But on the other side of the fence are the works which highlight the divide between the academic and the fan, and one such text in particular must be mentioned within the context of scholarship on *The Dark Tower*.

One of the most problematic texts concerning the study of King, specifically that of his *Dark Tower* series, is Bev Vincent's *The Road to the Dark Tower: Exploring Stephen King's Magnum Opus*. This text aspired to provide more direct discussion about King's *Dark Tower* series than previously published works, and, more to the point, it is touted as the first examination of the series in its entirety. However, the downfall of this book is its leaning towards summary, including reviews of each book in the *Dark Tower* series and examinations of the characters which do not go as far as some would like, especially as the observations provided in Vincent's text can certainly be gleaned by a passing acquaintance with the tale. And although Vincent's book has found favor among King's large fan-base, it does not provoke the same satisfaction among academics. Although a separation between the scholar and the fan may seem to be unnecessary, those who study King's work within a scholarly context can only do so much with the overly general observations and fan-oriented commentary from authors such as Stephen Spignesi (*The Essential Stephen King*) and George Beahm (*America's Best-Loved Boogeyman*). While I certainly appreciate the contributions that books like these and authors like Spignesi and Beahm provide for study of Stephen King, an academic voice is notably absent. In addition, *The Stephen King Universe* by Stanley Wiater, Christopher Golden and Hank Wagner looks at the issue of how King's tales come together into a fictional universe of interconnectedness, and although this volume does bring to light some of the more obscure connections among King's canon, especially through the second edition released *after* the *Dark Tower* series was finished, this text does not completely satisfy the academic mind.

Foregrounding the academic voice while attempting to sidestep the pitfalls of fan-oriented writing that tends to rely on summary with the occasional critical commentary, this text looks at *The Dark Tower* series through four primary identifying markers: Genre, Art, Evil, and Intertextuality. Most certainly, many of King's other works share common ground with these themes and will be discussed at appropriate junctures, but when thinking of a place to, essentially, begin scholarship on this collection of books, these four categories of analysis stand out. A plot review does no good, as is the case with extensive examinations of the characters, all of which should be known to readers, casual or otherwise, of both the *Dark Tower* series and this text. Moreover, this text operates on the foundation of hypothesis and speculation — offering views, opinions, interpretations and criticisms that look at *The Dark Tower* as a whole, and as a text comprised of select elements that seek to establish a place for scholarship devoted to and focused on the *Dark Tower* series itself rather than as an afterthought or side note to King's other fiction. And in response to the deficiency in focused, scholarly work, the doors to this book, and a few doors into *The Dark Tower*, now open.

Introduction

The Dark Tower—
A Literary Anomaly,
an Experiment in Horror,
or a True Mark of Literature?

STEPHEN KING'S EARLY AND LARGELY successful works such as *The Shining* and *The Stand* have received extensive treatment within academic circles—whether in terms of interpretation, observation, or outright critique—and scholarship on these texts mirror a trend within King studies to keep focus mainly on his first two decades of writing. Of course, for academics to stay current with King's writing is difficult as he is as active with publishing today as he was in the late 70s and during the 80s. But the lag in critical writings directed at King's more recent works, specifically concerning *The Dark Tower* series, does leave the intellectual doorway into King's universe as open as it was when King published his first novel, *Carrie*. While there may be little else to say on King's first several books, writers, students, scholars and critics remain enamored with the early volumes of his writing, constantly probing these texts and expanding the existing conversations of research and criticism, even to the point of excess. But as scholars and critics continue to write on King, voicing opinions from admiration to condemnation, the collection of novels which have begun to be considered King's masterpiece, *The Dark Tower* series, have yet to receive the attention typically devoted to the works of the gruesome, horrific and supernatural for which King is both celebrated and scorned.

It is the goal of this volume to provide a critical analysis on the entire *Dark Tower* series, especially as earlier criticism on these books lacks the complete context of the finished story. The focus will be on genre and

5

its relation to the gunslinger's climax, the artistic elements of both the fiction and the graphic novel adaptation of the *Dark Tower* series, primarily the initial run titled *The Gunslinger Born*, questions of evil and its constant permeation of the texts and characters, and the role of the *Dark Tower* series as the nexus of King's fiction. The aim of this introduction, however, is to explore the background of the *Dark Tower* series while discussing issues of readership and reception in an attempt to justify not only this examination of *The Dark Tower*, but also continued study of King's apparent magnum opus.

Horrific Foundations

Stephen King's reputation as a horror writer cannot be argued: haunted houses, vampires, apocalyptic landscapes, reanimated corpses, a telepathic prom queen and a deadly Saint Bernard have overwhelmed readers with fright and terror, which has led to the labeling of King as a horror writer. His audience grew and clamored for his style of writing, expecting continuous scares and frightening plots, and the successful film adaptations of King's fiction created an even larger audience for his stories as well as instigating continued interest in his brand of horror. Even among King's numerous cinematic surprises that did not satisfy expectations of a King film focused on horror, namely *The Shawshank Redemption*, *Stand by Me*, and *The Green Mile* which highlighted King as more than a writer grounded in horror, readers and viewers have continued to not only label King as the Master of Horror, but also have anticipated nothing else but additional novels, stories and films in the mold of the dark and dreary tale with skeletons, ghosts, and a variety of unexplained psychic phenomena. However, this began to change in 1983 when King published *Pet Sematary* and noted that he had composed a largely unknown novel the year before, titled *The Dark Tower: The Gunslinger*.

The Gunslinger had found a select and limited audience in the late 70s and into the early 80s with subscribers to the *Journal of Fantasy and Science Fiction*. The first section of *The Gunslinger*, titled "The Gunslinger," was published in October of 1978, and the gunslinger's tale, told in five installments, was completed in November of 1981. Then King published the entire story of his first book in *The Dark Tower* series the next year in 1982. But, the publication of *The Gunslinger* went almost entirely unnoticed as the publisher, Donald M. Grant, was a small press and not the publisher of King's other tales being published at the time. Yet, when King announced to his larger readership in *Pet Sematary* that there was a book many of his Constant Readers had not yet read, there were calls for making this text available to a larger audience as only 10,000 copies of *The Gunslinger* were originally available to the public. Even though the tale of Roland Deschain, the last gunslinger, was clearly a deviation from all other titles that King had written, demands for this novel did not wane even after discovering a noticeable separation in terms of plot and content from King's other writings, resulting in two additional printings of the first edition of *The Gunslinger* to appease the eager reader. Thus, the story of *The Dark Tower* was infused with life, and as this story became situated in the imaginations of King's admiring fans who waited patiently for him to take up his tale with the second volume, the figure of the gunslinger also grew in King's imagination and eventually found his way onto paper for the next installment of the *Dark Tower* series, *The Drawing of the Three*.

King went on to publish *The Drawing of the Three* in 1987, and with this second edition, the story of Roland Deschain had lived for nearly a decade in a published medium and for five years in hardbound editions, yet the story itself was actually almost twenty years old as King began composing the gunslinger's story in 1970. And although King's popularity as a horror writer continued to grow, readership of his *Dark Tower* series did not drop off despite the lengthy interludes between volumes or the move away from the horror genre that *The Dark Tower* displayed. Not even chiding book reviews, such as one which critiqued *The Gunslinger* as, "undergraduate-style goulash [...] [that] is, alas, merely sophomoric," kept readers away for long (Fuller BR22). Aside from the growing time involved in composing *The Dark Tower*, as well as reviews that hardly reflected any sense of admiration or praise, King's audience, however, largely received the strange landscape of Mid-World with open arms and eager eyes, as observed by King firsthand:

> My surprise at the acceptance of the first volume of this work, which is not at all like the stories for which I am best known, is exceeded only by my gratitude to those who have read it and liked it. This work seems to be my own Tower, you know; these people haunt me, Roland most of all. Do

I really know what that Tower is, and what awaits Roland there (should he reach it, and you must prepare yourself for the very real possibility that he will not be the one to do so)? Yes ... and no. All I know is that the tale has called to me again and again over a period of seventeen years [*The Drawing of the Three* 407].

As King continued to write, he gave readers the next two volumes of the *Dark Tower* series, *The Waste Lands* and *Wizard and Glass* in 1991 and 1996 respectively. Then, strangely and shockingly, King was hit by a van in the summer of 1999 while walking near his Maine home and the writing ceased. The gunslinger's tale then lay dormant for seven years, even though King wrote indirectly of the gunslinger's story in tales like *Hearts in Atlantis* just before the accident and in *Black House* two years afterwards. Still, readers waited, and not entirely with patience, for King to resume Roland's tale while having to be satiated with only allusions and distant references to the fate of Roland's ka-tet and the fate of the Dark Tower while King not only recovered from the accident but also searched for the story of the gunslinger in his imagination. King later delivered what his audiences asked for, although perhaps not entirely what the audience wanted, completing the *Dark Tower* series while also incorporating events that occurred during the interlude: the accident which nearly took King's life in the summer of 1999 and the events of September 11, 2001. Considering the importance that his accident and the attacks on the World Trade Center play in *The Dark Tower*, maybe the delay in composing the last three volumes of *The Dark Tower* was serendipitous, a necessary break from the tale required to complete the *right* story. On the other hand, readers can only wonder how *The Dark Tower* would have ended had the timing been different. Regardless, the tale is complete, and with all seven volumes finished, fans and critics alike have had much to say, albeit scarcely in a published medium. Observations and commentary stemming from the fan have certainly been given in greater volumes than the musings and critique from the academy, hence this volume.

Reviewing Readership and Reception

In looking back at the entire *Dark Tower* series juxtaposed to the rest of the King canon, a common question asked is, "Why did King write the *Dark Tower?*" Not only is this series of stories with a cowboy beholden to medieval ideals an odd shift from the rest of King's fiction which all seem to have some basis in reality with characters who, aside from ghostly presences and the like, could each be classified as an Everyman that constantly faces dire circumstances, but also the genres present in this tale, with the exception of the Gothic, rarely intersect with the realm in which King writes, or has been placed into by critics and fans alike: horror. As Andrew O'Hehir's curt and blunt commentary on *The Dark Tower* claims that the series, "sometimes seems like the awkward, left-footed stepchild of his [King's] work," he suggests that the move away from King's primary genre of horror, regardless of the accuracy or inaccuracy of this distinction, is one that is painful for his Constant Reader (B11). Still, do the questions and concerns regarding the singularity of *The Dark Tower* necessitate the designation of *The Dark Tower* as an anomaly, or even as a text that should be read and studied in isolation, away from King's more successful novels? Not at all.

With many readers and critics believing that *The Dark Tower* is certainly a peculiarity, including Richard Nicholls who has noted that, "while the books share with Mr. King's horror novels bizarre villains and frequent eruptions of violence, they are otherwise a distinct departure," the story functions as more than a literary outcast, a forgotten set of stories that are only related to the rest of King's writing by the author who wrote each tale (BR14). Knowing that the apparent magnum opus of King's fiction is a tale set against a post-apocalyptic landscape with a Western motif that conflicts and meshes with the Gothic undertones alongside science fiction elements that pre-date the epic and medieval themes found in the text, readers still wonder why King wrote this tale in the first place. Although King had, and continues to have, success under the canopy of horror, it may seem strange to have witnessed King writing outside of the horror genre and embarking on the literary experiment of *The Dark Tower.* However, even as the *Dark Tower* series can certainly be considered as experimental, the distinction of being an anomaly is a hasty conclusion.

Among concerns about King's experimentation in the *Dark Tower*, as well as questions focused on discovering why he wrote the gunslinger's tale in the first place, he begins to unveil the history and explanation for the *Dark Tower*'s existence when he says that the primary influence behind his story was J.R.R. Tolkien. Yet, King also says that aside from the inspiration he received from Tolkien, his purpose behind the *Dark Tower* was to create his *own* tale:

> The *Dark Tower* books, like most long fantasy tales written by men and women of my generation [...] were born out of Tolkien's. But although I read the books in 1966 and 1967, I held off writing. I responded (and with rather touching wholeheartedness) to the sweep of Tolkien's imagination — to the ambition of his story — but I wanted to write my own kind of story, and had I started then, I would have written his ["Introduction" xi].

Whether attempting to avoid plagiarism, or waiting for his muse to speak, King began his career with the tale of *Carrie*, along with several short stories that were published in a variety of men's magazines like *Cavalier* and *Penthouse*, and he let the *Dark Tower* rest for the time being. And with the growing popularity, or infamy, of his writing, he kept writing, publishing nearly a book a year and even creating another persona in Richard Bachman, all the while becoming labeled as a horror writer as death, monsters, and paranormal activity became mainstays in his writing. Yet the *Dark Tower* remained unfinished and barely begun, but the tale that Tolkien had essentially birthed in King's mind grew and drove him to write:

> I'm just saying that I wanted to write an epic, and in some ways, I succeeded. If you were to ask me *why* I wanted to do that, I couldn't tell you. Maybe it's a part of growing up American: build the tallest, dig the deepest, write the longest. And that head-scratching puzzlement when the question of motivation comes up? Seems to me that that is also part of being an American. In the end we are reduced to saying *It seemed like a good idea at the time* ["Introduction" xvi].

And, then, King wrote, composing nearly 4,000 pages of story that fulfilled the epic requirement of size. But regardless of the length of the *Dark Tower* series, and regardless of its acceptance among King's readers, the *Dark Tower* looms over the Stephen King canon as a mystery almost as great as the Dark Tower itself. It is a series that certainly displays the vast range of King's imagination, as well as his patience in that over thirty years of writing went into the composition of this tale, but is also somewhat problematic in its own range of themes and genres that constantly forces readers and critics to shake their head in disbelief, insisting that *The Dark Tower* is just another horror tale.

Or is it?

King as a Horror Writer

Not only does King's position as a horror writer limit his audience and often determine audience reception, *The Dark Tower* series is troublesome for the fan and the academic alike in that the horror King is primarily known for is quite scarce in this cycle of stories. Although evil and the supernatural are present in *The Dark Tower* as psychic characters, haunted houses (Dutch Hill Mansion and Black House), a witch (Rhea), nuclear freaks (the slow mutants), and a were-spider (Mordred Deschain) become essential to the storyline, the *Dark Tower* series, as a whole, escapes the boundaries of the horror genre. The presence of advanced technology and residue of medievalism may push *The Dark Tower* outside typical genre classification, but if one were to focus on these elements as indicators that King abandons the conventions and themes which are celebrated in his other works, there would be a rebuttal which denotes the elements in *The Dark Tower* as purposely aligned with those of the horror genre. As noted King scholar Tony Magistrale says:

> I have maintained that what is most horrifying in his tales has less to do with prehistoric creatures roaming the night or vampires cruising for nourishment. Rather, his deepest terrors are sociopolitical in nature, reflecting our worst fears about vulnerable western institutions — our governmental bureaucracies, our school systems, our communities, our familial relationships. In other words, King writes about horrors that operate on a variety of levels — embracing the literal as well as the symbolic [*Landscape of Fear* 1–2].

Magistrale's assertion suggests that King's writing is almost an atypical type of horror — that which captures the fright and shock of tales focused on monsters in addition to the desolation of the Gothic, but that is also shaped and appropriated for the social landscape of the current age. The horror, then, that King primarily focuses on is that of the human condition; more specifically, as King writes he creates scenes and scenarios which require mettle, sanity, perseverance, and hope in the face of both imaginative and original, or even outlandish and outrageous, settings and obstacles, all of which are not wholly unexpected in a horror tale which often poses such problems in phantasmal or paranormal masks. Additionally, Heidi Strengell suggests that, "it remains to be seen whether it [King's fiction] can even be labeled horror in the strict sense of the word," but believing in the necessary flexibility of fiction to adapt and prompt change within particular frameworks, strict adherence to or classification of a particular genre is unnecessarily parochial (27). But horror is the area King's writing typically occupies, and it is within this realm that another section of King's audience cries out — the academic, complete with exclamations that substandard writing consumes King's fiction.

King has certainly found great success as a writer of horror, and whether or not such a distinction is accurate, this particular category of literature has found a critical and reserved audience in the academic circles: "King seems to have pleased almost everyone except conventional mainstream literary critics" (Schweitzer 5). Despite the overarching resistance of King within the scholarly ranks, his immense popularity has nonetheless insisted upon study of his works. As the academy continues to appeal to the needs and desires of its students, it is not surprising to see students wishing to read popular literature in their elective literature classes — such fiction is not only familiar, but also enjoyable. Of course, as King's writing has begun to become more accepted within the classroom, he and his writing are typically classified as horror and is often studied alongside notable horror writers like Mary Shelley, Bram Stoker, Edgar Allen Poe and Nathaniel Hawthorne. Surely, each of these authors has influenced King and his writing, and the dialogue between these works is a discussion and interaction that has gained more and more attention as King's has continued to publish. And, for example, while it is certainly fascinating to examine King's take on vampire lore, as situated within the American small town, alongside Stoker's novel, King's fiction also serves as an accessible medium through which students can study other notable writers, including the parallels between King's demonic Randall Flagg and Milton's Satan from *Paradise Lost* which is certainly one of the more interesting comparisons that has surfaced. Still, reservations about King as a horror writer run rampant and are among the many causes behind the hesitancy to take King seriously.

Introduction

As King has astonished audiences with the versatility of his craft and writing, especially with works like *The Green Mile*, "The Body," and "Rita Hayworth and the Shawshank Redemption" (to name the stories which have been among the most successful cinematic adaptations of King's writing), he constantly surprises readers with the scope and range of his writing. Beyond the haunted house, troubled teens with telekinetic abilities or ghostly presences, King continues to experiment with his fiction writing, as seen with his mystery tale *The Colorado Kid* and even the nightmarish social landscapes of the Bachman Books. Even though the Bachman Books typically result in death or insanity for the protagonists, which solidifies the horrific label attributed to King, these latter tales are primarily speculative and fictitious sociological accounts of American suburbia. But whether or not King visits the small towns of Derry and Castle Rock or takes readers into familiar cityscapes, into the graveyard and into devious governmental and corporate institutions, or even ends his tale with a laugh or a cry, his breadth is best displayed in *The Dark Tower*. Even as King dabbles with a variety of genres, creates new faces of evil with Roland Deschain serving as anti-hero, and also utilizes metafiction, that, "smarmy academic term," in the gunslinger's story, any semblance of horror that is present in the *Dark Tower* is magnified to the extent that most everything else is washed away (King, *The Dark Tower* 843). The result is a constant misrepresentation of King that hastily places works like *The Dark Tower* in a single genre when readers of this tale understand that the classification of horror is overly restrictive.

In reviewing the blurbs that grace the back covers of some of the paperback editions of the *Dark Tower* series, there is an emergent pattern among the various praises attributed to King and his epic tale. In most every commendation for this story, the reviewers have had a tendency to insert phrases highlighting the presence of horror — indeed, the focus strayed from the tale itself and its fantastical elements as well as the technological presence that permeates the fiction, possibly to sell the books to King's established audience, those who wanted horror. To highlight these erroneous attributions, the following are some examples of the lauding phrases and brief plot summaries which are insistent upon King living up to his name as the "Master of Horror" within his *Dark Tower* series:

- "A magical mix of fantasy and **horror** that may be his [King's] crowning achievement"
- "Roland, the last gunslinger, is moving ever closer to the Dark Tower, which **haunts** his dreams and **nightmares**"
- "He [Roland] and his friends cross a desert of **damnation** in their **macabre** new world"
- "He [Roland] is a **haunting** figure, a loner on a spellbinding journey into good and **evil**"
- "Prime King, very **suspenseful** ... reams of virtuoso **horror** writing"
- "Set in a world of **ominous** landscape and **macabre menace** that is a **dark** mirror of our own"

With the constant attention given to horror either observed or foregrounded in King's fiction, it could be reasonably concluded that no matter how hard King tries his fiction will always fall under this category. On the other hand, one could argue that the continual genre distinction given to King, especially with regard to *The Dark Tower*, is done to avoid any confusion as to who King is as a writer and what he produces. Quite possibly, the focus on horrific elements in the *Dark Tower* series is meant to avoid the awkward consideration of these volumes as an anomaly in King's canon. Or, it may be the case that horror has become a blanket term to describe anything that escapes the realm of the norm or the stereotypical, which proves to be a misnomer when considering the content of *The Dark Tower*.

While books such as *The Stand, Firestarter, The Dead Zone, Rose Madder*, and *The Girl Who Loved Tom Gordon* all reflect, to some degree, the horrific elements one expects of King's fiction, these tales extend well beyond the shocks and scares that leave readers sleeping with the light on. Each tale contains a fairly close examination of the human condition when placed in extraordinary circumstances, which is somewhat formulaic when considering the basic plot element of conflict. But, the characters in these stories all receive such extensive analysis and treatment from King that it is needlessly limiting to merely focus on the horror — whether supernatural or realistic — that is assumed to saturate the fiction. The perseverance or defeat that these characters must display or endure transcends the boundaries of genre. And with King weaving in impossible circumstances, maddening dilemmas and the inevitability of failure alongside a glimmer of hope, examination of individuals like Stu

Redmond, Charlie McGee, Johnny Smith, Rosie Daniels or Trisha McFarland within the restraints of horror undoubtedly leads to incomplete and narrow readings of these characters. If King is purely a horror writer, and purposely utilizes elements of this genre to compose his writing and even dictate the climax of his tales, then his characters become nothing more than stock creations that fall prey to pre-established literary norms. In attributing the plot and characters of King's fiction to simple reflections of the genre in which King is purportedly situated, readers could certainly expect constant repetition of action, conflict and climax. However, this is not the case with King's fiction. There may be parallels among his writings and characters, but King is not bound by the genre which has been placed upon him, and the variety with which he writes suggests not only violations of genre conventions, but a genuine inventiveness that seeks a lens other than horror through which one may view his writing.

With many fantasy works focusing on the struggle of good versus evil, there is often a tendency to draw clear lines between these two camps in that the characters in these writing are aligned with one extreme or the other. In King's fiction, the question of evil is not reduced to a simple polar opposite to good, nor is it a force that receives consistent treatment and representation. With the demon entities King writes into the tales *The Eyes of the Dragon*, *Needful Things*, and *Storm of the Century*, Randall Flagg, Leland Gaunt and Andre Linoge, respectively, he may revisit the motif of the communal necessity to band together and rise up against the evil outside as well as the constant inhuman threat which seeks nothing less than destruction and devastation, but the variations among King's work suggests that the constraints of genre are not entirely applicable to his writing, especially regarding his antagonists. While it is often seen within a horror novel that good eventually wins through, usually with the loss of life or at some other great cost, King twists and manipulates the horror genre when he ensures that this formula becomes negligible in the aforementioned works. As Flagg is seemingly defeated in the end of *The Eyes of the Dragon* when the evil wizard disappears in a flash of smoke after taking an arrow to the eye, readers later come to know that Flagg was never truly defeated as he returns in *The Stand* and *The Dark Tower* series (and is alluded to in *Hearts in Atlantis*). The Kingdom of Delain may be rid of Flagg's treachery as *The*

Eyes of the Dragon closes, but Flagg is not gone forever; he even returns in the last pages of *The Stand* after being defeated in Las Vegas earlier in the novel. But Flagg's resurrection is short lived when Mordred Deschain kills him in *The Dark Tower*, suggesting that evil in King's fiction ultimately loses. Also to consider is that Leland Gaunt leaves the town of Castle Rock in ruins and later reestablishes his shop of wares in a new American small town at the end of *Needful Things*, reasonably suggesting that the atrocities and maliciousness witnessed in the story are not yet finished. And remember that in *Storm of the Century* Andre Linoge leaves Little Tall Island with his new apprentice, Ralphie Anderson, ensuring that evil will not die. Readers see that these examples of evil winning are not constant in King's canon as Flagg falls while the other demons endure to continue with their designs. Despite these variations in plot and climax, it is difficult for King to escape the boundaries of genre in that while his protagonists and antagonists both meet different fates in his writing, the constant struggles set against backdrops of horror perpetually place King and his fiction under the lens of the horror genre, which subjects he and his writing to the never-ending critique of the literary establishment.

The Canon and the Critics

In suggesting that King's writing is often needlessly classified and read through the lens of the horror genre, and in also claiming that King has at times labored to shed himself and his fiction of these figurative shackles, there remains the question of how genre functions within the *Dark Tower* series, especially considering that this cycle of stories consists of at least five distinct genres. But beyond the questions of genre in *The Dark Tower*, which will be addressed in the first chapter, are those which focus on Roland's humanity, his capacity for love, and what he will sacrifice to simply *see* his Dark Tower. The questions of compassion, the progress of technology, and the costs of a quixotic quest born out of the mind of a young, naïve gunslinger place the *Dark Tower* series alongside some of the traditionally canonical literary works, but this series has been, thus far, denied any classification beside the half-baked experiment of a writer who has little else to look forward to than the next paycheck.

Among these ponderings and musings are questions of what *exactly* makes a work worthy of the elevated position afforded to those within the literary canon. Or, as Greg Smith discusses, "the big deal in relation to Stephen King where academics are concerned, interestingly enough, seems not to be whether his books are dangerous, but instead whether they're *good*" (331). Additionally, Tony Magistrale concurs as he says that King is "a damn good storyteller, and this is one of the things that the academic elite is missing out on" (Davis, "Interview with Tony Magistrale" 121). And while other scholars and King's Constant Readers find him to be a skilled storyteller as well as a good writer, such overly subjective views and statements do little to forward the argument as to King's merits. At the same time, the support that King finds with his Constant Reader and the handful of scholars who appreciate and laud his craft suggests that there is some sort of quality, or even aesthetic, to be found in King's writing, which is certainly promising.

Questions of the literary canon have raged on for quite some time, and while the debate continues and while the canon also continues to face scrutiny and revision, one must wonder if King will ever be considered as a literary writer. King implicitly admits that his standing as a *popular* novelist may have some bearing on his possible exclusion from literary circles when he offers his own examination of the rift between the popular and the literary writer:

> I think novelists come in two types, and that includes the sort of fledgling novelist I was by 1970. Those who are bound for the more literary or "serious" side of the job examine every possible subject in light of this question: *What would writing this sort of story mean to me?* Those whose destiny (or ka, if you like) is to include the writing of popular novels are apt to ask a very different one: *What would this sort of story mean to others?* The "serious" novelist is looking for answers and keys to the self, the "popular" novelist is looking for an audience ["Introduction" xiv].

Although King has had an audience for his writing, and in mind, since he began his writing career, it would be rather hasty to neglect the serious elements of his craft. Audience is undoubtedly important to any novelist, and as writing that is created *for* an audience may gloss over some aspects of literary writing that prompt a distinction as being a serious story, King does find a balance between the two designated groups of writers. At the same time, King displays a keen awareness of the troubles associated with his particular leanings: "in writing popular, commercial fiction, there is nothing but danger. The commercial writer is easy to bribe, easy to subvert, and he knows it" ("Brand Name" 16). Whether or not King has "sold out" is a question just as debatable as the canon wars, but a more productive avenue to explore is that of King's attempt to bring together elements of the serious and the popular.

King's contribution to bridging the gap that exists among both the serious and literary writer is not a recent innovation or an inexplicable phenomenon as his predecessor, Robert Browning, navigated this dilemma with his poetry and fiction, although perhaps without the direct intention of doing so and without the success of bringing these two worlds together. Like King, Robert Browning's writing has endured questions of literary merit, and while Browning's poem, "Childe Roland to the Dark Tower Came," the work upon which King bases his tale, has also been treated as an anomaly in his canon, this distinction has not deterred scholars from offering a wide selection of criticism and scholarly examination. The opaque nature of "Childe Roland" serves as an appropriate work with which scholars can offer interpretations and critiques as it is suggested that educated and trained academics hold the keys to unraveling the deeper mysteries and enigmas of Browning's poem, a piece which positions the quester, Childe Roland, to not only seek the Dark Tower but also to discover himself though intensive introspection in the process. Moreover, as "Childe Roland" chronicles the adventures and dilemmas of its wanderer as he searches for the Dark Tower, a structure supposed to hold answers Childe Roland requires in order to better understand his identity and his position among his peers, Browning's work can be categorized as a serious work as it falls within King's distinction of being a writer that certainly seeks "answers and keys to the self." By the same token, if Browning's work is viewed as a serious literary work, despite its awkward presence in his corpus, it is not wholly unreasonable to consider King's *Dark Tower* series as having a serious side regardless of its popular acceptance and the proposition that these books are uncharacteristic of King's writing when compared to the rest of his corpus.

Much like Browning's Childe Roland, King's gunslinger is a character whose actions and motivations deserve close scrutiny: as Roland sacrifices his friends and companions for the Tower, murders his sons (both biological [Mordred] and surrogate [Jake]), and is possessed by an unwavering determination to reach the Dark Tower at all costs, King's tale certainly offers an examination of the self expected of a serious literary composition. Roland's deeds may earn him fame in Gilead and notoriety throughout Mid-World by means of the revolvers he carries, but King creates more than an enigmatic figure that is both revered and despised by readers and characters within the series. King creates a character whose inner demons and myopic world view are easily transcribed onto most any reader, prompting the examination of the self that seems to be the goal of most serious writing. The prideful pursuit of a quixotic goal without considerations for humanity and one's own soul are undoubtedly themes and makings of a novel directed at significant contemplations, but King's popularity still tends to overshadow the larger scope of his writing.

In light of the reception and criticism King's work has received regarding its popularity, Gary Hoppenstand, one of the leading scholars on King's fiction and film, suggests that readers, scholars and critics need to reconsider approaches as to how contemporary and popular writing should be received and judged:

> Here's a radical thought: perhaps the best type of fiction is that which entertains its reader. Perhaps the popular writer or a popular genre is self-selected by readers who aren't having their arms twisted by English Lit teachers armed with the dire threat of a looming, nasty essay test. Perhaps the popular fiction that can offer an escape while also communicating something important about the human condition might be vastly superior to literature that has to be propped up by the university professor, before it expires to self-absorption and obtuseness ["Country Club Literature" 795].

Viewing fiction as a means of entertainment, enjoyment and escape may seem like an overly rebellious call to alter the evolution of the novel and may seem to invite a regression of the art, but King's Constant Reader can only wonder, and even shudder, at the current direction the novel is seemingly being forced to take. Creating fiction that is appealing to the fan is certainly a boon for sales, and seems to prompt a return to the origins of the novel as being made for the entertainment and the pleasure of the reading public, which is aligned with King's own view of the novel as he claims that, "readable, interesting novels don't begin with a desire to teach but a desire to please" ("Typhoid Stevie" 14). In support of reading pleasure as opposed to pure didacticism, Jonathan Davis provides the reminder that King, "utilizes popular culture appeal to make his books fun for us to read, but if people take the time to read into the subtexts of his fiction, they will find that he is trying to tell us much, much more" (*Stephen King's America* 4). Yet, most attempts to promote these views within academic circles are met with resistance and scorn.

Whether approaching King and his writing from a holistic approach or one that examines the microcosms of the consequential subject matter aligned with canonical writing, there are those who tend to view King's writing though the lens of the eternal skeptic as influenced by King's inclusion of what is considered to be sub-literary content despite any compelling arguments to the contrary. Harold Bloom, one of the most widely recognized critics concerning matters of literature who has not been shy about his distaste for King's fiction, believes that, "the triumph of the genial King is a large emblem of the failures of American education" ("Introduction" 2). Bloom readily disregards King's sincere attempts at crafting literature that is both enjoyable and profound, suggesting that this combination is not what constitutes literature and even poses a danger to those who read and study fiction. As Bloom expounds his assertion by further claiming, "King will be remembered as a sociological phenomenon, an image of the death of the Literate Reader," he is met with resistance by not only King's readers who might take offense to Bloom's analysis of King's fiction and its affects on audiences, but also by other scholars who find King's work to be anything but the fictional quagmire that Bloom believes King's writing to be ("Introduction" 3).

Tony Magistrale, who has written at length about King's literary qualities, admits that King's popularity is certainly one of the deciding factors regarding King's literary position. However, Magistrale also suggests that much of this distinction can be attributed to the elitist nature of literary studies:

> There is little doubt that King's enormous popularity has damaged his reputation among academicians and literary scholars. There is a disquieting tendency among many English teachers and intellectuals in this country to view themselves as the final arbiters of "high culture," and any artist, regardless of his or her talent, threatens that exclusive *sanctum sanctorum* if s/he seeks admittance with a large, popular audience in tow [*Landscape of Fear* 3].

Introduction

Even if one were to accept that the largest offenders in debasing the popular novel are those within the Ivory Tower, all blame cannot be placed on these keepers of the canon. Although their critiques resonate throughout the academic world and are key factors in regulating the study of literature, their reach seems to also function as a catalyst that manipulates the products of the publishing world. With the horror genre receiving treatment as little else than fan-oriented writing that appeals to the short attention spans of the masses and the wallets of the publishers, other genres, such as harlequin romance and science-fiction, appear to remain satisfied with their established formulas and themes as the readership remains constant despite the apparently stagnating content. With this spiral being perpetuated by the academic resistance to popular literature, Gary Hoppenstand notes that this complacence limits the desire to create new and experimental literature:

> When speculative fiction was still somewhat disreputable, it also seemed to be more imaginative, more willing to take risks, more able to explore concepts and ideas not found in any other genre of fiction or popular culture. It appears that there are fewer and fewer wholly original talents at work today. Dan Simmons, the author of the magnificent *Hyperion* and *Ilium* science fiction novels is one, and Stephen King, author of the "Dark Tower" epic fantasy series is another, but many who could be creating the next fantasy classics are instead writing the 276th *Star Wars* pastiche, because that is where the money is ["Series[ous] SF Concerns" 604].

Again, as the popular novel appears to be dwindling rather than growing, whether in terms of academic rejection or because the money does lay elsewhere, King's boldness in writing *The Dark Tower* should be received as an honest effort to stay true to the writer's craft that opposes the growing trend to remain comfortable with a particular form rather than buckling beneath the burden of acceptance among a select group of literary judges, the oftentimes self-appointed custodians of fictional aesthetics. All in all, King still writes, and he delivered *The Dark Tower* to his salivating Constant Reader despite the constant pressures to avoid such, and in the process, though, King's willing experiment with genre, among other things, in *The Dark Tower* has resulted in an interconnected grouping of stories that, together, create what could be considered as the longest story in history.

21

Connections and Appropriations

With King's *The Dark Tower* series, readers are given the nexus of King's corpus, a work which purportedly connects all of King's writing — there may be several degrees of separation between *The Running Man* and *Bag of Bones*, but as readers discover Mike Noonan writing in *Bag of Bones* of a character named Raymond Garraty, it is seen that this character reference to *The Long Walk* connects the aforementioned novels through King's alter-ego Richard Bachman. As this is only one example of the minute, yet certainly present, linkage between two King novels that otherwise would seem to be completely disconnected, the theory that King's fiction all comes together to create a larger tale can be used as a lens through which readers can re-read and even re-contextualize King's entire body of work. But why create a tale through which an entire corpus of work can be connected? When King says of *The Dark Tower* that, "What I wanted even more than the setting was that feeling of epic, apocalyptic *size* [...] I wanted to write not just a *long* book, but *the longest popular novel in history*," it would seem that one way to accomplish this feat would to ensure that the story of the gunslinger was not limited to just the seven books in the *Dark Tower* series ("Introduction" xv–xvi). However, King implies that he did not necessarily intend for the *Dark Tower* series to end up as the center of his fictional universe:

> I have written enough novels and short stories to fill a solar system of the imagination, but Roland's story is my Jupiter — a planet that dwarfs all the others (at least from my own perspective), a place of strange atmosphere, crazy landscape, and savage gravitational pull. Dwarfs the others, did I say? I think there's more to it than that, actually. I am coming to understand that Roland's world (or worlds) actually *contains* all the others of my making; there is a place in Mid-World for Randall Flagg, Ralph Roberts, the wandering boys from *The Eyes of the Dragon*, even Father Callahan, the damned priest from *'Salem's Lot*, who rode out of New England on a Greyhound Bus and wound up dwelling on the border of a terrible Mid-World land called Thunderclap. This seems to be where they all finish up, and why not? Mid-World was here first, before all of them, dreaming under the blue gaze of Roland's bombardier eyes [*Wizard and Glass* 671].

Even though King discovered the grand-scale nature of his *Dark Tower* series after composing the first four installments, the final result is a tale that encompasses all others of his creation. Although King claims that only fifteen of the forty-four novels and collections outside the *Dark Tower* series are related to Roland's story, careful readers can distinguish connections among *all* of King's fiction; whether the connections be minimal like a recycled surname or allusion to events from another tale, King's entire canon resembles a spider-web in which each novel is connected to the other by one means or the other.

Although the placement of *The Dark Tower* at the center of King's fictional universe insists on its importance with respect to the remainder of King's canon, it is surprising to see how little critical attention these works have received. From an academic standpoint, as new articles and scholarly presentations are made on King's work, there is a noticeable resistance to examining the *Dark Tower* series. With the primary body of critical work on King focusing on his earlier works, or his "classics," the growing body of work on King and his writing remains narrow. With the difficulty inherent in creating original scholarly work on any author or novel, the easiest and most standard route for an academic to take is to simply expand upon what has been said. Still, as the *Dark Tower* series is either avoided or hesitantly approached, academic woes aside, the *Dark Tower* story continues to grow with each novel King publishes; the story has now been adapted into a graphic novel, *The Gunslinger Born*, and there is discussion that Roland of Gilead will soon grace the silver screen as well. With its growing popularity, and considering the monumental success King's novels have had regarding adaptation to the silver screen or the television set, the desire for a *Dark Tower* movie to be made certainly suggests a keen interest in this project, especially from the standpoint of the fan, but there are many problems awaiting on the horizon should Mid-World leap from the pages and onto the screen, adding another dimension to the already complex discussion surrounding *The Dark Tower*.

One of the primary problems that *The Dark Tower* series poses regarding cinematic adaptation is not the length of the series, but the *content*. For example, as King acknowledges a connection between this series and his novel *IT*, attempting to keep the connection between these two works, at least on film, would be nearly impossible. The primary link between these two works is the presence of the Turtle, one of the guardians of the Beam that the gunslinger and his ka-tet follow to the Dark Tower and the benevolent presence which aids the Losers Club in defeating It, at least *in the novel*. When the mini-series of *IT* made its way to television, the role of the Turtle all but diminished, which in turn eliminated the primary connection between this version of King's tale to *The Dark Tower*. As the dilemma of content and establishing, as well as reaffirming, the connections between *The Dark Tower* and King's other works remain as an obstacle for any potential director to trudge through, the concession to be made here is that any film adaptation of *The Dark Tower* will undoubtedly be seen as a stand-alone project, one that supersedes the intentional links among King's writing, which would likely defeat the purpose of the fiction itself in functioning as a lynchpin to King's canon, much like how the Dark Tower holds together time and existence in *The Dark Tower*.

Before *The Dark Tower* can be made into a film or mini-series, there is the graphic novel adaptation of this series produced by Marvel to discuss in terms of adaptation and its placement among King's canon. Although one can certainly appreciate King's openness to experimentation with a new medium for his tale, there are those who are dissatisfied with this new endeavor. With the graphic novel being dependent upon illustrations to forward the story in question, King may have intended to simply give his readers what they desired: an extension of the *Dark Tower* series, one that provides additional tales to supplement the original tales and additional visual depictions of the scenes and characters to aid the mind's eye in envisioning all that readers have come to know quite well through several thousand pages of reading. Aside from questions of art and its placement alongside fiction, which will be discussed at length in the second chapter of this volume, one might wonder as to why readers would want to read a graphic novel version of *Wizard and Glass*, especially one which drastically condenses the plot to the point of near incoherence. Regardless of the reasons for creating this latest installment of *The Dark Tower*, the story of Roland Deschain, like the rest of King's canon, continues to expand. And as this tale, much like the gunslinger's eternal quest, further develops, one can only wonder what King will reveal to his Constant Reader, or if the *Dark Tower*'s constant expansion will determine its final literary resting place: an anomaly, an experiment, or an attempt at crafting and re-crafting a distinguished fiction worthy of higher regard.

King's Future: What Does He Have Left to Prove?

After thirty years of successful publication, one might wonder what King has left to prove, not so much for his audience, but for himself. After mastering the horror genre, King may wish to continue his growth as a writer, constantly seeking new literary innovations and new themes in order to broaden his craft and solidify his legacy. As the tale of Roland Deschain returns to the Mohaine Desert where readers first discover the gunslinger, a return to the very first page and first sentence of the first book, the circular structure of this tale has continued to branch out, or rather, the tale has continued to draw in King's newer works: the reference to Charlie the Choo-Choo in *Cell* is but one example of the constant pull Mid-World holds over King's fiction, as is the alternative reality Boo'ya Moon in *Lisey's Story* as one that mirrors the multi-verse explored in *The Dark Tower* and the Territories of *The Talisman* and *Black House*. Although King claims that, "like it or hate it, the story of Roland is now done," the Constant Reader would do well to consider that he lies ("Introduction" xviii). With the *Dark Tower* series completed and King finished with his writing of this tale, "although perhaps not forever; the hand that tells the tales has a mind of its own, and a way of growing restless," his audience can still revisit Mid-World and enjoy a story that demands a second reading (King, *The Dark Tower* 817). Upon reading the first, and last, line King writes in *The Dark Tower*—"The man in black fled across the desert, and the gunslinger followed"—the circle that forms certainly asks that the future of Roland and his new journey be experienced again and again (*The Gunslinger* 3). It is not difficult to believe that readers will continue to follow Roland well into the future; after all, as Roland's quest for the Dark Tower appears to have no end, it would be a noble homage to King for his series to have a never-ending readership whether or not King hears the call of the Dark Tower once again, telling him that the journey may not quite be finished.

And as far as the academic is concerned, one could easily consider a tale with the largeness of the *Dark Tower* series to be a windfall for scholarship and criticism. It remains to be seen, however, if this series will draw in students and professors the way it has drawn in readers, especially those who are not considered to be among King's Constant Reader

Introduction

as the *Dark Tower* has attracted readers who are often not entirely familiar with the rest of King's fictional universe. Speculations and question of readership aside, attention now shifts to the function of genre, art, evil and intertextuality in *The Dark Tower*, which are only four of the numerous mysteries that lay behind the door to the Dark Tower.

The Ending Is Only
the Beginning:
Genre and Its Influence
on Climax

"*I'm like one of the old people's robots*, he thought. *One that will either accomplish the task for which it has been made or beat itself to death trying*" — Roland Deschain, from *The Dark Tower*

PERHAPS THE ONE QUESTION that is left in the mind of Stephen King's Constant Reader at the conclusion of the *Dark Tower* series is whether or not Roland Deschain will achieve some sort of victory at the end of his quest in that the gunslinger has repeated and resumed his quest many times before, losing his friends, lovers and even his own children while journeying for at least one-thousand years. With each renewal of Roland's quest to seek the Dark Tower, the world moves on and Roland brings with him not only a past that is nearly forgotten, if not presumed to be dead, but a sense of hope that he just might find something different than the sands of the Mohaine Desert behind the final door at the top of the Tower, the one marked "Roland." The gunslinger's near-eternal existence — "*May I be brutally frank?* You go on" — and his never-ending adventure keeps readers constantly wondering if Roland will ever find solace and if the world(s) must live on until he discovers whatever it is he needs to find in order to permanently keep the Dark Tower stable and safe from threat (King, *The Dark Tower* 828). But even among this repetition, the circular nature of *The Dark Tower* series that asks the Constant Reader to revisit the gunslinger's story, examining the text for clues as to how Roland may truly find an ending leads to the question as to why he seeks the Tower. Or, more to the point, for what *ending* does the gunslinger journey? To attempt finding an answer to this question, genre becomes the focus of this discussion.

Analysis of the various genres King employs in the composition of the *Dark Tower* story points towards some of the answers sought as examinations of the themes and formulas found within the distinct genres outlines reasonable expectations of Roland's quest, especially in terms of the tale's climax. Even though it has been suggested that, "*The Dark Tower's* generic and thematic impulses, in fact, typically disrupt the reader's pattern of expectations, offering him questions, not solutions," the search for at least an indication as to the overarching purpose and scope of Roland's quest is not unfounded or entirely quixotic (Egan, "Gothic Western" 100). Instead, the search for answers, albeit shrouded in mystery, speculation, skepticism and doubt, takes the curious reader down several paths towards termination points that may not necessarily be the original envisioned destinations desired by King. Yet, each generic route provides vital considerations for attempting to understand why the last gunslinger ventures into the waste lands and on to the Dark Tower of both his dreams and nightmares.

In attempting to answer the inquiry as to why Roland pushes on to find the Dark Tower, beyond the feeble suggestion that he must do so because Maerlyn's Grapefruit told him to do so as implied in *Wizard in Glass*, the various genres King employs in creating this tale provide a clue. But, it should be noted use of various genres in *The Dark Tower* has been a mild point of contention and worry instead of being seen as a pathway to some sort of interpretive conclusion. For example, one such criticism of the genres at use in the *Dark Tower* describes results of this experimentation as a rather strange creation, even by King's standards: "its choice of form and genre, its interweaving of reality and fantasy, and the backgrounds of its composition all break from King's norm, making *DT* an unusual book, even for a master of the unusual" (Collings and Engebreston 99). In conjunction with this, one book review of the third book in the series comments that, "*The Waste Lands* seems at times an uncertain hybrid of horror and fantasy," suggesting that the experimental implementation of genre King weaves into this story does not always succeed (Nicholls BR14). Considering how many types of fiction follow a general template, or, as Northrop Frye states that, "both literature and mathematics proceed from postulates, not facts," the formulas that King uses and alters clarifies the direction of Roland's journey (351). In short, if the various steps of a particular genre can be examined and applied to *The Dark Tower* and its ending, the expected conclusion within this selected genre becomes known, as well as the requirements that need to be fulfilled in order to reach such an end. With this approach, the first step is to isolate a genre, examine its structure and its expected ending, and not only see if Roland's tale fits within the framework, but also how the steps leading to the ending help to explain the rationale for endeavoring to accomplish the goal in question.

With King employing many genres in weaving together the gunslinger's tale with several variations and deviations, it is a moot point to simply say that the *Dark Tower* series is part Epic, part Western, part Gothic, part Post-Apocalyptic, and part Science Fiction and then show how the themes and markers of each genre can be identified in the work. For that matter, Linda Badley claims that, "King exploits the power of archetypes. He tells ancient stories, filtering them through modern Gothic and fantasy conventions" (102). Links between King and, say, Shakespeare and even the Greeks are not uncommon among scholarship on his writings, and, surely, such connections can be found within most any writer's fiction. But the sense of apprehensiveness that resonates in Badley's observation certainly suggests a lack of originality in King's writing, or at least a critique of his manipulation of the reading public by, presumably, presenting old tales under new guises. Yet, as James Egan suggests that, "in the broadest sense, a formula story provides its readers with 'a clear and reassuring regularity' and follows a straightforward and fairly predictable pattern of expectations," *The Dark Tower* series is noted as a collection of books that hardly follows any strict pattern, at least in the sense of genre, and further indicates a sense of inventiveness in King's writing ("Gothic Western" 100). Therefore, it is reasonable to conclude that with a heightened awareness of the genres King uses in the *Dark Tower* series, it can be better speculated as to what the outcome of Roland's quest might be due to the expectations each generic formula raises. In sum, within the many genres King writes into his tale, alongside the subsequent adherence to and manipulation of these templates, there is an answer waiting regarding to what the gunslinger's quest is aimed. However, it must be noted that some paths that are to be unveiled under the genres used in *The Dark Tower* are more revealing than others.

Preliminary Foundations

One of the earliest realizations any reader of *The Dark Tower* series comes to is that the story is an atypical work in that it does not easily or readily fit into just one genre. Readers start with a gunslinger, a cowboy apparently of the American West, but as the story moves on, it is discovered that the main character (the term "protagonist" is hesitantly used to describe Roland at any point in the story) lived his childhood in a medieval setting in which remnants of broken technology indicate an old and broken world. More to the point, James Egan notes of *The Dark Tower* that, "King's work can, perhaps, best be characterized as a blend of anti-technological science fiction, gothic horror motifs and dystopian premises" ("Technohorror" 48). But without any solid framework, or lenses, to guide an initial reading of the text, mystery is all that surrounds the tale. Suspense may be built into the tale through such vagueness, but the overwhelming ambiguity of the first book in King's series, *The Gunslinger*, whether in terms of defining and isolating genre or developing the characters, leads to several inquiries about the story, one of which is sustained all throughout Roland's journey: why does he seek the tower? A general response to this question is Heidi Stregell's assertion that, "King seems unwilling and unable to offer straightforward solutions to his protagonists' problems and spiritual ponderings" (120). Ambiguity and lack of clarity, of course, can be a part of the joy and journey of reading any book as it is not the author's job to give the reader all the answers. Then again, when facing questions of motive in fiction, readers can usually find answers within the text. But with King's *Dark Tower* series, Roland's motive is a mystery that equals the mystery of the Dark Tower itself.

An ideal place to begin with this discussion is Robert Browning's poem "Childe Roland to the Dark Tower Came" as it is the piece on which King's tale is essentially dependent. King references much of Browning's enigmatic poem in the story of Roland Deschain — his companion Cuthbert, the "hoary cripple with malicious eye" (Joe Collins/

Dandelo), and the anticipated winding of the slug-horn at the very end of the quest by the adventurer — but Browning's poem is just as problematic, if not more so, than King's story (line 2). Since the 1855 publication of this poem in Browning's collection *Men and Women*, literary scholars still have not derived a generally unifying interpretation of the piece. Still, some aspects of the poem are helpful as a starting point in the discussion on King's story. For an initial and general comparison between the two works and their respective adventurers, Heidi Strengell suggests that,

> Browning's protagonist has spent his adolescence dreaming of and training for the sight of the Tower. As a persevering knight, he presses toward this goal, disregarding the mental and physical dangers that he faces. King's Roland, too, seeks a vision he neither understands nor precisely knows where or how to pursue [120].

Here it should be noted that each Roland is introduced as an individual on journey; nothing more, nothing less. The reader in each case is immediately left with many questions to ponder through the duration of the adventure. Who charged each individual with the quest is unknown, motive remains unseen, and the overarching goal of the quest is never stated. However, readers of King's tale begin to understand why Roland thinks he must travel to the Dark Tower in the fourth book, *Wizard and Glass*, after Roland recovers from his first look into pink Wizard's Glass: "'the Tower is crumbling, and if it falls, everything we know will be swept away. There will be chaos beyond our imagining. We must go ... *and we will go*'" (King 581). Although it is actually quite foolish for Roland to wholeheartedly believe something he saw in the Wizard's Rainbow, it can be concluded that Roland gives *himself* the quest of saving the Dark Tower. In *The Gunslinger* Roland says of his quest that, "'To find the Tower is my purpose. I'm sworn,'" which does gain some context by way of the graphic novel *The Gunslinger Born* in which it is revealed that Arthur Eld's descendants are charged with protecting the Dark Tower (King 228). But, without the information provided in the graphic novel, the gunslinger's justifications for his quest beg the question as to why Roland swore, exactly to what he swore, and even if the act of locating the Tower is enough to satisfy the conditions of his journey, which once again raises the question as to *why* he seeks the tower.

Roland, like King's Constant Reader, may not entirely understand *what* he pursues, but in examining the thematic boundaries of his tale, and in looking at Roland as a crossbreed hero, readers are taken closer to an answer as to *why* he seeks the Tower, and, why the story ends as it does, with repetition, which hardly seems to be a conclusion informed by any genre.

The "Epic" Formula — Questions of Duty

The beginning point for analyzing the various genres and literary formulas at work in the *Dark Tower* series is with the classical, or rather the epic tale. Although many of the elements to be discussed fall into other categories, such as myth or romance, the term "epic" will serve as a meeting place, in name only, for these closely related variations in genre. To start, Thomas Greene suggests that, "the first quality of the epic imagination is expansiveness" (194). Immediately, this can be applied to Roland's quest as his journey for the Tower is for *all* of the worlds, not just his own. And as the stature of the epic quest suggests the importance of Roland's adventure, readers are nonetheless at a loss as to why Roland is the one chosen to undertake this important journey, and also why several others all fall while the gunslinger survives. Still, the gunslinger's continued existence and persistence in his quest can be explained, by the epic formula to which King adheres in places, as suggested by David A. Miller who says that, "a barebones scenario for the [epic] hero and his part in the quest would be: Someone extraordinary/ Goes or is sent/ To search for and retrieve/ Something important" (162). As Roland travels into the dangerous lands outside of Gilead to search for the Dark Tower, the nexus of space and time, it can be argued that Roland is merely following suit with respect to what is expected of a hero on an epic journey. Yet, is Roland an extremely special or an unusually endowed individual? *If* he is indeed such a character, one might see why he seeks the Tower: he simply has the mettle and wherewithal to undertake such a journey, and someone has recognized this in Roland thereby charging him with the quest, quite possibly just for the sake of the challenge. The story within the pages of the *Dark Tower* series, however, does not present Roland as this character, with the exception of his skills with a gun, but even this minute aspect of Roland's character hardly makes him extraordinary.

Expectations of Roland's position and status may be a bit over-whelming and exaggerated, but it cannot be denied that the gunslinger is, at the very least, one of the best "draws" who has ever lived. Roland's ka-mates — Cuthbert, Alain and Jamie DeCurry — all cannot believe how skilled he is with a revolver, but does this mean that Roland is truly extraordinary? Not at all, since, "the hero is always, *and must be*, a prodigy at weapon play," which suggests that the skills which mark Roland as not only a gunslinger but also an uncommon hero are simply expected of a man in his position and can be considered as normal within the epic scope (Miller 206, emphasis added). On the other hand, Roland is imparted with intriguing knowledge concerning his person when he resumes his quest at the end of book seven — "*You darkle, you tinct*" — suggesting an eternal nature exceeding the normal human boundaries which forces reconsideration of Roland's epic aptitude (King, *The Dark Tower* 828). Roland's state of near-immortality does place Roland in the company of the divine, but the source of Roland's almost-eternal exis-tence is neither extraordinary nor noble. Roland's repetitious journey and subsequent near-immortal status, stemming from one failure or another, is not a reward for an exceptional person who has lived an exceptional life, and his lengthy lifespan can neither be seen as an indicator of great-ness nor divinity, meaning that he is certainly not a noble warrior with god-like powers, meaning that he fails to live up to the epic expectation of a hero. Even holding to a more basic outline of the epic hero's quest which consists of, "departure/separation, initiation, and reintegration," there are still problems with the epic as a lens of reading *The Dark Tower* because Roland never truly becomes reintegrated into his world, espe-cially as resumption is not the same thing as reintegration (Strengell 121). Only once does Roland fulfill the requirements of this epic template: as a young man he leaves for Mejis, becomes initiated as a gunslinger with the defeat of Eldred Jonas and George Latigo, and then gloriously returns to Gilead. But this microcosmic triumph does not align with the impor-tance of epic size, and with Roland failing to fit within the basic formu-las of the epic quest, a shift in focus towards smaller components, such as the role of the hero within the epic framework, reveals more of the gunslinger's aims.

While conceiving of Roland Deschain as a remarkable hero is problematic, it cannot be assumed that Roland's quest is already out of the realm of the epic and that the climax of *The Dark Tower* is therefore inexplicable through this genre. In acknowledging King's deviation from the divine or wondrous protagonist as an acceptable move away from the expected formula of the epic hero, David A. Miller provides the following as an alternative guide as to what is reasonably expected of an epic hero on an epic quest:

> 1. The hero is unique and isolate. His mark is his strong and deadly arm, but a particular quest may demand a hero of cooperative venturing[...].
> 2. The hero is devoted to combat and confrontation: he must be prepared to seek out, or at least never avoid, those aspects of the quest[...]. He is both physically and morally prepared for such violence: a risk taker, superlatively courageous, honorable, single-minded in purpose — and probably, or necessarily, without much imagination. 3. The hero is detached from cultural and social place, is mobile and uncommonly swift [...] easily capable of taking up the challenge posed by time and distance in this world or another. 4. Precisely because the hero is easily detached from the social matrix, he is often as dangerous to the social fabric as he is useful in defending it. Indeed, in the end, he is more useful outside of society and displaying his excellence elsewhere — that is, on a quest [163–4].

While there are already reservations of denoting Roland as extraordinary, he is certainly distinctive in that he is a grudgingly likable antihero who kills his own mother and still earns the trust of his companions. Among all that, his nemesis Walter speaks of Roland's mind as truly unique: "'Your mind. Your slow, prodding, tenacious mind. There has never been one quite like it, in all the history of the world. Perhaps in the history of creation'" (King, *The Gunslinger* 228). As far as isolate, readers of the *Dark Tower* series find Roland on both page one of *The Gunslinger* and the last page of *The Dark Tower* all alone; and as the action between these pages is concerned, Roland may find people to accompany him along the way, but he admits to his companions Eddie, Susannah and Jake that, "'I am not a full member of this *ka-tet*'" which suggests that Roland's friends do not negate his isolation (King, *The Waste Lands* 259). Despite Roland's detachment from this group, they are necessary for his quest, which, according to Miller's model, is not uncommon. But as Roland adds to this when he says that, "'It may take a great many *ka-tets* to finish one picture,'" he suggests that the epic quality of isolation is not the key or the way to the Tower (King, *The Waste Lands* 259). To finish this line of thought on the role of the companion(s), Miller adds that, "The hero frequently has partners, companions, as a supporting cast *fitted* to his feats" (102, emphasis added). Roland might call it *ka* in order to explain the adept nature of his companions, but he is nonetheless a solitary individual who incidentally finds companions along the way and finds use for them as they are supposedly a part of his ka, people who serve particular functions for the larger story, or quest.

The second of Miller's heroic traits is the most interesting and telling of the four elements listed. With the epic hero "devoted to combat and confrontation," this is easily seen as a part of the gunslinger's code especially as the events in Calla Bryn Sturgis and Algul Siento play out. What is prominent about Miller's point is that the hero who faces danger without consideration of retreat does so as a matter of course, almost without thinking of any other option. In Roland's case, he does not travel to the Tower out of a sense of morality or even from a semblance of medieval chivalry. Roland's adventure moves out of the romantic offshoot of the epic as he is not one who follows the romantic form which, "purges life of impurities and presents chivalry in heightened and idealized form" (Pearsall 21). Assuredly, the gunslinger does not necessarily seek salvation or to heroically serve his fellow man; instead of functioning as a character who performs good deeds for the sake of securing a sense of nobility for his own character, Roland blindly journeys for the Dark Tower, and as this building draws him on, he becomes further separated from the romantic hero as romantic, "action has no external motivation" (Pearsall 22). As the distinctly epic hero whose motivation is not intrinsic and is aligned with Miller's second epic trait of being "single-minded in purpose — and probably, or necessarily, without much imagination" which describes Roland quite accurately — "'You have no imagination. You are blind that way'"— this purpose-driven individual melts into Miller's third point which says that the epic hero is culturally detached and able to move quickly from place to place; such would be easy, if not expected, of an individual who has a goal and whose field of vision focuses solely on achieving such an end (King, *The Gunslinger* 219). Last, as Miller says that the hero's position outside of society makes him a potential threat, the discussion arrives at a proposition that seems to fit Roland quite well.

As an outcast, as a loner who comes from a forgotten time, the gunslinger's anachronistic character is seen as a threat to the modernity of Mid-World as he brings outdated ideals to the world at large, but also has the guns and resolve to enforce his own incongruous views. As Miller suggests that the socially dangerous epic hero best serves his world on a quest, therefore consistently placed outside of the community walls, one must consider exactly what this means with respect to Roland's quest, especially if the purpose of Roland's constant questing is to keep him from inflicting harm on those he believes that he is sworn to protect.

As long as Roland continually resumes his quest, and succeeds in saving the Tower each time, then it appears that his purpose is to keep the Tower well and safeguarded, and maybe even for the well-being of all existence. This allows him to be truly beneficial for the world in which he lives because he constantly strives to save its existing communities. Yet, two critical issues arise which the benevolence of Roland's constant questing into question. First, as Roland repeats his journey for the Tower, the world has, "moved on since then. The world had emptied," which is to say that each repetition of Roland's quest does not truly begin back in the Mohaine Desert on the trail of the Man in Black *for the first time* (King, *The Gunslinger* 3). Each time Roland ends up back in the sands of the West and on the trail of the Man in Black, time has slipped away as evidenced by the assertions that Gilead is long gone to destruction and not recently brought to ruin. And Mid-World, as well as the universe, must endure continual existence, for good or ill, until Roland determines how to avoid repetition of his quest. As Roland repeats each quest, and as time slips forward each time, it is reasonable to believe that each journey is just a little bit different, with different players and different outcomes along the path which leads to the Dark Tower. When Roland resumes his quest, the world moves on and he does not begin at the true start, with the people of Tull still alive, Blaine still waiting in Lud, and Donald Callahan still traveling the highways in hiding. The next time through there will likely be no Allie, no Jake, no Andy the Robot — all have passed on, and have left Roland alone to find a new path to the Tower and with new companions who will most likely bear uncanny resemblances to Roland's former friends; Roland will remember Cuthbert, Alain and Jamie de Curry, but it is not far fetched to think that he will *not* remember Eddie, Jake and Susannah.

1. The Ending Is Only the Beginning

What this all implies is that while Roland journeys, supposedly serving his country to the best of his abilities by removing himself from the society to which he is a threat, he in turn endangers more and more people each and every time he travels only to climb the Tower and goes through the door at the top marked "Roland." As long as the gunslinger is on his quest, death and destruction will result; the danger may not be faced by the society of which Roland is no longer included, but death does result for others, which makes readers question whose lives are worth more. Perhaps death of those who reside outside of Roland's community is what he is to avoid in a successful trek to the Tower, thereby providing validity to Miller's last criterion of the epic hero regarding the gunslinger in that most everyone must benefit from the perpetual adventure of the hero. But, Roland is a constant threat to the general well-being of everyone whether he is questing or not, which suggests that Roland is not an epic hero and that his purpose cannot then be understood by means of the epic genre.

In a stark contrast to what has been proposed thus far, Heidi Strengell offers the view that Roland is a selfless individual whose journey does benefit humanity rather than serving as an imposition, one that situates *The Dark Tower* well within an epic framework. Strengell says, "As I see it, Roland chooses responsibility for humankind over personal wishes," but the extent of Roland's responsibility, especially for that of human kind, can be easily dispelled by his never-ending pursuit for the Tower (122). His reason for saving the Beams and thus the Tower does not stem from a deep-seated emotional tie to humanity; Roland only saves the Tower because it is his *duty* as a gunslinger, and because he feels the need to understand the Tower and enter it, which is a symptom of the epic genre as, "epic answers man's need to clear away an area he can comprehend, *if not dominate*" (Greene 194, emphasis added). Also to recall is that the duty that Roland has fulfilled comes as a matter of course as, "the central realities of heroic literature are not to love or honour but loyalty to one's kin or leader, revenge, and the imperative necessity of asserting self (especially self as embodying a nation or people) through acts of power" (Pearsall 21). As Roland cries the names of the fallen once he reaches the Dark Tower, he acknowledges that he has fulfilled his duty as a gunslinger, as a citizen of Gilead, as dinh of his ka-tet, and that his allegiance to his quest and his people has endured as he has accomplished the impossible by reaching the Dark Tower for the sake of those who have fallen during his quest. With this in mind, it should be concluded that Roland's quest is not a moral voyage at all. Besides, Roland's overarching indifference to death would seem to dispel any notions that he is worried about those who he encounters along the Path of the Beam as, "the hero deals in death, and for the most part he accepts that death will be his inescapable portion" (Miller 120). Or, when Roland says, "We deal in lead," he does not deny guilt and remorse as related to death and murder, but he does acquiesce to the necessity of death in his quest, which contradicts the overall scope of the epic quest, a seeking to ensure life instead of ending it (King, *Wolves of the Calla* 111).

Roland's desire to reach the Tower must be done so at any cost, and his responsibility for humankind is to contend with them in a manner that will ultimately help *him* along on *his* quest. After all, what is Jake to Roland but a means to an end, especially in the first book, despite Roland's evolving emotions and tearful goodbyes witnessed in later volumes? Heidi Strengell believes that Roland's initial relationship with Jake should be seen differently: "By sacrificing Jake, Roland has made himself worthy of a dream vision of the Tower and earned the right to continue the quest" (131). However, Roland's sacrifice of Jake does not make him worthy of any such reward; if anything, it justifies Walter's attempt to mentally ruin Roland through the vision of the cosmos at the golgotha in *The Gunslinger*. Roland had a choice regarding Jake Chamber's life, and the sacrifice of an individual for information is anything but noble. Also to consider is that Roland's journey(s) to the Tower need not take place on a single road. If anything, deviations from the path seen in the seven books of the *Dark Tower* would bode well for Roland in any future journey to the Tower. Therefore, Roland does not need to sacrifice Jake, or anyone else for that matter. So, does Roland venture forth to vanquish the evil tyrant for his king and his kingdom? Is the sacrifice of Jake worth the loss as a means for Roland to prove himself as a knightly figure merely performing the duty assigned to him out of a sense of honor for those he serves? If so, then it would seem that Roland's quest fulfills the ultimate goal of the epic quest: performing one's duty. But, seeing that Roland's journey has not entirely fit within this epic framework thus far, it should be little surprise to see that

Roland's quest, after all, is not reasoned or intended to be out of duty despite what he tells his companions and the reader.

Roland neither embarks on his journey out of a duty to a land that has passed nor for any sort of tribute or attempt at securing a particular reputation. Before the graphic novel versions of *The Dark Tower* were written, the original texts proposed that Roland charged himself with his quest, and that his duty was only to himself, which is an inversion of the gunslinger code as learned within the culture of Gilead. Roland also does not quest for the Tower for the sake of honor: storming the Tower, and even halting the destruction of Gan's navel, is not done for the sake of any one person, any one city, and neither is this quest undergone due to allegiance to an individual or an ideal nor is it for the sake of Roland's own personal distinction. While fame may be the goal for some epic heroes, as some might, "assume that the hero usually but very dramatically dies in the earnest hope of a kind of survival or even a persistence close to immortality, as a name to live on in fame and glory," Roland does not charge himself with saving the Dark Tower to restore a lost sense of nobility or to negate his infamous deeds as a youth, like sacrificing Susan Delgado and killing his own mother, Gabrielle (Miller 131). Were Roland truly an epic hero, one devoted to duty and the preservation of the well-being of the kingdom, he could be considered a champion of sorts. With this distinction, however, it must be understood that, "the first role of the hero as *champion* is to stand for the king; he is the hero festered into the structure of kingship, usually placed between the sovereign and external threat, or sometimes taking the place of the king" (Miller 182). But Roland does not necessarily function as a champion for any king or kingdom. Of course, Roland's homeland of Gilead is the land to which he feels a connection with, and a land for which he performs many of his questionable duties, especially as readers recall his war-cry in *Wolves of the Calla*: "'*For Gilead and the Calla*'" (King 679). Yet, it is impossible for Roland to fight for a land that has been dead for centuries; Roland may fight for the *memory* of Gilead, but he cannot claim that he truly fights for a land which lies in ruin, a place that, "has been dust in the wind for a thousand years" (King, *Wolves of the Calla* 30). In sum, Roland and his heroic quest may fulfill some of the epic requirements mentioned, and may merge into other similar genres, but his failure to adequately fulfill other expectations proves to be too problematic for utilizing the epic genre as a means of understanding the purpose of his quest.

Westward Expansion — In the Name of Civilization

When readers first meet the gunslinger on the trail of the Man in Black, he is witnessed as walking through the Mohaine Desert on the edge of civilization. Immediately, the reader begins to think that a Western is about to unfold finding a gun-toting cowboy leading a mule through a land that only shows smatterings of life: "He had passed the last town three weeks before, and since then there had only been the deserted coach track and an occasional huddle of border dweller's sod dwellings" (King, *The Gunslinger* 8). The sporadic and desolate presence of life and sparse civilization gives the story a Western feel as, "obviously, the Western takes place in the West, near the frontier," but more interesting to note is that Roland and his fellow gunslingers from Gilead always feared being banished from civilization, sent to the west and out of their homeland as failures (Egan, "Gothic Western" 96). Here, unfortunately, is the first problem with the Western formula: instead of encountering the promise of an underdeveloped land in need of the order and direction that a gunslinger cherishes and champions, the West of Roland's world is anything but a bastion of budding civilization. Instead, the West is a place for outlaws and failed gunslingers. In other words, as James Egan notes, "one expects clarity in a formula Western, but this is not the case with *The Dark Tower*" ("Gothic Western" 99). And while the formula of the Western is in some disarray when it comes to *The Dark Tower*, especially as the West is a locale of shame and of figurative darkness in the *Dark Tower* series, the Western formula does not completely fail in its potential in illuminating the gunslinger's ultimate ends. Or, at the very least, early problems noted in the Western should not halt an examination on this genre.

Although the West of Roland's world deviates from the ideal frontier of the stereotypical Western, much of the geographical aspects of *The Dark Tower* are undeveloped and in need of order. With this, Roland's presence becomes necessary in this setting as, "the Western hero of the early dime novels typically functions as an agent of civilization" (Jones 26). The frontier of Roland's West may not fit the expected mold of the American frontier, especially as the land has been inhabited before Roland arrives as evidenced by the abandoned technology found at the desert way station and beneath the Cyclopean Mountains. Yet Roland can function as a Western hero in that he comes from civilization and whose presence may prove to be advantageous to those living in the borderlands. Still, caution must be exercised in accepting Roland's perception of what constitutes civilization. Much like how the civilization of the Old Ones dies out due to overwhelming scientific innovation accompanied by a sense of hubris, the civilization which Roland represents and adheres to is long gone. Roland's role as a man of the civilized world who has come to spread a civilized way of life may be nothing more than a mirror-image of Randall Flagg's quest for dominance as clearly seen at the end of *The Stand* when the defeated demon stares down upon a new mass of people: "*They are simple folk. Primitive; simple; unlettered. But I can use them. Yes, I can use them perfectly well*" (King 1138). Flagg then goes on to say to his new herd, "'I've come to teach you how to be civilized,'" and the use of civilization as a means of dominance and control is seen, all of which Roland is guilty of using to further his quest, especially in marking his guns as machines of a civilization that has passed on yet which still exhibit a talismanic quality that affords a position of power (King, *The Stand* 1141). Roland is definitely known to most everyone he meets in Mid-World, identified as a gunslinger by the sandalwood grips of his firearms which tends to trigger a response of obedience or even reverence. But, Roland cannot be a man of civilization, its representative, when said civilization no longer exists.

Regardless of his failure to function as a representative of civilization, Roland can still fulfill the role of the Western hero in that he often acts on behalf of a town or a group of citizens who cannot defend themselves. And like the epic hero, many Western heroes employ a sidekick to aid in these harrowing situations, which Roland attains during his travels. With respect to the hero's role in the Western as a protector of sorts is the observation that, "the hero himself seldom stays to participate in the functions of that system he has helped to establish," and in a similar fashion, Roland, the champion of Calla Bryn Sturgis, and even Blue Heaven, moves on once his task is finished in each locale (Westbrook

39). Still, the Western hero serves as more than just a hired gun as Heidi Strengell suggests that, "in his roles as a diplomat, a mediator, a teacher, and a soldier, Roland does not depart from the Western hero archetype" (126). However, Roland's roles as diplomat and mediator are questionable. While Roland does act as a protector of the Rose in New York City and as a soldier for the people of Calla Bryn Sturgis, consider James Egan's assertion that, "at no point does he act as a mediator between conflicting groups, nor does he perceive himself as one. The essence of a formulaic definition of a Western hero, therefore, does not apply to Roland" ("Gothic Western" 99–100). Perhaps the quest of the Tower in and of itself prevents Roland from filling the role of the small-town hero as, "Roland and his quest go beyond the microcosmic battle of the Western to the macrocosmic proportions of myth" (Strengell 135). Roland may don a cowboy hat, wear weathered boots and carry the old-style revolvers of his father, but he is only a shadow of the Western hero. Still, the size of Roland's quest, beyond the small town and his departure from the triumphant and diplomatic hero of the people, suggests that within the Western formula the conclusion, the purpose of Roland's quest, overshadows the menial events of the common folk. Although Roland's quest occasionally necessitates the safety of the small town like Calla Bryn Sturgis, the safety of the Calla-folken is merely a means to an end as Roland needs to save the citizens of this town to ensure that the Tower remains standing for him to storm it. Whereas the Western hero might be satisfied with a job well done in the dusty streets of a dilapidated town, Roland decides to move on and forego celebration because there is more work to be accomplished, like the chase of the Man in Black.

Within the plot of the Western, pursuit constantly draws the protagonist on, which is present in the *Dark Tower* series as James Egan notes that, "first and foremost, the plot involves pursuit: Roland intends to learn the Man in Black's secrets by tracking him down" ("Gothic Western" 98). Roland's hunt for the Man in Black, and even the Tower, may be what pulls Roland away from any meaningful connection with the people he meets during his journey, so one may be able to neglect the fact that Roland escapes the microcosmic stature of the Western *hero* as he fulfills one of the formulaic aspects of the Western *plot* in his pursuit of the Man in Black. But, before Roland chases the Man in Black, he is supposed to have been a part of at least two other components of the Western novel: "In the dime novel adventure usually derives from a recurrent pattern of capture, flight, and pursuit" (Jones 137). Roland does fit within this pattern as he was captured in Mejis, only to be later freed by Susan Delgado and pursued Eldred Jonas. Also, Roland is later captured by the Little Sisters of Eluria and again escapes only to return to his pursuit of the Man in Black, who is caught by the gunslinger yet not necessarily captured. But, the plot of *The Gunslinger* and the rest of the *Dark Tower* books break the Western pattern mentioned in that pursuit becomes the most consistent and highlighted element of his quest, which does not assist with fully understanding Roland's quest in light of his constant pursuit of the Tower.

Although the West of Roland's world has been previously described as being in violation of the prescribed frontier of a typical Western, providing little assistance with the overall goal of discovering the purpose of the gunslinger's quest, a few pieces of Roland's tale can be placed into the Western template to better understand his journey by way of generic analysis. First, as the frontier has a tendency towards unrest and criminal activity; it is a place without order despite its resemblance to or attempt at forming some sort of community. And in Roland's West, the promise of civilization looks to be impossible to bring about as the primary culture is gone and dead. Yet, the disorder and chaos of Roland's West calls for attention, if not for the creation of a new society but for the sake of order. And order, whether in reference to a town or the Tower, just may be Roland's true purpose. With this notion of order, in conjunction with Heidi Strengell suggestion that, "the Slow Mutants and the residents of Lud [act] as the Indians or the outlaws," one might anticipate these characters as the general threat to stability in this underdeveloped landscape (127). Moreover, Roland himself proposes the idea that these outlaws and their rampages have benefited from the decay of the Dark Tower and that his quest for the Tower is not only about restoring the Tower itself but the land and its people as well. With the degeneration of the White, and the fall of Gilead and the kingdoms of the light, the Slow Mutants, the warring Pubes and Grays, or even the Wolves and those under the rule of the Crimson King all have risen to a dangerous level of power, which not only threatens various communities and the existence of peaceful people like those of River Crossing and Calla Bryn Sturgis but also the entire world. Roland's quest to save the Tower and halt the discord which is strewn all over his world may then be seen as a move to re-civilize the world. If this were true, it is tempting to embrace Daryl Jones's assertion that, "the Western may be viewed as a narrative construct whose unifying principle is the Western hero's quest to reorder reality in terms of his own vision of the ideal world" (137). But if Roland is attempting to bring a new order to the world, a new promise of civilization, it is likely that Roland is hoping to bring about *his* own view of what the ideal world should be, which suggests that this exercise of dominion and even authority is his ultimate goal.

Roland's conception of the ideal world would, of course, be highly subjective and likely take the reader and the citizens of Mid-World back to an age similar to that of Gilead; it is what Roland knows and what he mourns, which seems as likely of a goal for him than anything else. The promise of such a renewal may urge Roland on in his quest, but a quest to re-shape the world according to his own vision takes the reader from civilization and more towards tyrannical exercises of power.Roland's Gilead may have been a distinguished society, but even he cannot be sure that a return to this past is the best move to make and in the interest of *all* involved.

Civilization, in its varied forms and multiple settings, is, however, problematic for Roland's quest for the Tower. Roland's endeavor to restore his land, and even the line of Eld, appears to be a worthy quest, but it may be more appropriate to look to the horizon for a broader climax than the aspiration of re-establishing Gilead. To that end, Daryl Jones claims that, "altered, inverted, even parodied, the popular Western formula nonetheless survives. And it will continue to survive as long as it extends to humanity some glimmer of hope that a golden age still lies ahead" (168). What this suggests is that while civilization is the apparent ultimate end of a Western, *hope* is the key. Roland may *hope* for restoration of his broken world, and Roland's quest does prompt the reader to also hope that Roland will somehow avoid the continuous repetition of his journey coupled with the continued disintegration of Mid-World as the land, like Roland, is constantly moving on and moving forward because in the Keystone Tower world and Keystone Earth, "time [runs] just one way" (King, *The Dark Tower* 473). Additionally, the Horn of Eld does give Roland, and even the reader, a *"promise that things may be different […] that there may yet be rest. Even salvation,"* but while the Constant Reader may be hopeful that Roland's quest will one day come to an end, it is hardly appropriate to consider one man's success as the indication that a golden age is on the horizon (King, *The Dark Tower* 828). A personal golden age for the hero may come to pass, but what is to be reasonably expected of Mid-World's prosperity if Roland does find a way to succeed in his quest, or at least the quest intimated within the Western framework? Of course, Mid-World and its inhabitants would no longer have to endure Roland's treacherous and deadly adventures, but is this really something that can be considered as a golden age?

With the idea of the golden age on the horizon as being the ultimate end of a Western, the previous analysis of the frontier and the role of civilization as elements key to the formulaic climaxes of the Western genre is recalled in that this explanation lacks insight into to Roland's quest and motivations. As it were, if Roland's quest is to fit comfortably into the Western genre, the establishment of a new age would be Roland's goal, and if this was what drives Roland to seek the Tower, the Tower becomes a key to unlocking a new future, especially as Daryl Jones says, "often the plot of the dime novel seems nothing more than fast-paced, loosely connected sequences of fistfights, gunplay and hairbreadth escapes strung out interminably and tied together by a happy ending" (135). But, through all seven books of the *Dark Tower* series, the promise of the "happy ending" is not provided, in that Roland may have deluded himself into thinking that the Tower promises, with its restoration, the coming of a new age.

Without a guarantee of actual prosperity which stems from the survival of the Tower, Roland of Gilead becomes painted as a man who is ultimately out for power, an power unavailable in the Western but is nonetheless desired in order to mold the world according to his whims and even delusions that result in anything but a happy ending. Randall Flagg may have been the only character in the *Dark Tower* series to explicitly display aspirations of becoming the, "God of all," but Roland may not be too far behind (King, *The Dark Tower* 174). But, if the gunslinger is a character who hopes to find a means of shaping the world according to his own designs, he would need a way to accomplish this feat, and the road to this kind of dominance is not found in the realm of the Western.

The Gothic — The Dark Path to Power

Entering the realm of the Gothic, a focus on civilization is left behind with the Western. Within this new framework, that of, "the archaic, the pagan, that which was prior to, or opposed to, or resisted the establishment of civilized values and a well-regulated society," is the genre for which King is primarily known (Punter and Byron 8). Indeed, the *Dark Tower* series resonates with Gothic qualities, especially with the object of Roland's obsession being a dark building that is often portrayed as being a Gothic construction on the various book covers of the series and even in the paintings of the books. Focusing directly on the Gothic nature of the series, though, James Egan says:

> Several of the story's organizing motifs have a Gothic ring to them as well. Roland journeys into the nightland, into the dark side of existence, rather than into the bright sunshine and the Promised Land of the conventional Western. His journey involves a typically Gothic predicament — he sets out into an immense unknown destiny, and that territory is probably expanding, not stationary ["Gothic Western" 101].

Immediately Egan provides several key items of the Gothic novel to work with — the dark, the unknown, and the unstable. Thunderclap is the quintessential "nightland" with it being a land of eternal twilight as suggested by the artificial light beaming down on the Devar-Toi, and the "thinnies" in *Wizard and Glass* serve as evidence of an expanding land, one that even integrates parts of worlds other than Roland's own. In addition, one can reasonably expect Roland's tale to abide by the following guidelines of the Gothic: "In its rejection of moderation, regularity, compromise, simplicity, and stability, Gothicism embraces the erratic, the complex, the convoluted, the excessive, the abnormal" (Bayer-Berenbaun 144). Stated elements of the Gothic are certainly descriptive of Roland's, and Mid-World's, eccentricities, but like with the previous genres, but caution needs to be exercised before embracing the Gothic as the key to the gunslinger's quest.

In noting that, "the word 'Gothic' [...] originally conveyed the idea of barbarous [...] and antique, and was merely a term of reproach and contempt," it would be easy to consider Roland as a Gothic character (Summers 37). The extermination of Tull's citizens certainly helps to attribute a brutish nature to Roland, and as readers learn Roland is, according to Blaine the Mono, a "HATEFUL GUNSLINGER OUT OF A PAST THAT SHOULD HAVE STAYED DEAD," questions of the ancient are easily recognized in the gunslinger (King, *Wizard and Glass* 55). Also to consider:

> Where the classical was well ordered, the Gothic was chaotic; where the classical was simple and pure, Gothic was ornate and convoluted; where the classics offered a world of clear rules and limits, Gothic represented excess and exaggeration, the product of the wild and uncivilized, a world that constantly tended to overflow the cultural boundaries [Punter and Byron 7].

At first glance, the "chaotic," "convoluted," and "wild" side of the Gothic are clearly present in *The Dark Tower*. One need only to walk the streets of Lud to see a lack of order in the broken city, and the Great Western Woods traveled in *The Waste Lands* give a literal and figurative wild in which all things, especially mechanical, have come to ruination. However, if Roland's quest is primarily Gothic, it seems that the Western is appropriately undercut as civilization crumbles within the Gothic genre. But, as the gunslinger's stated goal is to save the Tower, and all the worlds, the inherent wreckage associated with the Gothic creates a dilemma because Roland's journey faces failure in a Gothic template, that which points towards destruction rather than salvation.

To provide an overview of what could be expected in King's tale which has ties to the Gothic and helps to explain Roland's quest, geography is an important focal point. As geographic instability is clearly seen in *The Dark Tower*, confirmation of the Gothic treatment of this theme is noted in the following: "What we find in the numerous conjunctions of Gothic and the post-modern is a certain sliding of location, a series of transfers and translocations from one place to another" (Punter and Byron 51). Instability in the landscape plays out as a constant imposition to Roland's quest, one that implies confirmation in that the Gothic genre is more of a determining presence in *The Dark Tower* series than other seemingly minor genre creations and integrations. In addition to the expansive and tumultuous landscape within the Gothic there is, "a certain attention to the divisions and doublings of the self" (Punter and Byron 51). Simplicity and singularity function as polar opposites to the Gothic which concerns itself with the ornate and various, which leads to the eerie pairings of characters in the *Dark Tower* series — Roland/The

Crimson King; Cuthbert/Eddie; Jake/Alain; Susan/Susannah; Sheemie/Bryan Smith — which suggests that Roland's final confrontation with the Crimson King is one of necessity as Roland must seemingly battle his double and triumph in order to proceed with his quest. Yet, the, "unimaginable final battle" which Roland is destined to fight is only a means to an end and not Roland's ultimate goal (King, *The Gunslinger* 231).

In continuing the search for Roland's purpose, other considerations of the Gothic novel must be looked at, including the suggestion that, "Gothic novelists are particularly fond of hypnotic trances, telepathic communications, visionary experiences, and extrasensory perceptions," which helps to contextualize the paranormal activities witnessed in the *Dark Tower* series as occurrences which may not necessarily be of the science fiction model (Bayer-Berenbaum 25). Even with the allusion to the science fiction aspects of the *Dark Tower* series, there is a Gothic twist added to the extraordinary mental states and scientific innovation as, "discoveries in the scientific only served to aggravate a sense of alienation and further disturb notions of human identity" (Punter and Byron 20). Science then becomes not solely a matter of speculation and the rational but an offshoot of the Gothic as the use of logic and technology leads the people of Mid-World farther and farther away from their own humanity, or what Roland calls the Prim. The Old Ones meet a Gothic ending in that their technology took over their lives and eventually destroyed them, and it is clear that the people behind the Sombra Corporation and North Central Positronics are taking the people of Keystone Earth in the same direction. While this is just one other instance of the repetitious nature of Roland's world and his quest, "for repetition is indeed a feature of many Gothic works," there must be some significant point to these Gothic connections and initial observations (Punter and Byron 284). As the Gothic can be viewed as a genre which fails to adequately sustain itself as something more than just a presence in the *Dark Tower* series, a genre which simply describes many aspects of Roland's journey, there is more to consider with regard to the applicability of this genre to the gunslinger's voyage. With confirmation that unstable geographies, double-identities/characters, exceptional mental abilities, repetition and the dark side of science are all present within the Gothic frame and are all witnessed in Roland's tale, there is most definitely something of importance to the climax of the story that can be concluded with this information.

With a prevalent theme of Roland's story being devoted to the Gothic, it stands to reason that his journey connects with that of the aimless wanderer, one who revels in the chaos and destitution surrounding him despite his sentiments to the contrary. This certainly keeps Roland's adventure in the realm of the Gothic as, "the Gothic quest is for the random, the wild, and the unbound," suggesting that Roland's journey for the Tower has little direction and it takes him from the security of being an apprentice gunslinger in Gilead to the uncharted territory of his world, a space in which he loses his friends and becomes the *last* gunslinger (Bayer-Berenbaun 29). One of the causes for the instability which Roland encounters is the crumbling state of the Tower and its effects on his world, and with the sickness of the Tower seeping out and causing disarray, Gilead falls to the rebel forces of John Farson. The defeat of the Gunslingers and the deterioration of Gilead at the hands of Farson and his men, presumably enabled by the deteriorating state of the Tower, eventually leads the Constant Reader to a lonely and calloused gunslinger, which comes about due to yet another Gothic twist as, "the Gothic novel has been continuously associated with revolution and anarchy" (Bayer-Berenbaun 42). As Roland witnesses such revolt and carries the affects with him, mostly in the form of nostalgia and even vengeance, his quest becomes devoted to restoring some sort of order. Yet, if the gunslinger were truly motivated and enamored with chaos and destruction, as might be expected of a Gothic protagonist, then the quest he describes to all he encounters as a journey to save the worlds brings about questions of the usefulness of the Gothic formula for discovering why Roland quests for the Tower.

It should be considered that, "the Gothic mind at once admires the tyrant and supports the collapse of institutions" (Bayer-Berenbaun 44). The gunslinger can be seen as a tyrant in his endeavor to possibly raise himself to the status of a god in his pursuit of the Dark Tower, but Roland's quest is primarily concerned with the restoration of the Dark Tower. If Roland can be seen as one who is consumed with desire for power, then the Gothic genre certainly illuminates Roland's character and his motive within such a position. However, the role of the tyrant, or specifically the Crimson King, who wishes to bring about the destruction of the Tower, becomes Roland's sworn enemy once the Crimson King's identity and intentions are made known. Still, Heidi Strengell suggests reconsideration of Roland's position as he, "also possesses qualities of the tyrant-leader at the beginning of the quest. He is ready to sacrifice anything to reach the tower and uses others as tools to achieve this goal" (134). Roland's perpetual questing has brought nothing but death and destruction, and the losses of those closest to him do not deter Roland from continuing on his journey. Stephen King says as much in *The Drawing of the Three*: "Roland loved her [Susannah] because she would fight and never give in; he feared for her because he knew he would sacrifice her — Eddie as well — without a question or a look back" (402). While this confirms Roland's lack of humanity, Roland reneges on this sentiment in *Wizard and Glass*—"'What you call "the bottom line," Eddie, is this; I get my friends killed. And I'm not sure I can even risk doing that again'" (King 664). What is telling about Roland here is that he is not entirely convinced of his new attitude toward the purpose of his companions as a means to the end of the Dark Tower.

Roland's indecision and vague indication of change, that being the transition from cold-hearted loner to loving *dinh*, does not entirely settle the intimations of the Gothic presence in his story as, "the characters in Gothic novels are usually hyper–self-conscious. They scour the depths of their own intentions, questioning not only their actions and perceptions but their motivations and fantasies as well" (Bayer-Berenbaun 38). Whatever Roland's ultimate choice — stoic killer or compassionate leader — remains a mystery to the reader, especially as he is more than willing to leave the Devar-Toi to save Stephen King moments after his friend and companion Eddie Dean dies, even though he also shortly afterwards shows a rare display of emotion when Jake Chambers dies, reluctantly leaving his surrogate son behind in the earth to, once again, move on in his quest. Even if Roland escapes the label of a tyrannical figure who seeks the Tower for his own personal ends, Roland still seeks the Tower despite the overwhelming uncertainty of what he will find at the Tower, and at the cost of losing his friends and companions. Death becomes an inevitable part of Roland's quest, with the exception of his own death, which is an implicit means of empowerment for the gunslinger. With Roland as the survivor, the most skilled of his class and the chosen leader of his ka-tets, the gunslinger is placed into a position of great power and even authority. In a Gothic context, this comes about as, "the Gothic fascination with death and decay involve an admiration for power at the expense of beauty" (Bayer-Berenbaun 27). With that said, the goal of the Gothic hero, at least concerning the *Dark Tower* series, is to attain power.

The Epic hero is primarily concerned with honor and duty, traits specific to the individual, usually acting for the sake and benefit of his community, and in the Western tradition, as civilization becomes the focus of the hero, the aim of the hero moves beyond the self to the development of the world around him. With the Gothic there is not only an inversion of previous traditions but that the primary end of the Gothic hero is not just a return to the individual, but a return that allows the hero to act for himself or herself, complete with a newfound form of power, suggesting that the purpose of Roland's quest is the attainment of power. The Tower is perceived to promise this power within Randall Flagg's mind, and Roland, too, looks have this thought in mind throughout the *Dark Tower* series. Unfortunately, the ambiguity of Roland's professed intentions prevents confirmation of this conclusion. For example, when Roland and Susannah reach the Castle of the Crimson King in the seventh book, it is suggested to Roland that he need not continue his search for the Tower despite his intentions and promise to do so: the Crimson King's steward Rando Thoughtful/Austin Cornwell asks Roland, "'To *whom* have you given your promise? ... For there is no prophecy of such a promise'" (King, *The Dark Tower* 610). Roland then indicates that his quest is self imposed, and is done so without any more reason than a child's response of *just because*: "'There wouldn't be [a prophecy]. For it's [the promise] one I made myself, and one I mean to keep'" (King, *The Dark Tower* 610). Even as Roland makes this promise to himself to seek and find the Dark Tower, and as Rando Thoughtful/Austin Cornwell seems to be genuine in his warning to Roland to "show sense before it's too late for sense and *stay away from the Dark Tower*," it is too speculative to conclude that Roland makes this promise for his own potential gain, or at least for the acquisition of power (King, *The Dark Tower* 617). However, when Tony Magistrale says of the Gothic genre that it is, "more than just atmosphere and indulgence; it is also a serious means of presenting the fundamental dangers — both personal and social — that are the consequences of amoral behavior," it can be concluded that while the gunslinger neither professes any desire to attain power nor directly plots to gain an elevated position, the atmosphere of morality linked to allusions of power is more revealing than a sustained focus on power itself within the Gothic template (*Second Decade* 145). All things considered, the gunslinger is a character whose morals and ethics come into constant question, but a study of his ideologies is almost as fruitless as the attempt to understand his motives and goals via the Gothic.

It may seem likely that Roland quests for power if his tale is isolated in Gothic restraints, but even more important to remember is the macrocosmic nature of Roland's quest — it is about more than one man and one world, and Roland admits this to Eddie in *The Drawing of the Three*: "There's more than a world to win, Eddie. I would not risk you and her — I would not have allowed the boy to die — if that was all there was" (King 405). If it is believed that Roland sacrifices the lives of his companions for a greater purpose, possibly negating the questions of morality connected with this genre, then the Gothic genre fails as a whole as the appropriate lens of understanding Roland's ultimate objective.

Post-Apocalyptic — A Time of Renewal

So far, three distinct genres have suggested three potential goals of Roland's quest — Duty, Civilization, and Power — and it has been claimed that none of these goals are the final aim of the gunslinger. Now that the progression has moved from the Gothic, a genre of the broken and deformed, the Post-Apocalyptic theme of the *Dark Tower* series enters the discussion with not a fascination with the broken in and of itself, but an examination and careful consideration of the causes and effects of ruination in the gunslinger's world. Early on in Roland's tale, readers see that the land through which he journeys has undergone some traumatic changes in the landscape and is also a scene in which various forms of technology have been rendered all but powerless. Even though Mid-World has seen its share of devastation and destruction, suggesting that Roland's world has already experienced an apocalypse of a sort, a better suited course of analysis is to view Roland's world as one that is in the middle of an apocalypse. In seeing the gunslinger's world leaning toward the End of Days, but not quite completely fallen to total destruction, his quest looks to be well placed within the *Post*-Apocalyptic novel by way of the allusions to some previous cataclysms. And the desolate land of the gunslinger's world implies that his quest of saving the Dark Tower is aimed at preventing the most common climax of an apocalypse — complete ruin.

Before focusing completely on the end of the world, it must be said that apocalypse is not just about a final judgment. As Heidi Strengell says, "although the apocalypse is frequently associated with the end of the world and the postcatastrophic scene, it also celebrates the birth of a new world" (132). What Strengell proposes is important in that as Roland may wish to prevent the end of existence by saving the Dark Tower, the anticipated result of his success is the salvation of Mid-World, complete with a hope that the saved world would prosper, similar to the golden-age promised in the Western genre. Even as the post-apocalyptic also deals with religious roots, there is a tendency to neglect the religious allusions of the apocalypse as it applies to Roland's world. Yet, considerations of religion lead to a clearer understanding Roland's world and his journey, especially as John R. May elucidates the necessity of religious exploration and clarification within the apocalyptic model by stating, "the import of the apocalypse as it developed in the Hebrew and Christian canons had nothing to do with holding the carrot of eternity before the believers' noses" (17). In thinking that the apocalypse does not represent an ending, or a completely religious ending, the conclusion that the apocalypse is more of a cyclical nature than one promising a true end may be believed, as suggested by John R. May's basic template of the apocalypse as being comprised of "judgment, catastrophe, [and] renewal" (209). Of course, the cyclical nature here seems to be a major influence on Roland's journey, especially concerning the last pages of *The Dark Tower*. Still, renewal and repetition are apparently inevitable in the apocalyptic/post-apocalyptic realm, especially as, "in Judeo-Christian apocalypse, time is irreversible" (May 210). The same is certainly true for the gunslinger: each time he resumes his quest—"'What do you mean, resume? I never left off'"—the world moves on with him (King, *The Gunslinger* 212). Gilead is never restored, Roland is not given a chance to go back to Jericho Hill to change the fate of his fellow gunslingers, or even pick up the Horn of Eld himself, and when he is seen in the Mohaine Desert once again on the trail of the Man in Black, he may not quite be exactly back at the beginning.

Traveling with Roland along the Path of the Beam towards End-World, a land that has seen its share of devastation, readers walk with Roland in an apocalyptic land that positions him to constantly move forward and yet still seek some sort of connection with the past. With the inevitable movement into the future — never backwards — the apocalyptic essence of Roland's quest takes on more than the typical feel of survival coupled with the constant questioning of *what went wrong*, or even what preventative measures could have been taken. In other words, "apocalypse is a response to cultural crisis. It grows out of that sense of loss that results from the passing of an old-world view" (May 19). If this claim is applied to Roland and his motivation for seeking the Dark Tower, readers would be essentially revisiting the role civilization plays as the ultimate end of the Western novel, but the twist within the post-apocalyptic thematic is that nostalgia and regret play more prominent roles than the attempted establishment of a particular way of life. While Roland may not be able to re-create the court of Gilead in Mid-World, the role he plays in adjusting and responding to the apocalypse may afford him an opportunity to at least renew the ancient way of life Gilead reflected, much like in the Western. But before accepting renewal as not just the second step in Roland's quest — the reformation of his ka-tet as implicated by the subtitle "Renewal" in *The Drawing of the Three*— the final destination and purpose of Roland's quest, and the basics of the post-apocalyptic genre, need to be examined.

Stepping back to see what leads up to the *need* and *desire* to recall a past that has been destroyed, the Post-Apocalyptic genre as a step-by-step progression initiates expectations of an apocalyptic text, and a ten-point template, as provided by R.W.B. Lewis, is as follows:

> 1. Periodic natural disasters, earthquakes and the like; 2. the advent and the turbulent reign of the Antichrist or the false Christ or false prophet; 3. the second coming of Christ and 4. the resulting cosmic warfare (Armageddon) that brings in 5. the millennium — that is, from the Latin, the period of one thousand years, the epoch of the Messianic Kingdom upon earth; thereafter, 6. the gradual degeneration of human and physical nature, the last and worst apostasy (or falling away from God), featured by 7. the second and briefer "loosing of Satan"; 8. an ultimate catastrophe, the end of the world by fire; 9. the Last Judgment; and 10. the appearance of the new heaven and earth [196–7].

1. The Ending Is Only the Beginning

Right away heavy religious implications are seen in this model, but with simple substitution — like John Farson in the place of the False Prophet, or even proposing that "the Man in Black's actions identify him as a manipulative demonic agent, the apocalyptic False Prophet" — this formula can be secularized, but even with a few creative twists and interpretations, skepticism comes as no surprise as failure has already occurred with the three previous genres in adequately determining Roland's actual purpose (Egan, "Gothic Western" 103). Nonetheless, the discussion begins with the first step in the apocalyptic progression, natural disaster, and the claim can be made that the Beamquakes Roland witnesses are an appropriate marker of the beginning of an apocalypse. Six Beamquakes will, as far as the Constant Reader knows, lead to the fall of the Tower and initiate the end of existence. Also, the thinnies Roland and his companions discover, "'places where the fabric of existence is almost entirely worn away,'" function as sporadic natural disasters of a sort (*Wizard and Glass* 66). The source of these disruptions in the natural order of Roland's world are easily recognizable and observed in the texts comprising the *Dark Tower* series, even including the presumed man-made disasters seen in the waste lands outside of Lud and in the badlands around the Castle of the Crimson King.

The second through the fifth points of the apocalyptic progression are ones that look outside of Roland's where and when and bring readers into the realm of the biblical where a stretch of the imagination is needed to find events and characters in the *Dark Tower* series to fit the post-apocalyptic mold and to foreground the end of renewal that has been suggested. With the arrival and the reign of the Anti-Christ, or the False Prophet, John Farson could represent this character. Farson's rhetoric — "'Ask not what the good man can do for you...'" — and the war he wages on the gunslingers places him and his politics well in the position of a False Prophet as he opposes the establishment, Gilead, and the sacredness and dignity for which this city stands to protect and honor (King, *The Gunslinger* 108). The third point in the apocalyptic model, however, poses a problem for the purposes of this exploration as the "second coming" of Christ does not occur in the *Dark Tower* series. Roland doesn't even hold to any faith worshipping this deity, despite the number of believers readers come across in Roland's journey. But, by the furthest stretch of the imagination, one might consider Roland to be a

Christ-figure, one who acts as a conduit for the Prim and the White to return to Mid-World which would make his quest appear as a second coming of sorts. Heidi Strengell takes the idea of Roland being a Christ-figure a bit further when she suggests that Roland and Jake are not completely separate characters, and that Roland's sacrifice of the boy Jake is almost like Roland sacrificing a part of himself: "Roland is also Jake. In this sense he sacrifices himself for human kind[...]. Like Jesus this Messiah is tempted: he could turn around and take Jake with him" (131). *If* it is accepted that the return of Christ occurs in King's tale through Roland, then the fourth point of the apocalyptic template can be approached as just another formula being adhered to in *The Dark Tower*: Armageddon.

The "cosmic warfare" that Armageddon suggests is usually the focal point of most discussions of the apocalypse as it is the event that brings about the destruction and desolation usually associated with apocalypse; also to note is that post-apocalypse typically implies a scene witnessed *after* the cause of the chaos has come to pass. In the *Dark Tower* series, however, the closest thing to Armageddon is the last stand of the gunslingers as Jericho Hill. Even though there are allusions to nuclear holocausts throughout Roland's story, these modern representations of Armageddon are never actually witnessed in *The Dark Tower*. Although it would be safe to say that these assumptions are most likely correct, the scale of these incidents becomes problematic for a general understanding of Armageddon, which would be *complete* ruin. However, Roland's world only experiences minor battles and events which suggest a miniscule reflection of what total Armageddon would cause. And as Roland's world does not necessarily experience Armageddon, there are further problems with the post-apocalyptic template in that the "millennium" which constitutes the fifth point in the apocalyptic progression never comes to pass. If there ever was a Messianic Kingdom in Mid-World, a period of roughly one thousand years of harmony, it might be considered the time of Roland's youth. But Gilead falls, and along with it a golden age ceases, which hearkens towards the sixth point of the apocalyptic template with the gradual degeneration of humanity. Various examples of the degeneration of mankind are seen as Farson comes to power in the West, the citizens of Mejis burn Susan Delgado at the stake in a display of mob madness, and even in what might be considered as an age of fidelity Gabrielle Deschain strays from her husband's bed and into the arms of Marten Broadcloack. But, going further back in time before the fall of Gilead, the social decline observed in the *Dark Tower* actually begins with the Old Ones, whose reliance upon technology replace an important element in the gunslinger's tale, that of faith.

When it comes to issues of faith, and not necessarily that of religious devotion, Cuthbert Allgood reminds readers that many of the gunslingers, those who are apparently charged with protecting the Dark Tower, do not even believe in the existence of this structure: "'There *is* no Tower, Roland,' Cuthbert said patiently. 'I don't know what you saw in that glass ball, but there *is* no Tower. Well, as a symbol, I suppose — like Arthur's Cup, or the Cross of the man-Jesus — but not as a real thing, a real building'" (King, *Wizard and Glass* 580). Even though readers and Roland later learn that the Tower does actually exist, Cuthbert's skepticism can be excused as the Tower was kept as a secret by the elder gunslingers. What this leads towards is an indication of the waning humanity in the court of Gilead as the gunslingers, perhaps shrouded in pride, would not let their own children know of the existence of the Dark Tower. While the senior gunslingers may be pardoned for this omission of information because there existed the possibility that their children would be sent west and possibly become threats to Gilead and the Tower, the implicit isolation of the gunslingers as the dominant individuals of Mid-World makes them susceptible to the onslaught of Farson and his men, who act on behalf of the Crimson King, a character some associate with the devil. As to whether or not the Crimson King's association with Satan and his plans for bringing the Dark Tower down fits the seventh point of the apocalyptical model — a return of Satan — is up to the reader to decide. But even as the last five premises of the post-apocalyptic model have proven to be problematic, the final three points of the apocalyptic model prove to be much more difficult to work with. As it stands, Roland's quest as seen in terms of the post-apocalyptic is certainly curious and interesting, but hardly enlightening.

In considering the last points of the post-apocalyptic model, Roland's journey into End-World shows no clear connection or even an allusion to a disastrous cataclysm facing the entire world, a Last Judgment, or even the appearance of a "new heaven and earth." Some may consider the scene at the end of the seventh book in the series when Roland is pulled through the door at the top of a Tower as a form of judgment, or even an accounting. Yet, even through a loose interpretation concerning the "catastrophe" and then considering Roland's resumption of his quest as a final judgment, it is difficult to regard the world in which Roland finds himself as one that is a "new earth." And although the *Dark Tower* is certainly out of place within a rigid adherence to the Post-Apocalyptic model, when Roland and his ka-tet liberate the Breakers of Blue Heaven and save the Shardik-Maturin Beam, the post-apocalyptic theme of renewal does come to pass. Additionally, with the regeneration of the Beams beginning, and the promise that the other Beams will begin to renew themselves in due time, Roland's quest comes to an end at this point in the Post-Apocalyptic genre. A new time is on the horizon, much like the "golden age" one comes to expect at the end of a Western novel, and Roland has saved the Tower. But this does not signal the end of the Post-Apocalyptic in *The Dark Tower*. Within the Post-Apocalyptic frame, there can be no renewal without the ultimate desiccation of the land by the "ultimate catastrophe" or the Last Judgment. Roland's quest, at this juncture, would have to be about salvation, and not necessarily personal salvation, as a true renewal cannot occur, theoretically, without the fulfillment of the final points of the apocalyptical formula. Renewal is at best a means to an end, but it is not Roland's climax, which is not saving the Dark Tower but entering it and even understanding its mysteries.

After four genres have been examined, and after four tries of attempting to find answers to questions as to why Roland seeks the Tower, one more genre remains: science fiction. And keep in mind that the progression of these genres also serves as a metaphorical template for Roland's own personal development: as each genre moves back and forth between a focus on the individual only to return to a concentration on the larger scope existing outside of the individual, a return to the individual waits on the horizon, and one of literature's outcasts will finally reveal what has been sought.

Science Fiction — The Pursuit of Knowledge

In nearing the end of the discussion, complete with previously unanswered questions concerning genre and its influence on climax, the realm of science fiction, unfortunately, poses plenty of problems as well. Above all else, Carl Freedman claims that concerning the science fiction genre, "no definitional consensus exists" (13). Moreover, Brian Stableford says that, "science fiction is something of an anomaly. There is no typical science fictional climax which exists in parallel with the typical climaxes of detective stories, genre romances, thrillers, Westerns, horror stories, or heroic fantasies" (8). While this does not bode well at its most basic level, especially as, "science fiction has no typical action or place," there are, nonetheless, various aspects of science fiction to work with in order to move on with a purposeful analysis (Gunn 6). In fact, science fiction is the most telling genre in terms of climax in *The Dark Tower* series.

First, there is the technological side to science fiction that asks for attention as Roland's adventure sees its share of scientific innovation — the Wolves, Blaine the Mono, Andy the Messenger Robot, and even the simple forms of technology like electric lights and gas-powered machines. But, beyond the common technological aspects of science fiction, consider the general foundation or beginning for most science fiction authors: "Most speculative writing is basically a response to the opening question 'what would happen if...?'" (Ash 11).

With this question, science fiction considers imaginative realms that are unfamiliar but not entirely surprising; science fiction takes what is known and what is conceivable, regardless of its improbability, and takes, "the reader far beyond the boundaries of his or her own mundane environment, into strange, awe-inspiring realms thought to be in fact unknown, or at least largely unknown, but not in principle unknowable" (Freedman 15).

Here science fiction takes on a mildly Gothic feel as the unknown comes into the picture, but, more importantly, science fiction delves into the realm of not simply what is unknown but rather what can be known and is awaiting discovery. In the context of Roland's quest, he may not be a scientist looking to develop or improve society through technological innovation, but as science fiction implicitly deals with discovery and knowledge, the mysteries of the Dark Tower ask for nothing less than exploration and contemplation if not outright comprehension. Also, Roland has promised himself to *find* the Tower, to discover it, and also to unravel its mysteries, and while this may not be what is typically expected of science fiction, it is certainly an appropriate lens through which his quest might finally be understood.

Science fiction should be treated and understood as not necessarily a genre which deals with future possibility, but one that places the characters in a scene which asks for immediate attention and uncanny cunning in order to survive a startling and surprising situation. While this view may be a bit convenient for the sake of application to the *Dark Tower* series, science fiction does involve, above all things, adaptability. In dealing with rampant machinery, questionable innovations, and even strange beings, all things one would typically expect in a science fiction work and things readers witness in the *Dark Tower* series, each of these scenarios involve the ability to adjust and adapt to a given scenario. As Carol Colatrella implies the same notion when she says, "while science fiction remains interested in the empowering possibilities of technology [...] it also tries very hard to figure out the mistakes we made getting here," science fiction is depicted as a genre that requires of its characters a keen curiosity aimed at embracing change and working to solve potential problems (562). Or, as Tom Moylan notes, "science fiction demonstrates our incapacity to imagine the future and brings us down to earth to apprehend our present in all its limitations" (42). Fortunately for Roland, "he had in his long life been nothing if not adaptable" (King, *The Gunslinger* 4).

Adaptability is nothing, however, without knowledge: in order for the characters in a science fiction novel to succeed, they must have knowledge that facilitates their adaptability. In order to defeat the forces run amok found in a typical science fiction novel, one would have to know *how* the machine works in order to find its weakness. Or, for Roland to save the Tower, he would need to learn *how* to save it. Even after he learns to do so as he becomes aware of the Breakers in *Wolves of the Calla* and concludes that the Tower itself is ailing because of the weakened Beams, the Tower still promises knowledge, which stretches beyond Roland's initial goal of saving the Tower. And this lure of the unknown is common enough to classify as a science fiction motif. Sidestepping the primary objective of a science fiction novel — knowledge — for a moment, it is important to look at some of the other components of science fiction to validate this end and to show how Roland's quest moves in this direction.

1. The Ending Is Only the Beginning

To start, "it is quite possible to class almost the entire serious side of the [science fiction] genre under divergent headings of 'utopia' and 'anti-utopia' writing, in which the future is seen as more (or less) agreeable than the present day" (Ash 3). In thinking of science fiction as a genre which deals with states of social perfection, or at least a preferable state of a specific community, and that the quest in this scene is aimed at achieving perfection by any means necessary and most likely through technological innovation, the story of the *Dark Tower* serves as a parallel to this template with the history of the Old Ones. The attempt to better the world before the gunslinger's time was achieved by technological means, and with the direction Keystone Earth takes in the series as prompted by the Sombra Corporation and North Central Positronics, the world of Eddie, Susannah, and Jake moves towards a science fiction utopia. Even though the literal definition of the word utopia — no place, no where — implies that such a state of existence is impossible, Roland's quixotic quest is nonetheless focused on setting up a new world order based on what he has learned (which certainly resonates with elements of the Western and the Gothic). But Roland lacks the knowledge to do so, and there is much placed in Roland's road which certainly limits his attainment of this information.

Science fiction brings to the table the formula of obstacle/response, or rather that of escape/resolution. Science fiction also suggests a scene of failure in some form and the resulting response of those who are faced with this breakdown. Not only does science fiction constantly ask "what if" when shaping the plot of a particular tale, science fiction seems to also ask, beyond the basic plot element of conflict, the question of how one would respond in a rather extraordinary situation. The end result, whether the hero wins through or not, is that knowledge is acquired. Of course, many threats in science fiction come about due to unwieldy knowledge, and as science, in general, attempts to harness knowledge by breaking things down into understandable units, the attempt at some manner of mastery serves as a constant form of motivation. And Roland becomes a character in the *Dark Tower* whose lack of imagination becomes one of his biggest impositions; Roland cannot be satisfied with saving the worlds by saving the Beams, and he cannot simply wonder at the marvel of the Tower in and of itself. And this brings up a key theme of science fiction to situate alongside knowledge: the theme of wonderment.

Characters in a science fiction novel often lack imagination — they are comfortable to a point in that most critical thinking is cast aside, both logical and creative. As Jonathan Davis implies of science fiction, the people in these tales tend to, "fail to realize what their mechanical babies will someday require of them" (*Stephen King's America* 71). In addition to this claim, Tony Magistrale asserts that, "throughout the greater body of his fiction, Stephen King addresses the dual genies of science and technology gone bad — the dim results of man's irresponsibility and subsequent loss of control over those things which he himself has created" (*Moral* 27). Therefore, it is the regeneration of the imagination, accompanied by a sense of responsibility, which allows the characters to win through; science put these characters into a dire situation, along with a clear misunderstanding or misuse of whatever threat is running rampant, and their humanity is what will help them to succeed. However, the movement from the rationality of science back to the emotional nature of the human needs some sort of catalyst, and readers see this play out in the *Dark Tower* series, first with the Old Ones who thrived in an age of innovation but later renounced their ways and tried to recapture the magic that they had abandoned because they witnessed the folly of their faith in technology. Readers also witness complacency due to rationality as they travel with Roland into New York as he chastises the citizens of New York for having no sense of awe or imagination to balance out their overly rational minds that have begun to take technology as a matter of course:

> Here he was in a world which struck him dumb with fresh wonders seemingly at every step, a world where carriages flew through the air and paper seemed as cheap as sand. And the newest wonder was simply that for these people, wonder had run out: here, in a place of miracles, he only saw dull faces and plodding bodies [King, *The Drawing of the Three* 366].

As Roland critiques the citizens of New York, he would do well to look at himself in the same light, but even if the gunslinger were to gain an imagination and a sense of wonderment that might aid him on his quest, one still must consider that Roland's enlightenment may not be needed, especially if it is suggested that the Tower *should* fall at the hands of the Crimson King and his son Mordred. With this thought, science and science fiction each seem to come with a cost/benefit scenario, and with Roland storming the Tower and ascending it, a backwards step must be taken in order to question what the cost of Roland's pursuit of knowledge is.

Knowledge, for all of its benefits within a science fiction model, carries with it some dangers and prompts caution. There is the idea that there are some things that individuals cannot or should not know, and that the pursuit of such knowledge is complete foolishness and encumbered with pride. If the Dark Tower is the great mystery of Roland's world, and if his quest is driven by knowledge more than anything else, questions arise as to whether or not Roland should even journey beyond the Castle of the Crimson King, if it is necessary for him to "'pass beyond ka itself'" (King, *The Dark Tower* 609). Perhaps the gunslinger may not need to actually enter the Dark Tower in End-World for his quest to be successful, which suggests that the knowledge Roland seeks by continuing his quest is not necessary, or that this knowledge is even purposely denied to Roland as each time he reaches the top of the Tower he is still left with all the questions he had at the foot of the building and no answers to take with him back into the desert. For the purpose of analyzing the use of knowledge in Roland's quest, his potential justification of seeking the Tower must be analyzed and critiqued to see if his search for knowledge is valid. With this prompting, focus shifts to what Roger Shattuck calls *forbidden knowledge*, the kind of knowledge Roland may be seeking, and of which Shattuck gives six categories: "1. Inaccessible, unattainable knowledge; 2. Knowledge prohibited by divine, religious, Moral, or secular authority; 3. Dangerous, destructive or unwelcome knowledge; 4. Fragile, delicate knowledge; 5. Knowledge double-bound; 6. Ambiguous knowledge" (327).

To explain the first category of forbidden knowledge, Shattuck explains it as follows: "Some aspects of the cosmos — of 'reality' — cannot be reached by human faculties [...] inaccessibility springs either from the inadequacy of human powers or from the remoteness of realms presumed to exist in ways inconceivable to us" (328). If the Dark Tower is the daunting enigma it is reported as being, a vessel which encompasses and maintains existence, then the goal of comprehending the nature of *everything* is understandable as such questions of existence cross most people's minds. Also, consider what Walter says to Roland in the golgotha: "'The greatest mystery the universe offers is not life but size. Size encompasses life, and the Tower encompasses size'" (King, *The Gunslinger*

221). And if the Tower encompasses size, it is certain that the Tower is the nexus of all the worlds and contains *everything* in existence. But, the knowledge that the Tower promises cannot be grasped by Roland as Walter generously warns Roland that, "'Size defeats us'" (King, *The Gunslinger* 221). If the Tower does promise knowledge of the infinite and the unknown, the adventurer who seeks such understanding may be better off knowing that, perhaps, "it is simply the nature of things, including ourselves, that prevents us from knowing everything" (Shattuck 328). The second category of forbidden knowledge that Shattuck provides, prohibited knowledge, makes sense within a civilized setting, but with respect to Roland's quest, nothing really prohibits him from attempting to gain the knowledge he believes awaits him in the Tower. Yet, considering the third category of forbidden knowledge, dangerous knowledge, one may hold on to the hope that Roland would exercise discretion at the prospect of learning what is to be learned, if anything, upon a successful completion of his quest that might prove to be perilous.

Regardless of the substance and nature of the knowledge Roland may find at the Tower, Shattuck states that, "simple prudence should impel us to take careful account of such dangerous forms of dangerous knowledge" (331). The unknown danger that may result in Roland's acquisition of knowledge, despite the potential benefits, lends credence to the claim that, "in some circumstances, the truth survives better veiled than naked" (Shattuck 331). If Roland were to learn of the great mysteries of the universe, and even comprehend them, his suspect nature makes it clear that he may not use his newfound knowledge for the best reasons. The gunslinger may not strive to be the godhead like Randall Flagg, but Roland's character is certainly questionable enough to wonder, with caution, as to what he might do with the knowledge he seeks.

Moving on to Shattuck's fourth category of forbidden knowledge, fragile knowledge, this is an area of knowledge with which Roland actually has much experience. He has dealt with this brand of knowledge several times throughout his quest, most notably concerning his knowledge of Susannah's pregnancy with Mia's child, Mordred. As Roland discovers Susannah's pregnancy before the others in his ka-tet, he keeps to his own counsel for the sake of keeping cover if Mia proves to be an enemy (which she does) and to keep his ka-tet intact as the information is certainly precarious. Roland undoubtedly knows that some knowledge is better left alone, or at least unstated, due to its volatility and potential for chaos, and he would then do well do remember that, "fragile knowledge finds its natural home in the domains of discretion and privacy" (Shattuck 332). The key word to this claim is "privacy," especially as it relates to the gunslinger's goal; Roland does not even consider that the reason for the Dark Tower's location, wheels and wheels from civilization, may be for the purpose of seclusion, which would help ensure the safekeeping of the fragile knowledge it presumably contains. However, Roland does not consider this as he pushes on to End-World in his never-ending pursuit of the Tower. Perhaps this can be explained by Shattuck's fifth category of forbidden knowledge, knowledge double-bound, or knowledge that seeks to reconcile the subjective and the objective. In this type of forbidden knowledge, Shattuck explains that, "we cannot know something by both means at the same time. The attempt to reconcile the two or to alternate between them leads to great mental stress. [For example] Losing culture while being immersed in another" (332). Roland's quest, and the knowledge he desires, comes from a completely subjective point of view. As he charged himself with his quest and initially learned of the Tower from no source but his own poorly-drawn conclusion as prompted by the Wizard's Rainbow, Roland then tries to present his quest from an objective standpoint. He believes he knows what he must do, but without the confirmation from an outside and impartial observer, Roland's quest is undertaken with the zeal and purpose drawn from within and with no true purpose other than what Roland himself attributes to the quest. And Roland does so even though, "hard as we may try, we cannot be both inside and outside an experience or life — even our own" (Shattuck 334). Still, the nature of Roland's quest tries to understand his quest from both positions. Even if Roland were to abandon his endeavor to be both inside his own life, the quest for the Tower, and outside of it, looking at it in an objective manner to give the quest purpose and even meaning, he would still be faced with the last category of forbidden knowledge, ambiguous knowledge.

Shattuck explains the last classification of forbidden knowledge as, "a condition in which what we know reverses itself right under our noses, confounds us by turning into its opposite" (335). Surely, there is no clearer indication of the futility of Roland's quest for knowledge it would have to be the ambiguous nature of the Dark Tower: it appears as a building, it is thought of as Gan's Navel, and while the Tower functions as both a symbol and a living being, every time Roland reaches the Tower it changes. Recall that as Roland ascends the stairs to the top of the Tower and looks into each room, they compose a series of snapshots of Roland's life, and assuming that each repetition of Roland's quest is at least slightly different than the prior journey, readers can also assume that the inside of the Tower changes to adapt to the new adventures Roland experiences on the road to the Dark Tower. Even though Roland cannot truly know what the Tower is because of its liveliness and its constant changes, he still moves on with the foolish hope that knowledge can be attained.

Although the genre of science fiction appears to be little more than a shrouded backdrop to *The Dark Tower* series with technological fear, robots, and travel between the worlds presented as commonplace and somewhat uninteresting when considering the larger scope of the series, the roots of science fiction are helpful for understanding the gunslinger's quest. Knowledge is needed for the gunslinger to fix the land which surrounds him, and the Dark Tower is supposed to contain and promise this knowledge, which suggests that a science fiction scenario takes place in the *Dark Tower* books. With information being the key to survival, at least within this genre, Roland's journey for the Dark Tower should not necessarily be seen as wholly ignoble or born out of pride. Yet this is not to say that neither pride nor fame are absent from the gunslinger's quest. In light of what the Dark Tower represents and what the gunslinger believes he can discover within this structure, the overwhelming question to ask is if anyone can blame Roland for trying to find the Tower and enter it, for going on a quest that he presents as one destined to save all of existence yet seems to be nothing more than a Faustian quest for knowledge at the cost of Roland's soul.

An Age of Anxiety

While it has been proposed that the ultimate goal of Roland's quest is for knowledge, despite the inherent dangers of seeking and using such knowledge, there are still questions concerning the role of the *Dark Tower* series as a lengthy volume concerned with the pursuit of knowledge within the contemporary society it was written. Although King's tale stretches across thirty years of real-time, half of Roland's tale — books V-VII, and even the revised version of volume I — is written in the 21st century, an age of information and also post–9/11 fears. This is important to consider as, "literature expresses and discusses under various shapes, as elegantly and masterly as its exponents are able, the prevailing ideas concerning the problems, material and metaphysical, of the current hour" (Summers 17). If the preceding is accepted, and if it is also accepted that the overarching aim of Roland's quest is for knowledge, what can be concluded of Stephen King's *Dark Tower* series? Can it be seen primarily as a reflection of contemporary insecurities and worries? Marleen Barr believes that this is the case as she says that, "science fiction permeates reality. Science fiction permeates literary fiction" (437). Within this reality that extends beyond fiction, James Egan also observes a link between make-believe and the world at large when he says that, "beneath the mayhem which permeates King's fiction lie interrelated, troubling questions about the power, extent, and validity of science and rationalism in contemporary society" ("Technohorror" 47). As it were, perhaps King is highlighting modern-day atrocities and horrors by way of the gunslinger, a character that seeks knowledge and the progression of his quest with little consideration for who is affected, neglected, and even cast aside in the wake of ambition and a myopic world view.

Literature has often been understood as a distant window through which people can look into for a glimpse of a given society or culture, and the window into the gunslinger's world looks right back into the world in which King lives and writes, reflecting an image of not only passion but unbridled zeal aimed towards questionable goals. As Stephen King departs from his typical style of horror — typical, that is, in the eyes of those who corner King as a horror writer — and brings in many different genres to compose what some consider as his magnum opus, it must be noted that the complexity of modern living cannot be encapsulated by just one genre. One analysis of the mixing and blending of various genres, complete with their cultural stigmas of a variety of anxieties and which blurs the reader's vision of a specific fear, is the idea that ambiguity and lack of overall structure is the most prominent fear facing contemporary society. Roland's blind quest, cloaked in an array of genres, themes and styles, seems to adequately reflect the state of the average individual, one who exists in a world of complication yet endless possibility; however, this structure of multiplicity promises no structure at all. Knowledge, then, promises some sort of control and stability of which Roland cannot be condemned for attempting to acquire, even though his aspirations lead to nothing but repetition. But one can still question whether or not Roland will learn what the cost of such knowledge is.

Again, if it is accepted that Roland endures the road of trials which mark the way to the Dark Tower — losing his fingers, his friends and even his humanity — for the sake of knowledge, then it is appropriate, like Roland, to return to the beginning of his quest. At first, most readers cannot decide whether or not Roland is a hero, a protagonist, or if he is an anti-hero, a despicable man who beds Allie in the town of Tull simply for information and lets a young Jake Chambers fall beneath the Cyclopean Mountains to catch the Man in Black for, above all, information. Back at this juncture of interpreting the character of Roland as one who the Constant Reader will cheer on in his adventure, or even as one that many may silently wish to fail, readers of *The Dark Tower* must also look at themselves as reflections of this ambiguous character. Tangled in a web of genres and paths to choose from, when readers are faced with decisions like Roland Descain — whether or not to seek knowledge that may be better left alone — readers must consider that in an age of information, if he or she would make the same decision as the gunslinger: to move forward though any obstacle, no matter what sacrifices are asked to be made, and to acquire knowledge in the hope that such information delivers enlightenment, relief or solace despite the awareness that these anticipated ends are never promised or guaranteed.

As a final note on the matter of information and climax, King utilizes the ambiguous, muddled and mercurial nature of the science fiction novel, in conjunction with a strange and inventive blend of other genres, to accommodate his designs for the ending of *The Dark Tower*, an ending that is surely unexpected for most readers and does not easily fit within any particular established generic categorization of climax. Perhaps King takes this route with his writing as, "expected endings function like magnetic north poles towards which the narratives always point," indicating that unsurprising or easily anticipated endings hardly make for good fiction (Stableford 1). Surely, overly aware readers rarely become immersed in a story that is too structured or notably contrived. Still, the conclusion which repeats the first line of the series is not solely a signal for a circular and repetitive continuation of the gunslinger's quest and the reader's following of this journey; it is also an appropriate continuation of King's experimentation with genre and writing within the series as a whole. Then again, the circular ending may be an escape King has sought with the conclusions of his other tales: "if we've learned anything about King by the close of this series, it's that he's terrified of endings" (Agger B14). However, with King balancing many genres and many possibilities concerning the outcome of the tale, it seems natural for the ending to truly be an original, a deviation from any previous norm that enriches the tale through its boldness and its call to re-read the story in its entirety as the circular nature of the text demands at least one subsequent reading. And while a true conclusion may be avoided by connecting the end of the *Dark Tower* tale to the beginning, the constant journey suggests that no knowledge or enlightenment is ever found, which then suggests that the gunslinger's quest does have a hint of horror to it. To discover that one's life quest is one of folly and purposelessness certainly seems to be in the mold of a Stephen King novel, which is marked by fiction that may seem to offer hope, but then pulls it away with little announcement whatsoever.

2

Illustrating Imagination: The Infringement (and Evolution) of Visual Elements in the *Dark Tower* Series and *The Gunslinger Born*

"the hand that tells the tales has a mind of its own, and a way of growing restless" — from *The Dark Tower*

IN HIS PREFACE TO THE Complete and Uncut version of *The Stand*, Stephen King admits that adaptation of fiction, specifically cinematic, affects imagination, saying that, "films, even the best of them, freeze fiction [...] That is not necessarily bad ... but it *is* limiting. The glory of a good tale is that it is limitless and fluid; a good tale belongs to each reader in its own particular way" (xv). Referring to the flexibility of a text and the lack of permanent meaning within a written word, it seems as if King's sentiments consciously note and carefully consider that, "as a rule, any transfer from one medium to another results in something being 'lost in translation'" (Gravett 184). Still, for a writer who has expressed concern over the diminished role and purpose of imagination as well as the problems of adaptation, King's readers have all too much been exposed to numerous visual representations of his work which severely limits the reading experience and the function of imagination when reading. The focus of this chapter is King's questionable use and reliance upon the illustrations presented for readers of *The Dark Tower* series to tell his tale, especially as these images have evolved into a rather problematic

71

graphic novel series that infringes upon the imaginative perceptions of his Constant Reader who now must face *established* visual conceptions of particular characters and events which are better left to be conveyed by the solely written word.

In the *Dark Tower* series, King teams with several artists to create illustrations depicting specific scenes in each novel, yet with the variety of artists involved in this project (seven books, six artists), and through the ubiquitous and constantly changing visual elements in *The Dark Tower* series, he defiles the imaginative consciousness that he claims to champion. The inclusion of illustrations to accompany the seven texts of the *Dark Tower* series serve as teasing glimpses into the author's own imagination, as well as the imaginations of the artists behind the artwork, but the inevitable variations between the artists who worked on these texts in relation to King's envisioned landscapes, characters and creatures is noted as unavoidable. Even among any consistencies among the inconsistent visual representations in the series, like how the Dark Tower is depicted as both a brick and mortar medieval structure and an ornate, decorous Gothic creation, and regardless of the intent behind these artistic representations of the gunslinger's journey to the Dark Tower, their placement in the graphic novels, otherwise referred to as comic books in come circles, is questionable at best.

The meshing of King's craft with that of visual art insists that he remain grounded in his primary profession — that of fiction *writing*. While most graphic novels display exceptional plots set against thrilling and fitting illustrated backgrounds, King's adaptation of his work to the medium of the graphic novel is inconsistent with the original story, imposing to the imagination, and even incomprehensible in places. As with most adapted stories, primarily those which are transferred from book to screen, prior knowledge and familiarity with a story provides a clearer and fuller view into the entire story. Similarly, while many film adaptations remain, typically, coherent to the point of cohesiveness without prior exposure to the story, King's *The Gunslinger Born*, as well as the follow-up installment *The Long Road Home*, is an experiment in adaptation that fails to present a fully developed story, one that is not easily accessed by the new reader for whom one would assume the graphic novel is written as, "the 'popular' novelist is looking for an audience" ("Introduction" xiv). Yet, alongside the array of missing elements and absent scenes essential to fully understanding the plot of the original tale, the move from fiction to a fully-illustrated text severely restricts and even confines one's reading of the tale, whether by means of imagining the characters and action or through attempts at reconciling the inconsistencies between the two mediums, and whether such is an initial reading or a review of the story.

Adaptation and Initial Criticims

Among the question of adaptation comes the concern of *mediums* of adaptation, especially regarding King who is an author, a filmmaker, and is now working with graphic novels. With movies adapted from fictional texts, and music videos, for example, bringing a visual element to music itself, some sentiments expressed are those which look at each and every adaptation as a stand-alone project. In this isolated nature, that of a particular adaptation escaping worries of intent and even purity, King's graphic novel adaptation of his *Dark Tower* series is a work that is portrayed and reported as a new version of the books on which it is based, a project that can stand on its own. When considering the additional series that follow the initial installment, *The Gunslinger Born*, all of which are reported to bring new elements and tales into the *Dark Tower* mythos, it is not ill-conceived to think of the graphic novels as an entity unto themselves, a story that is self-contained and functions as almost a satellite to the *Dark Tower* series — a story that adds to the original tale, with some pull and sway, but which does not fundamentally alter the original fiction. Yet, believing that the graphic novels based on *The Dark Tower* are stand-alone tales that can easily immerse a reader is a belief that necessitates reconsideration.

While *The Gunslinger Born* and *The Long Road Home* seem to function as stand-alone tales that warrant no previous acquaintance with the *Dark Tower* series, there are several issues with the medium of a graphic novel as it relates to the solely written word that pose many problems for this experimentation with form and story. As it would be all but impossible for King and the staff at Marvel to give, in its entirety, the original tale of *Wizard and Glass* in a condensed format, the problems of size and scope loom large over this project. Also to consider is that the *consistency* of the tale to be relayed, that within the graphic novel as it compares to the original text of *Wizard and Glass* as well as select scenes from *The Gunslinger*, is questionable albeit forgivable as *The Gunslinger Born* seeks to be its own project, its own story with no fixed ties to any outside sources or references. But the *incompatibility* that this story shares with its founding tale is cause for woe and worry among casual readers, fans, purists, scholars and critics alike. Although *The Gunslinger Born* is derived as a series that does not ask for any outside knowledge of King's *Dark Tower* series, designating these graphic novels as stand-alone is hardly accurate. Even though it is impossible for those who are familiar with King's fiction series to eliminate such prior knowledge of the gunslinger and his tale when approaching the graphic novels, there are still instances during reading that *any* given reader will stop and question either the context, the actual plot, or the clarity of the story.

Although these early critiques allude to a sense of superiority of written word over visual elements, it is hasty to deny the proposition that, "pictures can stimulate the imagination every bit as much as words" (Gravett 10). Yet, with pre-existing pictures in the novels that tend to compete with the images brought forth in the graphic novel, the illustrations provided for the *Dark Tower* series and *The Gunslinger Born* are quite burdensome on their own and are even in competition with one another. Among the questions and criticisms discussed so far, King does display an awareness and foreknowledge of many of these issues that have been raised. In an attempt to justify and explain the experiment of *The Gunslinger Born*, King addresses anticipated concerns of his Constant Reader by first saying that, "I'm always curious, and open to seeing what new formats can do for old works" ("Open Letter" 44). While this is not an unreasonable interest for King to pursue, as he has done so before with not only his films but his first graphic novel project *Creepshow*, he also suggests that there is no danger to his writing by doing so when he says of the *Dark Tower* books that they, "are unimpeachable, beyond change. So there's really no risk, is there?" ("Open Letter" 44–5). King, however, not only neglects to see the constant function of a reader's imagination and its place in the reading process, one that often re-reads a text with new eyes and new images that are controlled by the reader which suggests a constant flexibility with any text, but he also forgets that his endeavor to unify all of his writing has resulted in constant re-workings of his fiction that certainly suggest his writing is anything but unchangeable. While the written word of King's *Dark Tower* series remains the same now as it was when King first published the series, the meanings effectively face change with every reader, every variation in the artwork, which is particularly witnessed in *The Gunslinger Born.*

Setting aside concerns of the artwork in the graphic novels for the moment, the add-on stories that accompany the graphic novels con-tribute very little to this venture in that they are simply additional sto-ries provided to appease readers wanting information over plot. As most stories ultimately move towards a climax, or even some sort of purpose other than simply completing the tale at hand, the stories like "Charyou Tree" and "Welcome to the Dogan" that are found in *The Gunslinger Born* and *The Long Road Home* are problematic attempts to fill in informa-tional gaps that King created when composing the original *Dark Tower* tale. Naturally, every particular scene or occurrence mentioned within the pages of *The Dark Tower* does not always contribute to the progres-sion of the plot, i.e. the reference to a Not-Man in *The Gunslinger* as this invisible being is only mentioned in passing and has no function other than to help establish the mystical and magical nature of Mid-World. Exploring this off-stage reference might be entertaining for read-ers, as it also might be somewhat satisfying in discovering how the gunslinger lost the belt his mother made for him and tried to present to him on the day he killed her, but exploring this particular side-story would have done nothing to take readers closer to the Dark Tower, and neither do the graphic novels. This is not to say that the graphic novels serve no function or do not realize some sort of lofty or even arbitrary standards relating to their aesthetic or literary merit. Rather, in conjunc-tion with the need for mildly clearer explanations regarding the plot and dialogue to add missing context, the critique of the add-on nature of the graphic novels is to suggest that the gaps and inconsistencies which are created between the original tale and the graphic novels is more than merely observing and noting places in which the various pieces to this *Dark Tower* puzzle do not quite fit. In looking at *The Dark Tower* and its graphic novel counter-part, sharp readers are able to see past the spec-tacle of the graphic novels and note that the grudging kinship between these two separate projects results in a story that hardly needs more muddled plot, unceremoniously dropped references, or an overabundance of story that finds difficulty in holding itself up.

Returning to the artwork and beginning to look at the general foundations and guidelines for graphic novel development, Dennis O'Neill provides several suggestions to keep in mind for those who write graphic novels in addition to those who look at the final product presented to the public eye. First, O'Neill discusses the various ways a graphic novel may begin and warns, "what you never, never want to do is open on an inanimate object — a building, for example — unless it is so unusual that, in itself, it excites curiosity. People are interested in people, not things" (37). To this degree, *The Gunslinger Born* succeeds in instantly immersing readers into the mysterious nature and story of the main character, Roland Deschain, the gunslinger. Although the opening pages of *The Gunslinger Born* are a bit too ambiguous with the introduction of the gunslinger for some tastes, the mystery and suspense that is created does serve as an overall smooth beginning for the story. Also, with respect to general guidelines and expectations of the graphic novel, O'Neill also suggests that any graphic novel should, "have enough story to fill the allotted number of pages" (86). With *The Gunslinger Born* based on a novel that approaches 800 pages of story, it is certainly safe to say that the seven installments of this mini-series has ample story to fill the pages. But, with the writers of *The Gunslinger Born* attempting to reduce several hundred pages of text into seven graphic novels consisting of forty-eight pages, there is actually too much story. While it is certainly difficult to think that a book which is originally 781 pages long could be fully adapted in a seven-volume graphic novel series, the writers of these texts have actually accomplished this feat, albeit at the cost of eliminating much of the original tale in addition to altering pertinent information and facts that noticeably conflict with the fiction. But, as is the case with graphic novels, the story must move somewhat quickly, and in the case of *The Gunslinger Born*, the speed at which the story progresses loses much in the process. With the sacrifice of plot advancement through imprecise and informal narration, *The Gunslinger Born* necessarily focuses on art and the visual representations offered by the medium of the graphic novel at the cost of clear storytelling.

King may insist upon the power of the artist in the *Dark Tower* series, especially through the character of Patrick Danville whose pen rids

Mid-World of the Crimson King, but the visual artist has no place in the *Dark Tower* universe as King suffices as an adequate storyteller. With the woes of adaptation and the pre-existing story of *The Dark Tower* influencing reader response and reaction to the graphic novel, it is impossible to say that the images included clearly convey a singular message or meaning. While art, like fiction, is subjected to multiple interpretations by many people with different backgrounds and within different contexts, the pressure on the artist to create straightforward art is overwhelming to the point that it may be ridiculous to expect the artwork in *The Gunslinger Born* to function in any other way than an imposition on imagination as shaped by the fiction that precedes the artwork. To wit, David Carrier provides the following critique of art and its lofty goals within the medium of the graphic novel:

> The artist's aim is to enable the spectator to form some hypothesis about what is depicted. If that process is successful, the spectator's hypothesis matches the artist's intention, and that viewer sees illusionistically represented what the artist desired to depict. When, rather, the artist's image is visually ambiguous — capable of more than one plausible interpretation — then he or she has failed to communicate [14].

Whether or not the artwork provided in the pages of the graphic novels has fully or accurately communicated particular messages and meanings to the reader is open for debate. However, in noting that the illustrations provided do conflict with descriptions of characters as found in the original story, the visual elements of the graphic novels are seen as lacking. As Will Eisner states that, "comprehension of an image requires a commonality of experience. This demands of the sequential artist an understanding of the reader's life experience if his message is to be understood. An interaction has to develop because the artist is evoking images stored in the minds of both parties," he suggests that a certain level of agreement between reader and writer/artist needs to be reached (13). Yet, among the images presented within the graphic novel and those described, there is a wide chasm existing between the words King penned and used to create images of his characters and settings, there is the problem of constantly changing and shifting artwork from book to book, and there are the graphic novel images which attempt to bring together the words and images already presented to faithful readers but fail in such an endeavor.

With graphic novels relying on artwork to portray characters and actions, albeit in select and still scenes, dialogue becomes an important element to telling the tale within the pages of a graphic novel. With the role and function of the narrator necessarily minimal, the words of the characters in the pages must reflect a sense of genuine and believable dialogue, and these conversations must provide information typically reserved for the off-screen interruptions of the narrator. But, dialogue in *The Gunslinger Born* is not sufficient in forwarding the plot. While readers are certainly given the words spoken by the characters, and some background and context to inform the reader as to the feeling and sentiment behind these words, the complexity and comprehensive nature of King's writing as being grounded in extensive detail is missing in the graphic novels, resulting in minimal insight into his fictional creations in the adaptation. Moreover, as, "we cannot look inside another person's head; we can only infer that person's thoughts from their outward expression in words and gesture," dialogue that fails to provide information and even a certain sense of closeness to the characters in a graphic novel results in confusion and perhaps even disdain and distaste (Carrier 40). While this sentiment certainly suggests the importance of a narrator within the graphic novel to convey those thoughts which cannot be expressed through speech, it has already been noted that the narrator has a purposely reduced role in graphic novels, especially considering that excessive narration in the graphic novel creates a separation between the reader and the artwork that is supposed to compliment the dialogue and adeptly tell the story at hand.

The narrative voice that dominates almost one-fourth of the actual story in the first issue of *The Gunslinger Born*, and later insists upon its importance and influence on the reader with whom it attempts to create a perpetual and necessary link, takes the story away from the characters of the graphic novel who, through their speech, give life to the story in this particular medium. Fiction may rely on the presence, role and function of the narrator to convey events, thoughts and back-story within a particular tale, but graphic novels operate within not only a limited number of pages but foreground action above development from an outside source; graphic novels allow the characters to tell their own stories in their own ways, and often the dialogue exchanges are constructed in a manner to reveal as much as a reader needs to know about a particular individual's idiosyncrasies, complexities, and predilections. In *The Gunslinger Born* and *The Long Road Home*, King's characters are adapted into a medium that necessitates an abundance of developed dialogue, enough to advance the story and hold it together while also forming the characters in the panels, yet the fictional foundation on which Roland Deschain and his friends rest creates characters whose speech need not be as elaborate and intricate as that which is found in graphic novels.

Also, regarding the role and function of the narrator in *The Gunslinger Born*, one item of concern extending beyond the overly personal interaction that the storyteller attempts to establish is that the original narrator for the events of *Wizard and Glass*, as well as the tie-in scenes from *The Gunslinger*, is Roland himself. While the actual narration of these memories from the gunslinger's youth are literally conveyed by Stephen King, the third-person omniscient narrator whose words are seen on each page of the *Dark Tower* series, Roland is the narrator of such stories within the pages of *The Dark Tower* as he tells Jake of his youth in Gilead and tells his ka-tat of Eddie, Susannah, Jake and Oy the story of his days in Hambry while huddled around a campfire on the Topeka turnpike. But, much like the characters within the fiction of *The Dark Tower*, the audience that reads the graphic novels needs a narrator similar to the gunslinger, one who covers every corner of the tale, one who does not drop any references, and one who does not fail to contextualize the story being told. However, because of the medium of the graphic novel and the limitations imposed on narration, the audience must learn to be satisfied primarily with dialogue. And while some audiences may be able to follow the story through what the characters say, the audience of the graphic novels does not always receive the best storytelling, whether by way of narration or dialogue, and is often left wondering as to what, exactly, is occurring in the story itself.

Audience is always a key consideration for any type of writing, whether it is academic or entertainment-oriented, and with *The Gunslinger Born* the writers claim to have a specific audience in mind — King's Constant Readers who are already knowledgeable of the *Dark Tower* story and acquainted with the particular selections of plot, narration and dialogue present in the original text. With such an audience in mind, it would be rather harsh for anyone to condemn the graphic novels for their content in that these tales are not necessarily meant for new readers of *The Dark Tower*. However, it would be very difficult to envision *The Gunslinger Born* as a project solely meant for those who have read the entire *Dark Tower* series; such an esoteric and even surreptitious product would likely fail to draw in outside readers as it is hard to believe that this series was planned and constructed to remain within a particular reading circle. As Dennis O'Neill says, the job of any graphic novel writer is to, "[tell] your story as clearly as possible. I emphasize clearly because one of the recurring and embarrassingly valid criticisms of modern graphic novels, particularly the adventure and fantasy titles, is that they are extremely difficult to understand on the most basic level" (24). And while there are certainly moments of clarity in the graphic novels, there are also numerous instances in which confusion looms over one's reading rather than understanding. To that end, in assuming that *The Gunslinger Born* is primarily meant for initiated readers as well as the unlearned, the chasm existing between these two reading groups is hardly reconciled at any point in the seven issues of *The Gunslinger Born*.

Although a complete focus on the artwork is suggested by the title of this chapter, the parenthetical notation focused on the "evolution" of the artwork is a beckoning to not only the illustrations in the texts of *The Dark Tower*, but also the graphic novel project *in its entirety*. Art, in this case, is accompanied by the necessary narrative boxes and dialogue bubbles common to sequential art, which, alongside some rather burdensome and questionable illustrations regarding consistency with the original tale, must necessarily include a heavy critique on the story that is conveyed in the seven issues of *The Gunslinger Born*. To start, with a *Star Wars*-esque introduction to the first issue of *The Gunslinger Born* reading, "In a world that has moved on..." the graphic novel does ambiguously and enticingly ease readers into the story despite the uncreative beginning (David, et al 1). Of course, these introductory words mean something more than a vague sentiment, or catch-phrase, that is used to open the story at hand as the underlying meaning and importance of the opening line to the *Dark Tower* series is that the decayed and destitute world in a distanced and defeated land is an image of King's world. However, as is the case with much of this project, unexplained phrases and dropped references are quite common. Yet, such is not exactly a detriment to the assumed readership that this series is suspected to draw, although the use of familiar phrases and plot elements from the original text that are rarely, if ever, explained in the course of the graphic novel. Even though *The Gunslinger Born* is a graphic novel series that insists upon a pre-existing relationship between the reader and the narrator(s) of the visually-represented adventures of a young Roland Deschain, the informational and contextual chasms impede any reader.

Beyond the concerns of the opening words in the *Dark Tower* graphic novels, the actual beginning of the tale to be told and visually presented in the series is as taxing as the first seven words all readers are greeted with. The first page of illustrations meets the reader with select words from a narrator, a presence that later abandons the third-person omniscient position and utilizes second-person references which creates a forced and counterfeit relationship between the speaker and the reader, a relationship that is as imposing as the artwork and one that is lacking in King's texts. Then again, in the Coda of *The Dark Tower*, King precedes the final scene of his epic tale with a personalized disclaimer that breaks the fourth wall and directly addresses the Constant Reader, and even chides the reader who only cares about the immanent ending instead of the story in and of itself. To look at this from another angle, it is not lost upon readers with prior knowledge and exposure to *The Dark Tower* that the main character, Roland Deschain, is certainly a complex character that cannot be reduced to a few simple blurbs or fully explored with only a few pages at the beginning of a graphic novel series. And it is certainly understood that the rest of *The Gunslinger Born* will unveil layers of the gunslinger's history, persona and psyche through the story contained in the pages following the brief and metaphoric introduction that uses ambiguities to introduce an enigmatic character. But when considering that this series would do well to adhere to the accepted norms and standards of other graphic novels yet does not, the leniency and ready forgiveness for the unorthodox beginning is abandoned. However, there are still key issues to examine from the other six installments of *The Gunslinger Born*. Aside from the insights that these graphic novels do impart upon the reader, including revelations concerning Marten/Walter's ever-changing face to suit his particular company and his easy ability to travel from one place to another through a magic doorway by means of chalk and a crystal, too many problems surface for any clear or comprehensive reading of these graphic novels.

Even among the gaps in information and the guessing that becomes almost inherent in reading through *The Gunslinger Born*, the explanations provided in this story as it relates to the kinship between not only the gunslinger and the Dark Tower but also the Crimson King and the Dark Tower is helpful in understanding and recontextualizing the original story. When readers learn that, "the new high king [Arthur Eld] pledged his life and the lives of his descendants to protect the Tower," it is easily concluded that Roland Deschain's link to the Dark Tower, especially by way of his guns which had once belonged to Arthur Eld, is one of necessity and ancestry (Furth, "Maerlyn's Rainbow" 33). Additionally, discovering the Crimson King's union with the Dark Tower is appreciated: "As his father had sworn, the Red Prince was bound to the Tower. But whereas a human child would have been bound to defend it, Arthur's monstrous child was determined to destroy it" (Furth, "Maerlyn's Rainbow" 34–5). Yet, even with these explanations provided to clarify content from King's fiction and the story that is spun in the graphic, the careful and speculative reader will find fault with these illuminations. For example, when Roland mentions that his quest for the Dark Tower is a promise that he has made for himself, and is a promise on which he will never renege, he insinuates that his quest is not only born out of his own mind but that his blind and unbridled passion will be his undoing. But, when it is suggested that Roland's quest for the Dark Tower is promised and unavoidable, the gunslinger's actions and decisions become largely insignificant — as long as he fulfills his destiny and seeks the Dark Tower, Roland Deschain's rationale and zeal are inconsequential. At least this is what is proposed in the story "Maerlyn's Rainbow," whereas the actual text of *The Dark Tower* suggests that Roland's thoughts and actions are of importance and are the keys to salvation instead of repetition and resumption.

In addition, the first four pages of the first issue utilize and even rely upon the assumed and supposed kinship between reader and writer, those presumed to be bound together as if in a fraternal order through their love of the *Dark Tower*, by means of short, obscure sentences that seem to foreshadow an exciting and even frightful opening. This only culminates in the introduction of a single character, the gunslinger, who is bluntly discussed as one who should be known to the reader no matter what prior reading experience has been had, if any: "If the gunslinger looks familiar to you, well, that as may be" (David, et al 3–4). Also, as pages four and five of the first installment of *The Gunslinger Born* display the gunslinger, in a single panel, posing like a superhero with the sunset as a backdrop with his gaze looking off into the clichéd distance, several narrative boxes describe the gunslinger and the object of his desire, the Dark Tower, with quick and murky discussion and additional phrases that seek to create a partnership between the reader and writer — "praise the Man Jesus," "do ya kennit," "Ka is a wheel," and "a father whose face must never be forgotten" — it is difficult to see any real advancement of the story or any genuine attempt to describe and explain who the gunslinger is (David, et al). Most stories rely upon some sort of hook to attract and maintain audience attention, for which, "comic writers have a page or, at best, two," to immerse the reader in the story at hand (D. O'Neill 37). With *The Gunslinger Born*, however, the story is absent as the first six pages present simply a progression of images and allusions to the story that is about to unfold, all of which does little to bring the reader into the story, much like the illustrations found in the *Dark Tower* books.

The Artistic Progression of the Series

The inclusion of illustrations to accompany the seven texts of the *Dark Tower* series serve as teasing glimpses into Stephen King's imagination, but also function as imaginative obstacles for the Constant Reader to overcome. The variations between the artists who worked on these texts in relation to the envisioned landscapes, characters and creatures in the original books is certainly noticeable, but their placement in the series is questionable at best, regardless of intent. In short, for first time readers of *The Dark Tower* books, the story becomes effectively ruined as many of the illustrations reveal events of the story that are meant to be suspenseful but become known simply by glancing at the artwork. Of course, the paintings in the *Dark Tower* series do not tell, in and of themselves, the tale in its entirety, but the artwork is too revealing of particular plot elements that would be better shrouded in secrecy and relayed through the written word rather than visually. With a look at the last illustration in the *Dark Tower* series, the very same picture which graces the cover of the first edition of this last book, Roland is found to be alive and ready to storm the Dark Tower of his dreams and adventures. For those who may have thought that Roland would not enter the Tower, this illustration then unveils that the final chapter, the climax of this cycle of stories, has the gunslinger positioned to enter the Tower. This is unfortunate concerning questions of suspense in that as King, back in the second installment *The Drawing of the Three*, attempts to create some tension and mystery for this series when he discusses the *possibility* of Roland achieving his goal instead of the *inevitability*: "Do I really know what that Tower is, and what awaits Roland there (should he reach it, and you must prepare yourself for the very real possibility that he will not be the one to do so)" (407). While the speculation as to how art can effectively alter one's reading of the *Dark Tower*, not only in terms of imagination but also concerning plot development, is only speculation and surely does not summarize most reading experiences of this series, art must still be considered as a problematic inclusion in the stories, with the Dark Tower itself also becoming victim to the various artistic representations of this structure.

As King experiments with genre in his *Dark Tower* series and includes elements of the Gothic, the Medieval, and that of science fiction, he not only creates an innovative conglomeration of formulaic conventions to create his tale, but also injects a troublesome blend of methods which creates mass confusion among his readers. As Roland quests for the Dark Tower, the supposed nexus of space and time, visual representations of this structure vary from an elaborate Gothic construction, which signifies a dark and deadly conclusion for this tale, to the basic brick and mortar medieval tower, which alludes to nobility and chivalry. The conflict between these two basic depictions of the Dark Tower force readers to continually alter their impressions and interpretations of Roland's quest, and although the malleability of the Dark Tower, which is also described as a living umbilicus as well as a contemporary sky scraper, is essential to understanding the true nature of this building, King nonetheless limits the reading imagination and further restricts the aesthetic nature of literature as the graphic novel *The Gunslinger Born* provides unchanging faces for King's characters and story, faces which, as he implies in *The Dark Tower*, should be left for the reader to imagine: "'If there's stuff in the rest about coming to the Dark Tower — or not — puzzle it out by yourself. You can do it if you try hard enough, I reckon. As for me, I don't want to know'" (695). With this sentiment, ambiguity and obscurity are depicted as essential aspects to the *Dark Tower* tale, a story which relies upon the imagination and interpretation of the Constant Reader. But, imagination is nearly halted as the words written upon the pages of *The Dark Tower* are constantly interrupted and affected by the illustrations included in each installment.

Before devoting complete focus to the graphic novels based on *The Dark Tower*, a brief review of the illustrations included in the books is needed. To that end, consider the following quick critical overview of the artwork in the *Dark Tower: The Gunslinger*— the first view into the gunslinger's world by way of Michael Whelan's fantasy-oriented art is that which sees cartoon-like characters roughly playing out parts in a story that has yet to find its way; *The Drawing of the Three*— a book for which there are two sets of illustrations, each being a noted deviation from the fantastic mood portrayed in the first novel; however, the illustrations continue to portray the characters as cartoon-like creations rather than realistic people; *The Waste Lands*— artwork which sees a return to the fantasy style of illustration found in the first book, but becomes rather boring with images that include a plain depiction of Blaine's travel on his monorail in addition to two illustrations which show the strange creatures in the blasted lands whereas one painting might have sufficed; *Wizard and Glass*— illustrations of a seemingly avant-garde and experimental nature yet which are a wholly dark influence indicative of the tale of woe and loss contained therein; in short, the artwork marks a move from typically clear depictions of the characters and settings to something a bit more muddled; *Wolves of the Calla*— a return to fantasy artwork reminiscent of comic books, of which one critic says that they are, "done in a broad comic book style, which strive to rob the story of whatever subtlety it might possess" (O'Hehir B12); *Song of Susannah*— artwork which recalls the somber mood of *Wizard and Glass* with pictures that are largely comprised of dark colors, but also finds criticism among reviewers concerning their placement in the text: "the hokey illustrations, by Darrel Anderson, don't help untangle things" (Sisario 16); *The Dark Tower*— a return to the original artist, Michael Whelan, and a return to the fantasy despite the constant blurring and blending of fiction and reality, and a final stop on the roller coaster of imaginative constraints placed upon the reader from the very first book.

These critiques may seem harsh in their judgment and perhaps overly reductive, but the artwork is overwhelming and even distracting when reading through *The Dark Tower*. The darker illustrations in *Wizard and Glass*, as well as those in *Song of Susannah*, tend to mirror the story being told, providing a non-intrusive backdrop for the story. However, the cartoon-like and fantasy-oriented paintings for the other five novels remind readers that they are reading instead aiding with immersion into the story. Perhaps the only illustration in the entire series that does not directly interfere with the imaginative interaction with the text is the depiction of Charlie the Choo-Choo in *The Waste Lands*. With this illustration, it is almost as if the reader is looking through Jake's eyes into a real book: the haunting grin on the locomotive and the tears of the children in tow easily matches the description in the pages of the text. But one picture out of seventy-seven is not exactly impressive. And just as the illustrations in *The Dark Tower* fail to perform as much more than a distraction, the graphic novelization of *The Dark Tower* is a project that fails to impress in much the same regard.

The Gunslinger Born: An Imaginative Imposition

One of the most noticeable elements of *The Gunslinger Born* is its reluctance to develop characters. Many of the players in this tale, along with their relationships, their idiosyncrasies and their foregrounded features — physical, mental and spiritual — are mentioned in passing but do rely on prior knowledge of the *Dark Tower* story for full understanding. With Randall Flagg, as well as Rhea the witch, *The Gunslinger Born* does provide a few select instances of character development, both informative for the reader in terms of context and detrimental to the original story. But first, consider Robin Furth's statement from the second volume of her *Concordance*: "characters are kind of a thought-form. An author creates them (or facilitates their passage into our world), but then the characters exist in the minds of many" (5). While such a view into the nature and imaginative power of writing implies an intrinsic flexibility with fiction, the multiplicity of interpretation and imagination is not necessarily a reflection of a writer's detriment. Varying views and varying visions of a story's content certainly do not translate to inadequate writing that fails to create a uniform understanding of fiction and the elements within that can become visible in the mind's eye. A little ambiguity is the beauty of fiction, and is an aesthetic appeal of the *Dark Tower* series as King does not burden his readers with overly extensive physical descriptions of his characters. While particulars, like Roland's haunting blue bombardier eyes, are mentioned and often referred to as specific markers of his character, there is not enough information and description in King's actual writing for a sketch artist to create a completely accurate portrait of anyone from the story. The illustrations that are included in the texts negate the necessity of these details, but their presence and eventual transformation into the *Dark Tower* graphic novels comes with numerous problems and issues.

Moving into a more specific critique, *The Gunslinger Born* does provide a few select instances of character development, both informative for the reader in terms of context and yet detrimental to the original story. Although *The Gunslinger Born* seems to solve the debate regarding Clay Reynolds' hair color — "his curly red hair hanging about his ears" or he "with the black hair" — and gives this Big Coffin Hunter dark black hair, this series does create an inconsistency with one other minor detail of hair color with reference to Roland's friend Cuthbert Allgood (King, *Wizard and Glass* 173; King, *Wizard and Glass* 226). In the third illustration from *Wolves of the Calla* titled, "Gunslingers, to me!" Cuthbert is depicted as having blonde hair. In addition, when Roland receives from the *character* Stephen King a copy of Robert Browning's "Childe Roland to the Dark Tower Came" and reads from the sixteenth stanza, "I fancied Cuthbert's reddening face/Beneath its garniture of curly gold," Roland does not deny this description of his lost friend (lines 91–2). Yet, with *The Gunslinger Born* the young Cuthbert Allgood is shown to have straight, shoulder-length black hair. Of course, such notations are of little consequence when discussing the story and plot behind the *Dark Tower* series and its relation to the graphic novel, yet the finalization of established visual creations of the characters does not afford any sense of individual imaginative autonomy with King's magnum opus.

More importantly, as the character Cuthbert is known for his sense of humor, or at least his juvenile approach to most issues bordering on the serious, he is referred to as, "'that laughing donkey,'" and it through this dominant trait of humor that the gunslinger not only remembers vividly his lost friend but also begins to understand Eddie Dean, another character who cherishes and hides behind humor (King, *Wizard and Glass* 649). Further foregrounding Cuthbert's predilection towards laughter in the novels, he dies while laughing at Jericho Hill: "*He can feel Cuthbert's burning body, its suicidal trembling thinness. And yet he's laughing. Bert is still laughing*" (King, *Wolves of the Calla* 171). Yet, in *The Gunslinger Born*, every depiction of Cuthbert that attempts to display any trace of hilarity fails. While some of his speech, and some of the description imparted by the narrator, suggests a leaning towards facetiousness, Cuthbert becomes little more than a background character who happens to accompany Roland on his early travels. Indeed, the young gunslinger whose humor was constant and infectious is replaced with a character that lacks more than just artistic dimension.

Moving on to the gunslinger's mortal enemy, Randall Flagg — in the guise of Walter — makes but one direct appearance in the original tale of *Wizard and Glass*, a meeting between he and Eldred Jonas, yet in the graphic novels his role is extended to one that reveals Walter is in fact Marten, a suspicion that is not confirmed until the seventh book of the series when a stranger bearing a name-patch with "Randall Flagg" stitched into it is referred to as Walter. As Walter speaks with Mordred in *The Dark Tower* and reveals that he loved Roland's mother, "'or at least coveted [her],'" this indicates that Walter is actually Marten, the man who seduced Roland's mother in *The Gunslinger*, the man whom Roland identifies as such in the Green Palace at the end of *Wizard and Glass* who also calls himself Flagg in the very same scene (King, *The Dark Tower* 179). Once all three of these characters are reconciled as being one individual, the scope of the story changes, but this information is not revealed until the seventh book in the original series, and the perpetual mystery associated with what are assumedly three distinct characters through most of the primary tale is dismissed unceremoniously in the graphic novels. And regarding the visual representations of the gunslinger's nemesis, the many faces of Walter in the graphic novel almost function as a gimmick. His role as "the Good Man's underliner" is undercut by the knowledge of Walter's primary allegiance to the Crimson King and the need for the disguises as he positions himself in Gilead's court under the moniker and face of Marten but as the pale-faced and sardonic Walter in the other realms of Mid-World (King, *Wizard and Glass* 423). The man Jonas meets in the original text is described as, "a man of medium height, powerfully built [...] with bright blue eyes and the rosy cheeks of either good health or good wine [and that] his parted, smiling lips revealed cunning little teeth," yet the Walter of *The Gunslinger Born* does not resemble this individual (King, *Wizard and Glass* 406). Walter and his other manifestations of Marten and Flagg both display a dark wit and love of silliness in the original texts, but readers encounter, rather, a fairly one-dimensional representation of this three-faced creature in the graphic novels, one who solely functions as an agent of evil instead of one with an intricate back-story and a reliance upon humor and wit to mask the disturbingly malicious character behind his ever-changing visage as the one behind the destruction witnessed in *The Stand* and who has endured the sufferings of being a rape victim.

Beyond Cuthbert Allgood and Randall Flagg, with respect to the distorted picture that has been formed through myriad visual depictions and disjointed storytelling, is the witch, Rhea of the Cöos. Described initially as a physically unimposing figure with, "cold flesh spongy and loose on the bones, as if the woman to whom they were attached had downed and lain long in some pool," Rhea is a character who becomes even more of a physically deformed individual in the original text (King, *Wizard and Glass* 118; King, *Wizard and Glass* 126). What is given in the graphic novels resembles an old crone as Rhea is portrayed as less of a witch and more of an old frontier woman, with plain dress, a full but grey head of hair stylishly twirled into a bun, and at times with a white bonnet donning her skull instead of the, "white hair standing out around her head in dirty clumps" described in the original book (King, *Wizard and Glass* 118). Additionally, in the graphic novels, Rhea never becomes the individual described in the original text as one that, "was so scrawny that she resembled nothing so much as a walking skeleton [...] [with] Sores clustered on her cheeks and brow" (King, *Wizard and Glass* 488). The original text of *Wizard and Glass* also juxtaposes these disgusting images against a the side of Rhea that extends beyond visual disgust in that when Susan Delgado spies Rhea looking into the Wizard's Glass in the original story she sees, "the face of a young girl — but one filled with cruelty as well as youth, the face of a self-willed child determined to learn all the wrong things for all the wrong reasons" (King, *Wizard and Glass* 128). This description of Rhea is certainly of little variation from the sentiments expressed in the graphic novel when discovering information about Rhea's youth and eventual infection by Maerlyn's Laughing Mirror, a device that amplifies her spite which is fully accounted for in the mini-story within the graphic novels that hinders King's tale more than it helps. Still, this woman, one whose childhood was filled with hate and malice which only becomes magnified, is of little consequence to the larger tale of *The Dark Tower*. By attempting to explain and explore the evil that grows and resides in Rhea Dubativo, the witch does gain a layer of understanding, if not sympathy, from the reader. As Rhea's leaning towards evil is reported to not entirely stem from within herself, the resulting ambivalence, that of despise tempered by mild empathy, incongruously and overly influences readings the original text. Rhea, as the individual who orchestrates Susan Delgado's death by fire and by the hand of her aunt Cordelia, needs to be positioned and constructed as a wholly evil character whose selfish and spiteful ways are necessarily contrasted against Susan's victimization. Any attempts to explain and explore Rhea's youth while also seeking to justify her abhorrence of the world around her critically challenges the primary tale.

Consider the initial meeting between Susan Delgado and Rhea of the Cöos during which Rhea must determine whether or not Susan is "honest," or a virgin. Within the graphic novels, readers are given a few verbal exchanges between the witch and Susan, along with an image of Susan *beginning* to disrobe as nudity, even comic nudity, appears to be taboo in the graphic novels. The dialogue, though, in the second issue of *The Gunslinger Born* does include crude references to Susan's body, as well as the comment that she is "caulked tight," but without the context provided by the original story, a new reader cannot begin to understand why Susan develops a particular hatred for Rhea, and vice-versa (David, et al 24–6). While the graphic novel does include the scene of hypnosis from the original text in which Rhea instructs Susan to cut her hair upon losing her virginity (supposing that this will happen after Hart Thorin has bedded Susan), there is no explanation in the graphic novel as to why Rhea would wish to see Susan humiliated. Regarding the artistic depictions of this scene, while *Wizard and Glass* does include an illustration of Susan enduring Rhea's examination of her purity, the inclusion of artwork, which is a bit more risqué than that found in the graphic novel, does not relay to the reader any semblance of violation that occurs in the fiction. When reviewing the original *text* of *Wizard and Glass*, however, a clearer understanding of the relationship that grows between Susan and Rhea is clearly established.

When "proving honesty," Rhea must inspect *all* of Susan Delgado's body, including her bowels and genitals. The first examination, when Susan, "felt one of those corpse-like fingers prod its way into her anus," is absent from the graphic novels while serving as an intrusive and foreboding preview of the key element of Rhea's services in the primary story (King, *Wizard and Glass* 132). The implicit reference to Susan's virginity ("caulked tight") in *The Gunslinger Born* is present in both the fiction and the graphic novel, and is notably sufficient for indicating that Susan is inexperienced with sex. But what follows this invasion, Susan's first vaginal penetration, is an exchange in which Rhea molests Susan and which resembles a lesbian scene of such twisted and unrequited lust that clearly positions Susan and Rhea as enemies, at least within *Wizard and Glass*. For further detail, as Rhea finishes with her examination, "the hag's withdrawing fingers closed gently around the little nubbin of flesh at the head of Susan's cleft," and Rhea begins to masturbate Susan for what proves to be an enticing yet disgusting sexual experience, one that cannot be illustrated (King, *Wizard and Glass* 133). With Susan's, "arms and belly and breasts breaking out in gooseflesh," at the touch of the old woman, she quickly commands the witch to stop, and at this order, as Rhea is not ready to halt either her molestation or figurative rape of Susan, the hatred begins (King, *Wizard and Glass* 134). No picture or simple dialogue is able to convey either the sense of violation that Susan endures or the subsequent hatred felt by Rhea who is not one to take commands. And it is with this scene of such heavy emotion and critical plot elements which are unfathomably removed, whether by choice or by necessity of the graphic novel medium, which further suggests that *The Gunslinger Born* certainly offers little to the expanding story of *The Dark Tower*.

Also to consider in the way of character analysis in the graphic novels is the rebel John Farson who is finally given a face, at least one behind a mask, in the third issue of *The Gunslinger Born*. As this enigmatic character is argued to be just another guise of Walter as Robin Furth suggests in the first volume of her *Concordance* that, "in the new *Gunslinger* we find out that Farson was just one of Walter's many masks," it is rather curious to see Farson meet face to face with Marten, who is actually Walter as readers witness each one physically altering his face to take on the visage of the other (60). This scene is not necessarily highlighted to provide yet another example of the many inconsistencies among King's tale and its venture into the illustrated text, but rather Farson, as a character finally brought to life, is an awkward character to bring into *The Gunslinger Born* in that he never comes onto the stage of the *Dark Tower* tale. Farson is always referred to as if he was almost a ghost, an insane man with high aspirations, yet one who never directly crosses Roland's path and never receives any treatment other than through the mouths of other characters or the narrator. For Farson to finally be given a face and a voice removes the mystery that this character carries all the way until the last page of *The Dark Tower* when it just might be possible to accept that he is another incarnation of Randall Flagg.

Another noticeable flaw found in *The Gunslinger Born* comes in the fourth issue just before Susan's rape-like encounter with Hart Thorin. With the set-up for this scene being that Susan is trying on a dress, the problematic content is not Susan's sensuality or sexual allure but the description of Susan's garment as her "Reaptide gown" (David, et al 28–2). The issue to take with this reference is that there is no prior mention in the graphic novel as to what "Reaptide" refers to. Readers familiar with *Wizard and Glass* are aware of the holiday and festivities, as well as the moon phase, that marks Reaptide, but the details concerning the background and context of this term, especially as such is a key element in fully understanding Susan's death by burning at the stake, is as dreadfully vague as the "Charyou Tree" phrase that is abruptly inserted into the tale just prior to Susan's death. And speaking of Susan's death, while initiated readers are easily able to recall that Susan's peers, the people of Hambry, tied her to the stake at which she is consumed by fire, there is yet another distressing gap in the story as readers of *The Gunslinger Born*'s seventh issue witness the speeches from Cordelia Delgado and Rhea of the Cöos in which it is heavily *implied* but not actually stated that some sort of justice befall Susan as she "'freed three killers [...] and murdered the sheriff'" (David, et al 27–2). The story in the graphic novel then takes readers to the scene at Hanging Rock in which Roland, Cuthbert and Alain have lured George Latigo and his men into the thinny at the bottom of Eyebolt Canon, and after several pages detailing the progression of events in this scene, Roland begins to gaze into the Wizard's Glass and sees, as the reader sees, Susan burning at the stake — but neither Roland nor the reader fully understands why this happens, or even how this happens.

Moreover, as the graphic novel only depicts the image of Susan burning to death as the only vision Roland sees in the Wizard's Glass, the Dark Tower that is mentioned at the very beginning of the graphic novel series which Roland sees in Maerlyn's Grapefruit well before learning of Susan's demise in *Wizard and Glass* is absent. The ultimate goal of Roland's questing is teasingly mentioned in the opening pages of *The Gunslinger Born* but no further references are made to the Dark Tower in the graphic novels, much to the discredit of the series as the guidelines surrounding graphic novels, as stated by Dennis O'Neill, include the decree that, "by the time your tale is done, your readers should have a sense of completion: all conflicts resolved, all questions answered" (91). Although there are plans to continue with this series and compose upwards of thirty installments, with the third installment titled *Treachery*, what readers actually have right now barely constitutes completion, especially with the structure of the Dark Tower serving as a happenstance reference that only means something to readers who have read outside the graphic novels.

As *The Gunslinger Born* progresses to its fifth issue, readers find Roland and Susan finally joining in a carnal embrace, although the professions of love in this seem rather quick and surprising considering the little amount of attention that this affair receives throughout the previous issues. Without delving too far into Roland and Susan's love, this fifth issue makes its mark with Rhea's knowledge of Susan's first sexual encounter with Roland. Although readers of *Wizard and Glass* come to know that Susan was to cut her hair upon losing her virginity, and that such was supposed to be a mark of shame and embarrassment for defying Rhea's advances and command while Susan endured the test of proving her honesty, *The Gunslinger Born* reveals no such information. As Rhea watches Susan with Roland in *Wizard and Glass*, readers are reminded of Rhea's distaste for Susan as the witch anticipates Susan butchering her golden mane — "*let's see how sexy you feel in a few minutes, you snippy bitch*" — and the intentions behind Rhea's commands are made quite clear (King 320). Yet, the graphic novel fails to fully re-create the tension and hatred these two women have for each other, and when Susan finally loses her virginity yet fails to carry out Rhea's command. In this fifth issue of *The Gunslinger Born*, readers see only a calm and mildly disappointed Rhea — "'The little one does the hokey-poke, but her hair's still on her head. Why didn't she do as I told her? Seems other steps need to be taken, so they do'" — instead of a spiteful and venomous witch who hates anyone or anything that defies her command (David, et al 11–2).

To add to the list of challenging elements of *The Gunslinger Born*, concerning the writing now as opposed to the artwork, the graphic novel makes a bold move with Eldred Jonas revealing to his companions that he is a failed gunslinger. In the fifth issue of *The Gunslinger Born*, Jonas mentions that, "'I trained as one [a gunslinger], after all,'" showing no signs of regret, remorse or even shame in his declaration (David, et al 18–1). However, Jonas' humiliation associated with being a failed gunslinger is pivotal to the plot of *Wizard and Glass*. Jonas's reputation relies on fear, and with his advanced age and "quavering voice," he understands that his physical appearance needs to be trumped by his intangible qualities, those that cause fear, meaning that any sort of weakness would be better hidden than displayed to the public (King, *Wizard and Glass* 174). As *Wizard and Glass* reaches the scene in which Roland and his friends are arrested for the murder of Hart Thorin and Kimba Rimer, and as Roland finally realizes that Jonas had once lived in Gilead and sought to win his guns yet did not do so, Roland boldly declares to Jonas that, "'The soul of a man such as you [Jonas] can never leave the west'" (King, *Wizard and Glass* 479). Infuriated that his history has been unveiled, Jonas almost kills Roland right there, but with a surprising show of composure, Jonas does not pull the trigger. His emotions do continue to boil as, "he'd believed no man had known [of his exile]. Roy and Clay suspected, but even they hadn't known for sure" (King, *Wizard and Glass* 480). Yet, why the writers of *The Gunslinger Born* ignored this key piece of information when drafting and crafting the graphic novel is unknown, but the criticism is that this alteration to the storyline is certainly detrimental to the subtext of the original story.

The fifth issue of *The Gunslinger Born* also brings into the *Dark Tower* mythos the second and third installments of the story behind Maerlyn's Laughing Mirror. In the add-on stories from this issue, readers learn that Rhea of the Cöos and Eldred Jonas are bound together by much more than hate and an attraction to the pink glass of Maerlyn's Rainbow. Here readers learn that both Rhea and Jonas have been cut by the Laughing Mirror and carry a small piece of this in their bodies. Of course, the back-story regarding both Rhea and Jonas's exceptional and extensive ability to hate is as entertaining as it is informative, yet the attempts at closing the gaps included in King's primary story leave more questions than answers. As it is made known that Rhea made a pact with a demon to lengthen her life, her end of the deal, regarding the foretold union of Roland and Susan, is to, "ensure that no child was conceived, and if a child did kindle in the girl's belly, then it had to be destroyed" (Furth, "Laughing Mirror Part 2" 32). However, this tale of Rhea's early life inadvertently attempts to re-write *Wizard and Glass* by adding context to Rhea's involvement in Susan's eventual demise, yet this information cannot be applied to a text that is finished and closed. Even though the *entire* story of King's *Dark Tower* series receives an accessible and somewhat fruitful expansion through the graphic novel adaptations as well as the add-on stories included in each issue, the writing to be found only provides additional disparities that arise with the condensing of an 800-page novel into seven graphic novels.

Regardless of the benign intentions behind the conception and delivery of *The Gunslinger Born*, the final product is one that resists proper integration into the *Dark Tower* story by means of its revisionist approach in that many scenes in this series attempt to amend and alter the original story by including new events that went previously unstated and unexplained or necessarily excluded. Indeed, the stories included in these graphic novels resemble fan-fiction more than genuine inclusions of the *Dark Tower* mythos. When Robin Furth writes of the Dark Tower's first encounter with its enemies, her writing does convey a sense of knowledge about the history of Mid-World, but it is also betrayed by some rather convenient and even cliché writing afterwards: "Though his injuries were terrible, Gan would eventually heal. After all, every magical being has the ability to endlessly regenerate" ("Laughing Mirror Part One" 36). Not only does the latter part of this passage reflect a contrived style of story-telling, these words pose a multitude of problems for *The Dark Tower* series and Roland Deschain's quest. If the Dark Tower, or Gan, is fully capable of healing himself, then it is conceivable that the Dark Tower will stand no matter what threatens its well being. If one were to mention the Beams which supposedly hold the Dark Tower steady and safe, Robin Furth's explanation of the Beams in "The Laughing Mirror Part One" suggest that the Beams are of little consequence when considering the Dark Tower's well-being and survival: "he [Gan] divided the universe into multiple, parallel realities, and set six magnetic Beams in place to maintain the alignment of time, space, size and dimension in all of them" (32). As the Beams support the stability of all the worlds which spin around the Dark Tower, their function, as described here, seem to have little importance regarding the Dark Tower itself. Even though the continuation of the universe(s) requires the constant hold of the Beams, the Dark Tower itself seems to be completely independent of the Beams for sustained existence.

Another point of consideration and contention is that of geography. To be sent west, in the *Dark Tower* story, is the most feared punishment that any potential gunslinger faces. To the west lies exile and life among the harriers and uncivilized who thrive on chaos and discord. The Western Sea, and its beach on which Roland journeys during *The Drawing of the Three*, is the western-most edge of the world as it is known to Roland, which is confirmed in *The Gunslinger Born*, but the discussion of geography that takes place in "The Sacred Geography of Mid-World" from the first issue of this series raises more problems than answers questions. For example, when a failed gunslinger is sent west, it can be safely assumed that the westward direction and designation of the outcasts is to place these potential threats to the Dark Tower farther away from the actual structure, suggesting that the Dark Tower lies east of Gilead. But, with the Tower presumably residing in an eastward direction from Gilead, a few issues with consistency as well as flawed writing arise, even though King provides an explanation, or a cop-out, when he mentions that, "'the directions of the world are also in drift'" (*The Waste Lands*, 80). In *Wizard and Glass*, Roland and his friends are sent to Hambry, which is east of Gilead. Moreover, when Roland later enters Maerlyn's Grapefruit and first sees the Dark Tower, "*the pink storm [...] bears him west along the Path of the Beam,*" this suggests that the Dark

Tower is not only west of Hambry but west of Gilead, in the land that is overrun by failed gunslingers and those who would seek to harm the Dark Tower (King, *Wizard and Glass* 570).

Further, in "The Sacred Geography of Midworld," Robin Furth tells the reader that Gilead lies directly on the Eagle-Lion Beam, one which would connect the numbers 3 and 9 on the face of a clock, or true east and west. In this story when the gunslingers' tutor, Vannay, shows his students the Path of the Beam by placing a needle in a cup of water and then positioning himself directly under the Beam, "the needle rose and floated to the surface, spinning lazily for a moment before pointing east," this suggests that the Dark Tower lies in the lands opposite to those to which exiled gunslingers are sent, or in the east (Furth, "Sacred" 44). The trouble with this element of Furth's story is that it suggests the Dark Tower is somewhere between Gilead and Hambry. With Hambry bordered to the east by the Clean Sea, and as Mid-World is essentially an island—"On all sides it [Mid-World] was bordered by water—the Western Sea, the South Seas, the Clean Sea, and the frozen, ice-capped Northern Sea"—Hambry marks the eastern edge of Mid-World as there is no land, no Tower, farther to the east, only ocean (Furth, "Sacred" 40–1). Furthermore, as Roland, Cuthbert and Alain travel the lands between Gilead and Hambry and fail to encounter the Dark Tower, it would seem that something within the story of Mid-World's geography is certainly askew. Also, when discovering that Roland knew of the Beams as a young gunslinger, that Gilead was constructed underneath the path of one of these Beams, as well as the Guardians which stood at the ends of the Beams, this contradicts the apparent search Roland had embarked upon, as he says in *The Waste Lands*, "'I think now that I've been look-ing for one of the Guardians ever since I began my quest'" (King 40). As Roland's quest for the Dark Tower primarily required knowledge as to where any single Beam was located, "The Sacred Geography of Mid-World" tells the reader that Roland knew of at least one place to start— Gilead—even though *The Dark Tower* books clearly indicate that Roland did not possess this knowledge that the graphic novels claim he had.

For the final examination of problems posed by *The Gunslinger Born*, focus shifts to one of the key add-on stories included in the back pages of the series' issues, the tale titled "Maerlyn's Rainbow." In this tale, readers are given a rather extensive history of the Dark Tower itself as well as the relationship the gunslinger has with this nexus of existence. This story, also written by Robin Furth, details the account of the Tower's creation and the attempt by the Great Ones (creatures that preceded the Old People) to conquer the Dark Tower by way of re-constructing it through mechanical and scientific means:

> When the architects, electricians and builders arrived in End-World, they were amazed by what they saw. Not only was the Tower more imposing than they had realized, but what they had taken for stone was actually hardened flesh. Still, they wanted to earn their glory, so they set to work. But no sooner did the first wrecking ball hit that imposing edifice than the ground was rocked by an enormous tremor ["Maerlyn's Rainbow" 30].

Beyond this brief account of the initial failure to alter the Dark Tower by the Great Ones, those in league with the infamous and malicious Maerlyn, is the note that, "despite the horror and havoc, the Tower survived" (Furth, "Maerlyn's Rainbow" 30). In detailing this survival and eventual recuperation, however, the intimation is that the Dark Tower could take care of itself and protect itself from any outside harm, which seemingly negates the need for assistance and succor from the last gunslinger. Additionally, the tremor described when the Great Ones attempted to reconstruct the Dark Tower is denoted as a Beamquake, but such would be impossible as a Beamquake is specifically noted as an earthquake-type of cataclysm which occurs when one of the six Beams holding the Dark Tower break. Still, it is declared that Roland Deschain would seek to enter and save the Dark Tower, despite the apparent needlessness of this action: "As a warrior of the White, he [Roland] would destroy the Outer Dark. Unless he was destroyed, he would kill the Crimson Prince and rein in the power of the Prim forever" (Furth, "Maerlyn's Rainbow" 35). Aside from the statement that the last gunslinger is surely the key to saving the Dark Tower, the idea that Roland Deschain's quest would restore the magic needed to sustain the Dark Tower is quite surprising as no such promise is ever given in *The Dark Tower*. To be sure, speculating as to the result of a successful journey for the last gunslinger, one in which he either purposefully remains outside of the Dark Tower or finds something other than the sands of the Mohaine Desert behind the door at the top of the Tower, is just that: speculation.

As the flaws and foibles of *The Gunslinger Born* are numerous, even though many of the complaints railed against the graphic novel are minor, it cannot go unstated that this project does relay an incomplete story that is conceivably problematic for first-time readers as well as those who are privy to the origins of the *Dark Tower* tale. For example, in the first issue of the graphic novel as Roland discovers his mother's indiscretions with Marten, Roland leaves his mother's quarters as Marten says to Roland, "'best of luck in finding your hand'" (David et al. 17–4). While this certainly mirror's Marten's words from the original text in *The Gunslinger*—"'Go and find your hand'"—these references to Roland's appendage make little sense in and of themselves (King 172). With no context, no explanation of why Roland needs to discover something attached to his body (for a literal interpretation), these lines are ridiculously cryptic. Yet, as it is revealed in *The Gunslinger* that the reference to Roland's hand is an allusion to masturbation as Roland walked by his mother's apartments to find solitude on the roof, "where a thin breeze and the *pleasure* of his hand awaited," one can only wonder what the writers of the graphic novel were trying to accomplish with an enigmatic line that might be understood as a condescending and mocking send-off from Marten but, in all likelihood, is read as one of numerous lines, references, and scenes that make little sense among the choppy, episodic and lackluster storytelling (King 170, emphasis added). With the many inconsistencies and enigmas brought forth in *The Gunslinger Born*, one might expect the second series, *The Long Road Home* to be a clearer project, one that relies less upon the established story of *The Dark Tower*. But, unfortunately, the second run of the *Dark Tower* graphic novels is just as problematic as the first series.

The Long Road Home: More Story Does Not Equal Better Story

With *The Gunslinger Born* almost entirely comprised of events and actions from the fiction of *The Dark Tower*, the second run of graphic novels which tell the tale of the young gunslinger, *The Long Road Home*, attempts to fill in the gaps between the death of Susan Delgado and the return of the gunslinger and his friends to Gilead. Since the source material for *The Long Road Home* is minimal when compared to the source material for *The Gunslinger Born*, it could easily be assumed that there would be fewer inconsistencies in this series as there is little previous or established information from the *Dark Tower* books to compete with the information ultimately presented in the graphic novels. The action of *The Long Road Home*, along with the additional add-on stories in the mold of those found in the first seven graphic novels, provides more story to the eager reader as the journey to Gilead from Hambry only receives passing treatment in King's novels. However, as is the case with *The Gunslinger Born*, there are inconsistencies and problems including the fact that not much happens in the way of plot in this run of the graphic novel. The action of *The Long Road Home* shows that Roland and his friends leave Hambry, cross a river, and return to Gilead, which is information already gleaned from *The Dark Tower*. And while much action in *The Long Road Home* does take place inside of the Wizard's Rainbow and does provide a few original scenes that are not touched upon in the fiction, there is very little in the way of revelation, enlightenment, or even story to be encountered. Readers may come to see that Marten is as crafty and sleek as originally depicted, and there are a few moments of action that move the story along, such as Alain's entrance into Maerlyn's Grapefruit, but with the minimal and often bothersome narration used to move readers from one scene to the next, this series is not exactly an improvement on the first seven issues. With *The Long Road Home*, the writers had much more space in which they could work as the details of the gunslinger's return to Gilead are a bit muddled in *The Dark Tower*. Of course, a few facts regarding this journey were made known throughout the course of King's series, but the limitations posed by *Wizard and Glass* on the first series, which were largely ignored and thereby created discord instead of harmony between the graphic novels and the books, were less of an imposition on these next issues.

However interesting the new information presented in *The Long Road Home* is, such as the revelation that actual eyes inhabit the Wizard's Glasses and that Sheemie was not a naturally skilled "Breaker," the storyline is met with some resistance from the original texts and the overall product is not entirely remarkable in terms of the story it tells and adds onto the larger *Dark Tower* story. As the first installment of *The Gunslinger Born* closes with the last two issues, the inconsistencies and troubles begin to wane, but not so much that they should escape a critical eye that has the benefit of looking at *The Long Road Home* for comparison. For example, as the sixth issue of *The Gunslinger Born* finds Roland and his friends imprisoned for the murder of Hart Thorin and later rescued by Susan, readers find these four met outside the jail with their horses ready to ride with Sheemie who had prepared the steeds. And while this is consistent with the novel, the absence of Sheemie's meeting with Susan just *before* she frees Roland, Cuthbert and Alain is cause for concern. As Susan is startled to find Sheemie conveniently prepared for the escape and willing to assist, Susan questions his knowledge, or seeming foreknowledge, that his help would be needed, to which Sheemie replies, "'I just knew,'" (King, *Wizard and Glass* 506). Although these three words seem inconsequential, they are, as the Constant Reader comes to discover, a foreshadowing of Sheemie's exceptional skills, which come to include the ability to teleport, suggesting that Sheemie is not as much of a dullard as one might come to believe in the early pages of either the original fiction or graphic novel. And while Sheemie's mental capacity for supernatural skills is not germane to the plot of *The Gunslinger Born*, it does pose problems for *The Long Road Home*.

As it is noted in *Wizard and Glass*, Sheemie finds his way to Gilead after his separation from Roland and then Susan: "'he followed us. [And] it couldn't have been easy for him'" (King 624). Further details of the difficulties faced on the road to Gilead are found in *The Dark Tower* when Roland and his friends cross a bridge spanning the Xay River, and Roland mentions of this passage that, "'there was only the one bridge, a thing made out of ropes, and once we were across, Alain cut it. We watched it fall into the water a thousand feet below" (King, *The Dark Tower* 271). Jake Chambers then concludes that Sheemie, while following Roland's trail, must have teleported across the chasm with no bridge to continue his journey to Gilead. Although this scene may appear to be minute, an in-depth examination of what is revealed in the original texts and what eventually appears in the graphic novels raises even more concerns. In short, as Sheemie is shown in *The Long Road Home* as directly receiving some sort of catalyst from one of the Old People's robots which triggered his ability to teleport, this undercuts the uncanny intuition Sheemie displays in *Wizard and Glass*. While the scene in the graphic novel does provide at least an explanation for the plot which readers anticipated, this also undercuts the foreshadowing provided in *Wizard and Glass* as Sheemie is depicted in the graphic novels as not just a peculiar and slow character, but one who is hardly special by his very nature.

In addition to the inconsistent portrayal of Sheemie as a character artificially imbued with his mental abilities, *The Long Road Home* depicts Sheemie as an individual capable of a great many things that create a dilemma when compared to the original fiction. Key among these is Sheemie's apparent ability to heal not only others, but also himself. This becomes problematic considering the death that Sheemie meets in *The Dark Tower* as a mild infection received from stepping on a piece of glass ends his life, which seems rather strange considering that the graphic novel shows Sheemie being able to recover from being shot — twice. Additionally, in the fourth installment of *The Long Road Home* readers see Roland Deschain taken to the Castle of the Crimson King where the gunslinger not only meets the self-proclaimed "'Eater of Worlds,'" which is certainly a forced and faulty link between the Crimson King and It even though Ralph Roberts from *Insomnia* seems to look into the Crimson King's deadlights (a phenomenon typically reserved for It), but Roland also learns of this creatures existence (David, et al., *Long Road* 12). The latter point here is important because when Roland's new ka-tat sees sign of the Crimson King in *Wizard and Glass*, the gunslinger gives the following response to questions as to who he is: "'I know not'" (King 666). In this instance, it could be suggested that Roland's experience in the Wizard's Rainbow is not entirely remembered, but to forget meeting one's arch enemy seems rather convenient, or the substance of lies. And even though the Constant Reader is aware of Roland's deception, or even keeping his own council when it suits his needs, the mystery behind his initial lack of knowledge as to who the Crimson King is, along with the gunslinger's strangely acquired information as to who the Breakers are in *Wolves of the Calla* and where Le Casse Roi Russe lies on the Path of the Beam, such mysteries become less and less untwined as the graphic novels continue to be published.

Still, there is a sense of excitement and anticipation as to where the remaining graphic novel series will take readers and what will be revealed along the way. And such considerations of the audience are addressed in the final installment of *The Long Road Home* when writer Peter David acknowledges the reader when looking back on the first two series and generously mentions that, concerning the content of these graphic novels, "the results are, of course, ultimately up to you, the reader, to decide," ("Comments" 40). At this point, after the first two story arcs have been published and have not been entirely successful, David's awareness of the potential problems of this series and commentary on the attempt to somewhat appeal to the reader does provide a glimmer of optimism that perhaps the remaining story to be told will be better than what has already been presented to the public eye. After all, with each series following *The Gunslinger Born*, there is less and less of a dependence upon *The Dark Tower* for information and plot, suggesting that the writers of the graphic novels have all the leniency they need to create a fully stand-alone tale that does not conflict with the original story. But, at the same time, there is enough detail provided in the original books to at least give a mild structure of expectation as to what will take place, which could result in the additional installments of this project falling prey to the same criticisms discussed here. For the time being, the hope is that with less and less direction from *The Dark Tower*, the graphic novels will begin to stand on their own and adeptly add to the existing story rather than detract from it.

The Pen vs. the Brush

As Stephen King notes in the forward to the first volume of Robin Furth's *Concordance* to the *Dark Tower* series, "unabridged audio forces the reader to slow down and listen to every word, whether he or she want to or not. It also lends a new perspective" (viii). The audio book functions much in the same manner as the graphic novel in that it does provide a new angle by which one can appreciate and approach a given story, but hearing a story in a textually-oriented culture is just as oppressive as viewing a story in a graphic novel when the original tale was created as text. But, for a purposeful shift into other concerns regarding changes in medium, the problems of adaptation concerning Stephen King's fiction is most notable in his films. Much of the commentary on King's film is only analogous at best concerning adaptation and the venture into the graphic novel, but the same critiques that cinema faces hold true for the graphic novel. As Michael Collings suggests that, "what we see in King, then, is a novelist closer than most to the visual arts, incorporating film references into his prose, structuring episodes on filmic techniques, and drawing on his readers' reservoir of images from film and television," it would seem that King's writing is meant to be seen outside of the reader's imagination (*Films* 11). Also, as critics like Harold Bloom have declared that King is primarily a visual writer, one whose writings tends to evoke particular imagery and often by means of referencing the actual world of his readers, it appears that King is certainly a writer who does write for the screen, or perhaps even the graphic novel. Regardless of the apparent appropriateness of visual mediums and their purported compatibility with King's writing style, there are certainly issues to consider beyond simply providing visual representations that the mind's eye of the author has envisioned.

In essence, the graphic novel adaptations of *The Dark Tower* almost function in the same manner as a cinematic adaptation of King's writing as the transfer of his text to the screen is rather problematic despite any box-office success, such that often results in a, "beautifully produced, eye-popping spectacle that does absolutely nothing to you emotionally" (Magistrale, *Hollywood* 19). Further, as Stephen King admits in Tony Magistrale's *Hollywood's Stephen King* that, "the difference between books and movies is that when I have you in one of my books I want to move you emotionally, to establish some kind of intense emotional reaction [...] With films, every time you add another layer of production, the surface gets blunted more and widens," it would seem that King would prefer to avoid adaptation and side-step the problems of translating and transferring one medium to another (19). Of course, this is not the case, which is not surprising considering the *commercial* success of King's films, or sarcastic criticism from Harold Bloom who says that King's books, "are visually oriented scenarios, [which] tend to improve when filmed" ("Afterthought" 208). However, beyond the financial considerations that inevitably trail King's cinematic ventures, as well as the condemnatory commentary that suggests King's writing is actually meant for film, there are criticisms that suggest there is more to King's success at the movies than monetary gain, implying that adaptation can relay a coherent and genuine product as Tony Magistrale asserts, for example, that, "of all the telefilms adapted from Stephen King's fiction, *IT* is arguably the most faithful rendition of the novel that inspired it" (*Hollywood* 188). An actual look at the film would suggest otherwise, and serves as another example of critique that that is deservedly extended towards King's adaptive practices and his recent move into the graphic novel arena.

In the mini-series version of *IT*, the figure of the Turtle is noticeably absent, which may seem inconsequential to the story of *IT* itself, but when considering the positioning of this novel in King's fictional universe as a *Dark Tower* related story, it would seem reasonable to assume that such an important figure would endure. The novel *IT*, as it relates to the *Dark Tower* series, relays to the reader the larger tale and context behind the Turtle totem that serves as one of the Guardians of the twelve portals that mark the edges of Mid-World. The Turtle is a benevolent force that guides the Losers Club in its battle against It, is the source of cosmic origin —"*I'm the Turtle, son. I made the universe*"— and the Turtle is the only Guardian in the *Dark Tower* mythos that receives any treatment beyond just an animal distinction and a name (King, *IT* 1009). With no placement of the Turtle in the television version of *IT*, this exclusion, at least regarding Stephen King's cinematic universe, removes *IT* as a film from the *Dark Tower* story (if this story does end up on film; other related tales such as *The Mist* have made attempts at creating a link between the film and the world of the *Dark Tower*). Such not only creates a regrettable separation between the novel *IT* and the film version, but also solidifies the proposition that the function of adaptation is quite limiting, that no matter how well King's films or projects within other mediums are completed, the larger context of his canon that he has purposely created through his *Dark Tower* series serves as constant interjection and rejection of King's inability to keep all his creations working together as one single tale as he purportedly intends with his fiction.

While the preceding certainly implies that reading be left solely to the reader, there are problems that arise when wrestling control away from the author. However, to take imagination away from the reader, as is the case with the graphic novel version of *The Dark Tower*, is just as taxing as an author who abandons his work and leaves it entirely in the hands of his audience. Still, as Orson Scott Card says, "though the printed page can last for years, the story only lives when someone is reading it" (229). And, surprisingly, the popularity of this series has sustained itself, and has even drawn in new readers to the *Dark Tower* series. Despite this acceptance, exploring *The Gunslinger Born* and *The Long Road Home* reveals too many enigmas and inconsistencies to be considered as either a complete project or even an adept or coherent one. The fan-fiction feel that arises from *The Gunslinger Born* is more of a burden than a boon for serious scholarly attention regarding King's *Dark Tower* series, which is not to say that graphic novels are devoid of any scholarly or academic worth. But, among the concerns outlined and discussed here, it is a wonder as to how the graphic novel series has remained popular among readers.

3

The Face of Evil:
Behind the Hood and
Under the Cowboy Hat

"The guilt of worlds hangs about his neck like a rotting corpse" — from
Song of Susannah

EXAMINATION OF THE GUNSLINGER and his growth throughout the *Dark Tower* series is certainly a common task for the reader to take on, especially when considering the complexity involved concerning questions of emotion, motivation, morality, autonomy, and sacrifice. Although these categories through which one begins to analyze Roland Deschain are only a few of the possible paths leading into the gunslinger's psyche, each of these routes tends to point in one primary direction — towards the realm of evil. Labeling the gunslinger as a wholly evil character, however, is erroneous, but attributing evil to him is not exactly misleading. More importantly, the overwhelming presence of evil, or an absence of decency and compassion, is found in most every character in *The Dark Tower*. Even Oy cannot escape at least a mild designation as an evil character. Loosely used here, applying the term *evil* to Oy comes from the perspective of his origins, as a presumed outcast from his own family, suggesting that the billy-bumbler is cast aside for some sort of violation among his kin. In speculating that Oy's evil in this instance comes from an inability, or unwillingness, to conform to the norms and standards of his brethren, labeling this character as evil is a bit inaccurate. Still, this character, or creature, one that is often forgotten among the council held by Roland and his ka-tet, a being that sacrifices itself so Roland can continue on his quest for the Dark Tower, should not be seen as an individual completely aligned with innocence and goodness. Oy, like the gunslingers he follows, adheres to the codes of the Eld, which hold killing as a largely minor offense, suggesting that his allegiances position him as evil not so much by the deeds he performs but by association with Roland and the others. Perhaps the overwhelming presence of evil and altered perceptions regarding, say, murder, reflects the decay of Mid-World rather than a conscious decision by many in *The Dark Tower* to stray from the White and into the Black. On the other hand, most signs point towards the implication that with *The Dark Tower* Stephen King has composed a tale in which hope and redemption are merely glimmers in the background that constantly dwindle and fade as the characters in these books consistently and consciously choose evil over good, in capacities both large and small.

When Orson Scott Card declares that, "no one is so good that he is untouched by evil," he suggests evil is so ubiquitous that it infringes on everyone's life in some way or another (226). In the *Dark Tower* series, King sees to it that evil becomes a constant presence in the story, but he avoids the pitfalls of attempting to create wholly good or entirely evil characters as he blurs the lines between such distinctions, creating a tale that consists of not groups or individuals as simply polar opposites to one another but rather a selection of characters whose transgressions garner little sympathy with the reader. With the main character, Roland Deschain, functioning as an anti-hero who unquestioningly kills anyone obstructing his path to the Dark Tower, and even sacrifices his friends in order to achieve his ends, he is nonetheless the only hope for Mid-World, and the entire Stephen King universe. And this duty, or burden, to ensure the safety of the Dark Tower and ensure the continued existence of time and space is frighteningly placed into the homicidal hands of the gunslinger.

Much like how the gunslinger is positioned as a protagonist but is also depicted as an antagonist, as the Crimson King is described as "Hell, incarnate," it cannot be said that he is the epitome of evil — he may be an individual whose designs of conquering the Dark Tower places him in a position that is certainly aligned with that of evil intentions and evil ancestry, but his eventual insanity alleviates the attribution of evil (King, *The Dark Tower* 785). Also consider that Randall Flagg, the demonic wizard from *The Eyes of the Dragon* and the satanic wanderer *The Stand*, escapes the designation of an entirely evil character — when it is learned in *The Dark Tower* that Flagg was raped as a young man, speculations arise as to whether or not Flagg's actions are truly those of purely evil intention or those which stem from a victimized mindset that seeks a sense of equilibrium to counterbalance the atrocity he endured. Yet, the purpose of examining the multitudes of evil is not to simply note the constant gray-area that King's characters in *The Dark Tower* occupy regarding their ethicality and morality, but to investigate the varying degrees of evil in this series as a means of understanding the purpose and cost of creating characters with which readers do not easily identify. With no clear protagonist in *The Dark Tower*, King offers a fictional rarity in that the forces and people battling one another in this tale all seem to be cut from the same cloth, which can be interpreted as a bold experimentation or even as a distressing critique on the typical fantasy figure.

Among the ideas promoted thus far which depict King as a writer who is mostly focused on the seemingly realistic portrayal of everyday life and everyday people who are caught up in some form of evil or another, or at least very trying circumstances, various critics offer contrary views. First, Deborah L. Notkin believes that, "Stephen King is one of the few writers today, in any field, whose primary theme is one of hope and survival, despite the odds" (142). Additionally, as Notkin provides the suggestion that King is, rather, a writer of optimism and perhaps even that of faith, she also suggests that, "the overwhelming impression to be gained from reading King's books is that the kinks and the sadists are the exception, not the rule," implying that the less than savory characters readers constantly meet in King's fiction are likely foregrounded and brought into the fiction as a counter-point to the struggling yet undismayed characters who comprise a population of generally good and sympathetic people (132). Even though the previous proposition can be easily met with skepticism, another point to consider is the argument of authorial design forwarded by Heidi Strengell. Concerning the question of evil in King's fiction, Strengell says that, "the body of King's fiction is strongly marked by the various types of determinism" (187). In suggesting that King's role as an author is of more consequence than the actual plot readers encounter in one of his books, it looks as if Strengell's view on evil is that which does not deny its presence but rather seeks to excuse it. The determinism for which Strengell argues lessens the evil found in King's characters, especially if they are pushed into evil instead of lured and tempted. But, rather than offer a rebuttal to this argument, Strengell gives one herself when she says that, "King's characters always have the choice between good and evil," suggesting that the argument for determinism is not entirely convincing (189). At any rate, while arguments concerning the nature and purpose of evil in King's fiction continues, little scholarly attention regarding evil in *The Dark Tower* has been explored.

In *The Dark Tower*, it has been noted that the gunslinger functions mainly as an anti-hero, a character that is neither the protagonist nor the antagonist, but still serves as the main character. In this individual that is the only character to be present in each and every book in the series, Roland serves as the closest thing to a hero that these books have to offer — readers follow the gunslinger's adventures and exploits, with particular attention given to the many actions and choices that hardly seem befitting of a character that garners attention and perhaps even is created to elicit sympathy to sustain readership through all seven texts. But, in purposely delaying an in-depth examination of Roland, it must be mentioned that the gunslinger is not alone in what appears to be a character comprised of mutually-exclusive traits, those of clarity and ambiguity. The gunslinger is no different than any other character readers meet in *The Dark Tower* in that every individual offers both desirable and despicable qualities. With the focus on evil and the negative traits that these characters exhibit, Tony Magistrale's assertion that, "the shape evil takes in Stephen King's fiction is as varied as the creatures that populate it," rings true in that the hero of *The Dark Tower*, the villains, the side-kicks and the background characters primarily share similar masks of cruelty, malice, and corruption, at least to certain extents (*Moral* 25). And there is no better place to begin an initial analysis of evil run rampant in *The Dark Tower* series than with one of the more likable characters, the lone child in Roland Deschain's ka-tet, the one named John "Jake" Chambers.

Within the *Dark Tower* series, Jake must learn to survive in the adult world, one of which he is quite skeptical and even fearful. From his father's overly vested interest in his work, along with an occasional snort of cocaine, and his mother's constantly drugged existence in which she is transparently unfaithful to her husband and inattentive to her son, Jake voluntarily leaves this family life for one of equal discord. Although Jake is much happier as the gunslinger's surrogate son, and as the pseudo-sibling of Eddie and Susannah Dean, his time in Mid-World is such that sees him not only grow into a young adult out of necessity for survival, but also ensures that he remains a lost child in a world governed by adult forces: "most of his [King's] fictional adolescents find themselves enmeshed in the dark complexities of an adult world; they are not responsible for either their parents' divorces or governmental errors in judgment, but they are nonetheless forced into coping with the consequences of such events" (Magistrale, *Landscape of Fear* 73). Jake, consequently, becomes little more than a puppet whose strings are pulled by the gunslinger. And with Roland not only teaching his students, or disciples, the ways of the Eld, in addition to his own brand of emotion that is consumed by a lack of compassion, Jake becomes a reflection of the gunslinger as he adapts to the way of the gun. Or, as Jonathan Davis claims, "children to King are like lumps of clay on a potter's wheel waiting to be sculpted into the individuals they will later become; they are the most impressionable beings in the human chain" (*Stephen King's America* 48). While this suggests that Jake is merely a child that naturally and purposefully follows the orders and examples of his elders, his views of adults and adulthood show a stark awareness of the charades and façades surrounding adults. Even though Jake is wont to adhere to Roland's teachings, views and opinions, his decision to follow the lead of the gunslinger undercuts any sympathy that may be felt, or any view which sees him as purely innocent. He is a child who wishes to abandon childish things, yet in his quest to appeal to his father, and perhaps even become like him, Jake is still often easily manipulated for purposes beneficial to the gunslinger's quest. Despite the initial distrust Jake develops as Roland sacrifices him to catch the Man in Black in *The Gunslinger*, Jake is the most developed gunslinger in Roland's new ka-tet. It may seem that Jake's tendency towards the unsavory is alleviated by his position, as a shadow of Roland who may not necessarily be held accountable for his actions because he is a child. However, Jake's autonomy as exercised by the choice to trust the gunslinger and open his heart to his dinh's command suggests that regardless of his tendency to slip towards innocence and an absence of guilt, his decision to follow the path the gunslinger has set before him aligns the young gunslinger with a brand of evil that would sacrifice anyone and anything to achieve one's goals.

Stepping away from Jake Chambers and the depictions of this child as a monster in the mold of Roland Deschain, many have noted that evil serves as not only a rather tempting option, but also as a mirror into which readers must look. And while King's particular brand of evil in *The Dark Tower* that extends into every character brought forth for the reader, one begins to question what norms King attempts to establish through this tactic. One suggestion comes from Tony Magistrale who says:

> King often places his protagonists in situations where they encounter the reality of evil, and from this encounter they must make choices which will influence the remainder of their lives. How his characters react to the loss of innocence is a central theme in King's work; their ability to survive is dependent upon what they learn from the fall from grace ["Hawthorne's Woods" 126].

With King, then, providing a fictional mirror for his readers to hold up, and creating an image that reflects the agony of choice alongside the difficulty of survival, readers encounter evil as a common presence that typically instigates a chance to turn away from negative influences despite inevitable loss looming on the horizon. With evil being a constant presence, or threat, to King's characters, evil cannot be shunned or ignored — decisions must be made, and if the wrong path is chosen, hope is not lost entirely as King offers means of survival and even levels of redemption for his characters. That is if an awareness of particular transgressions is gained, or if the opportunity to correct a select wrong or injustice is provided. However, identifying evil from both within and without is difficult in that, "for King, the strength of evil often lies in the element of secrecy and masquerade" (Winter 84). With this claim, it appears that evil generally has the upper hand within King's texts; awareness and action are often delayed, if ever achieved, as unveiling evil is a rather difficult task. And the complexity evil displays, which often serves as a means of keeping the secrecy of evil intact, runs rampant through *The Dark Tower*.

For an example of the intricacy of evil in *The Dark Tower* as a tool for further concealing the truth, readers are given information as to what the gunslinger says his quest is — to save the Dark Tower and thus all of existence. But, one of the first obstacles to consider with this reportedly simple quest is whether or not the gunslinger can be trusted. Of course, the completion of Stephen King's *Dark Tower* series allows for several theories and speculations as to why Roland must repeat his quest for the tall, dark edifice, many of which focus on the gunslinger's honesty and nobility. Questions arise as to whether or not Roland has learned to love again, which some suppose to be the true key to the room at the top of the Tower, and some question the death of Roland's companions believing that his ka-tet, and not just the gunslinger himself, are supposed to enter the Tower with the gunslinger. Setting such questions aside, however, one must consider that the gunslinger's quest is one that involves death, with matricide, murder and sacrifice being among the most atrocious of Roland's crimes, but these are often forgotten as he touts the quest for the Dark Tower as a journey in which the ends seemingly justify the means. The rationale behind this view is certainly shadowed by the gunslinger's limited discussion on the matter, and his misleading and even duplicitous conversations on the subject result in additional objectionable actions. Mia, daughter of none, suggests that Roland's evil is certainly intertwined with deception as she provides her own view of the gunslinger's quest to Susannah:

> "Not even your gunslinger friend hopes to *prevent* it [the Tower's Destruction]" Mia said, "only to slow it down by freeing the Breakers and — perhaps — slaying the Crimson King. Save it! *Save* it, O delight! Did he ever tell you that was his quest? [...] No," Mia went on, "for he won't lie to his ka-tet unless he has to, 'tis his pride. What he wants of the Tower is only to *see* it [...] Oh, perhaps to enter it, and climb to the room at the top, his ambition may strike so far. He may dream of standing on its allure as we hunker on this one, and chant the names of his fallen comrades, and of his line all the way back to Arthur Eld. But *save* it? No, good lady! Only a return of the magic could possibly save it, and — as you yourself well know — your dinh deals only in lead" [King, *Song of Susannah* 111].

Here readers come to a crossroads in *The Dark Tower* series in that they are asked to consider viewpoints from two distrustful sources — Roland and Mia — and then decide what the truth of the matter is. More importantly, readers are pushed to sort through the declarations of characters who have displayed evil intentions and actions, and then decide from which of these two untrustworthy sources they will draw their conclusions.

Within the constant struggle that King writes into his fiction with respect to deciphering evil and also observing evil in one shape or another at almost every turn and in almost every corner, hope appears to be minimal. Perhaps this can be attributed to the horror label under which King has been placed, for the constant presence of evil certainly produces horrific effect in the text and despair in the reader. However, for those who see an absence of hope and resolution in King's fiction, there is seemingly little fear as Orson Card states that, "fiction isn't fact. Fiction is lies. Those people are made up" (225). Yet Card also asserts that, "any depiction of life without evil is a lie," which reminds readers that even though King's stories may be heavy-handed in their treatment of evil, these tales nonetheless resonate with a sense of truth and accuracy that reminds readers that even though the content of any King story is made-up, the lies that are presented open doors into harsh realities that fiction often aims at unveiling (226). At the same time that evil reigns and lingers in King's fiction, it also brings about a sense of sympathy in that no evil is portrayed as purely evil. Yet, the boldness of King's *Dark Tower* series is that it seems to imbue all of its characters with a noticeable semblance of evil that is both recognized by the reader, author and characters in the text, and that this evil is more often than not neither forgotten nor forgiven. Indeed, believing that there may be a delicate balance between good and evil in King's fiction and in *The Dark Tower* is a conclusion that should not be readily drawn.

Even more frightening than the ever-present evil readers encounter in *The Dark Tower* is the sense of blindness that the characters have towards evil. Moreover, as Jonathan Davis says of King's characters that, "when acting on behalf of reason, they believe they cannot be wrong," he gives a reminder as to the fine line between sanity and insanity in King's body of fiction (*Stephen King's America* 45). Sanity, in the loosest sense of the word, entails the ability to recognize and face one's downfalls, whereas insanity recalls a refusal to see any personal ills. The lean towards insanity, or the immense draw of evil considers the costs and benefits of battling evil as, "the discovery of sin can frequently be overwhelming; it does not always lead to a higher state of moral consciousness," which suggests that the practice of evil and remaining within the circle of evil promises a sense of progress or accomplishment that alignment with goodness does not (Magistrale, "Hawthorne's Woods" 126). Even as this alludes to the claim that, "the dark forces in King's fiction almost always derive their power from the weakness and vulnerabilities of their prey," that evil often runs rampant as it first feeds off frailty and then depicts a return to righteousness as one that promises nothing in return, evil is thusly painted as a force that is subtle in its craft but also very persuasive as the promise of power by way of evil juxtaposed to an empty existence on the other side of the spectrum unsurprisingly recruits several of King's characters (Davis, *Stephen King's America* 41). But among the discussion of evil and the lenient use of this term calls for a deeper look at the nature of evil before looking back at King's writing and the characters of his creation.

Evil Itself

Throughout his career, King has given numerous indications as to how he views evil and how it functions in his writing, saying that, "my definition of evil is 'the conscious will to do harm'" (Perakos 66). Here King claims that evil stems mainly from personal volition, a decision to perform a certain action or to follow a particular path. Even though King suggests that, "the ultimate thing about evil is that it leads to nowhere," readers find that his characters often take the course of evil, either out of an inability to see the folly of evil or from an unwillingness to see the error of evil (Gagne 95). Consistent with this interpretation of King's words, that evil is a choice individuals make, is his statement that such concerns of a moral, ethical, or even religious nature, "proceed from the *inside*" (Perakos 65). Of course, the author himself determines the choices his characters make, but the overarching message that King primarily delivers is that evil is not necessarily a phenomenon that happens *to* people but rather something that happens *because* of people.

Beyond the autonomous individual, one who either practices evil or shuns it, is the community and culture that influences its citizens, adding another dimension to the question of evil's nature. Tony Magistrale considers the element of forces acting upon the actor, and suggests that while the basis of evil is mainly founded in individual desires and actions, evil cannot be completely reduced to personal choice:

> in King's novels, the concept of evil is rooted in both the individual himself [...] and the social community that surrounds him. Individuals in his fiction who succumb to the temptations of evil usually do so of their own volition. But King also acknowledges the existence of outside forces — particularly a malefic fate — that often bears some responsibility for the victimization of an individual [*Moral* 14].

Considering that, perhaps, King's characters escape the deterministic limitations critic Heidi Strengell sees in his fiction, views offered by King and Magistrale provide a glimmer of hope in that choice does not seem to be entirely dictated in King's fiction. Additionally, with the decision of the individual tempered by outside factors like community and likely upbringing, characters who display a predilection towards evil often garner a level of sympathy from readers. However, beyond questions of determinism and extenuating factors like one's environment are views which place full responsibility on individuals.

In contrast to claims that suggest evil is certainly a complex notion that involves more than simply decisions made by particular people, Daryl Koehn suggests that evil is mostly found within a given individual. Moreover, Koehn depicts evil as something that can be defeated with awareness of the self as attained by mere thought: "Individuals achieve self-knowledge only by thinking" (6). More to the point, Koehn says that, "evil is a failure to develop," which implies that *thinking* is the key to battling and resisting evil (45). Although this is certainly a reduction of Koehn's complete argument, these sentiments do sum up her overarching view that thought, or perhaps common sense, can turn evil aside. But contemplation is not always enough to eliminate evil. Thinking is similar to the sufferings that result in evil actions and deeds in that facing oneself and coming to terms with accepting and knowing the individual outside the mind is a frightening task, one that is generally avoided by King's characters. Also, as Jonathan Davis notes that, "often in King's stories, people are faced with the moral choice of whether to selfishly appease the self in acquiring personal gain regardless of the consequences or to surrender that gain for the sake of righteousness and the well-being of others," the implication is that thought alone, especially that which looks beyond the individual, is not always a convincing means to denying evil (*Stephen King's America* 77–8). Thought does not even guarantee the possibility that evil can be mastered and controlled, whether for good or ill. But thinking as it leads to awareness is at least a positive step, which is a step that is generally avoided by characters in *The Dark Tower* series.

As a final thought before starting with an extensive look at the gunslinger, he of questionable values, it should be said that morality and ethicality, certainly, become altered over time and suggest a relativistic foundation rather than an absolute one. However, if this examination is grounded in King's consistent treatment of less than desirable actions as performed by questionable individuals, as well as his constant use and positioning of evil as a counter-balance to his more agreeable characters, the issue of evil can be approached by means of reference to King's representations of evil instead of projecting outside views onto his fiction. Assuredly, the function of evil in *The Dark Tower* series serves as a persistent and pervasive aspect of the story that merits careful attention, scrutiny, and treatment as a presence that is inescapable, and one that permeates every character brought into the tale.

Roland Deschain: Anti-Hero

The gunslinger of *The Dark Tower* is almost universally recognized as an anti-hero who displays genuine emotion and utilizes carefully considered rationale before making any decision. But he also typically acts in a manner that limits sympathy and even results in outright disgust and despise. As one reviewer of *The Gunslinger* bluntly asks of Roland Deschain, "this mass murderer is the hero?" (Fuller BR22). Although it is easy to reduce the gunslinger to a homicidal quester, one who is a mere product of a society which treasured blind obedience in conjunction with training for skilled killing, he is more. Even though Roland Deschain is mainly a killer who treks to the Dark Tower with little explanation or reason, he is, "a simulacrum of the classic elements of heroic mythology: a lone, relatively amoral seeker wandering a dark wasteland for a purpose he has not yet realized" (Winter 66). But beyond the configuration of this character as informed by the author and established literary elements and formulas, the gunslinger is a character marked by haunting and troublesome decisions made throughout *The Dark Tower.*

Roland is quite the cerebral character, one that must often keep his own council whether he is alone or accompanied by his friends and followers. When James Egan says that, "Roland must confront a series of intricate choices, several of which have ambiguous, long-term consequences for him and for the human race itself," he confirms Roland's position as one that must exercise extreme caution in all that he does ("Gothic Western" 100). However, the gunslinger's actions hardly reflect care or concern for anything that hinders his quest for the Dark Tower, and he is a character who should garner little sympathy. But this is not to say that he is an uninteresting character because of his unsavory deeds and actions. To the contrary, casting the gunslinger in a role as an anti-hero who constantly moves between the role of the hero and the villain creates an exciting story, one in which no reader can be comfortable for too long. The moment a reader feels any sense of worry or sympathy for Roland, he says or does something to negate these feelings. But, the gunslinger is a character that is so mysterious and even bothersome which helps *The Dark Tower* to be consumed and read: "He who writes about happy people in a happy world [will not] last long as a writer. Nobody cares about that happy stuff. Evil is intrinsically more interesting. More entertaining. Evil *sells*" (Card 225). And as King has certainly created an engaging if not entertaining character, he has also performed a service for his readers by instigating close examination of a character that exhibits traits from each side of the spectrum of morality and ethicality, so much so that the gunslinger appears to be just like any person existing outside of the text who also straddles the fence of good and evil. But, of course, evil seems to be the direction towards which the gunslinger generally looks and acts.

Some scholars who have perused the pages of *The Dark Tower*, however, see the gunslinger in a more flattering light, that which depicts Roland as a character carrying guilt for his misdeeds and doing the best he can when placed or positioned into a given situation that calls for questionable actions. Oftentimes the gunslinger is absolved of his atrocities because he is purportedly pushed into facing certain dilemmas rather than voluntarily engaging in such maddening scenes. Among those who view the gunslinger with a sympathetic eye is Heidi Strengell, whose views on the gunslinger suggest that he is certainly a character who deserves sympathy and should be removed from any judgmental sights, says that, "although Roland is violent and carries guns, he nevertheless avoids needless killing" (127). On the other hand, the gunslinger is one who admits that he deals in lead, and nowhere is this better seen than with the murder of his own mother. Although the killing in this scene is not premeditated, Roland constantly finds himself faced with instances in which his guns act before he even considers alternatives to death: "in Gilead, the sons of the aristocracy trained to be an Eye and a Hand, an aim and a trigger, before they were trained to be a heart and a mind. And often, as Roland found to his later distress, such training meant that the hand could act before the mind had time to think" (Furth, *Concordance* 1: 7). Also, in the same vein that sees the gunslinger as a somewhat innocent character, Heidi Strengell also claims that the gunslinger, "is *forced* to sacrifice the people he loves" (130, emphasis added). Strengell's portrayal of the gunslinger is rather forgiving when considering his history and evolving emotions, those which are expected and anticipated as eventually reaching a capacity to love. Perhaps it is with this large-scale scope in mind that Strengell stands firm in her view of the gunslinger as a sympathetic character, one who journeys not for the self but for the world. Although the larger picture and scope behind the gunslinger's journey resonates with at least a mild sense of concern for the world and its stability, the text of *The Dark Tower* series suggests that Roland's motivation for questing is certainly grounded in his own whims and desires. Although the graphic novel *The Gunslinger Born* indicates that an element of Roland's quest is that of duty, a responsibility to ensure the Dark Tower's safety that is placed into the hands of Arthur Eld's descendants by way of Eld's promise for all of his kin to be beholden to protecting the Tower, the gunslinger nonetheless exercises and displays a sense of pride that implies his quest for the Tower is conceived within his own mind, on his own terms, and without any acknowledgement of his imposed obligation. Therefore, little, if any, personal growth is ever reached for the gunslinger. Assuredly, a veil of ambiguity surrounds the gunslinger's motives and actions, as well as his supposed repentances, and it then becomes appropriate to label the gunslinger in the same manner that Rhea and Mia do — as a man of remorseless death.

Sacrifice litters the trail Roland takes to the Dark Tower, with the sacrifice of Jake Chambers being the first discovered in the series. Leonard G. Heldreth suggests that Jake's death is not entirely to be blamed on the gunslinger as, "the death of Jake is a combination of predestination and conscious action" (143). However, the only real sense of determinism found in the *Dark Tower* series is that which can be traced back to the designs of the author. Of course, the books direct readers towards the possibility that Roland is nothing more than a pawn on a cosmic chessboard and is moved without making any decisions himself. This would certainly clear the gunslinger of any charges brought against him by the reader, but the sense that the gunslinger is active in his quest and, more importantly, the decisions he faces and makes, places him outside the grasp of destiny and determinism. Unsurprisingly, when the gunslinger is faced with his actions and the reality of his autonomy in choosing to murder and sacrifice, among other crimes, Heldreth also claims that, "it is Roland's knowledge of his conscious act that haunts him," which suggests that even though the gunslinger recognized the wrongs he has perpetrated, allowing Jake's death is of less consequence and nearly absent of guilt to the gunslinger as the sacrifice itself is not what haunts him but rather the realization that he has performed evil (144). And it is with this minute yet key element of the gunslinger's person it is seen that the evil which surfaces in his deeds are less important than the recollection of his offenses; the choices the gunslinger makes as well as the actions he executes are troubling in and of themselves, but to conceal and contextualize these events as mere occurrences, the gunslinger fails to face his own propensity for evil. Even when the gunslinger says to himself in the final scene of *The Gunslinger*, "'I loved you, Jake,'" it seems as if this announcement is one of many attempts to lessen the pain he knows he should feel but, alas, does not (King 230).

Roland may display a sense of thinking that is required of those who are to turn evil aside, but he never seems to go beyond his own mind when considering evil. As the gunslinger is certainly aware of his misdeeds, their affect on his quest are limited to his own mind — his thoughts rarely, if ever, materialize as a deterrent for avoiding questionable scenarios in which his training has him act in a manner that is dubious. This cognitive dissonance that Roland faces sums up the *Dark Tower* quite well: even as Tony Magistrale notes that, "the gunslinger wants to believe in the righteousness of his westward quest, but he is sometimes bothered by the practices he must engage in during this quest," readers are reminded that despite Roland's mental worries, any other woes are absent as he continues to journey to the Dark Tower (*Second Decade* 144). Even if Roland is bothered and pushed into feeling a mild sense of guilt for his actions, he still moves on and often repeats the sins of his past. The Dark Tower looms over the gunslinger's journey, and no matter how many times he shows glimpses of humanity or even awareness that perhaps a little remorse would serve as a means of instigating more thought and less action, "he is relentless in his quest, and will not stop at massacring the entire town [Tull], even the girl for whom he had developed some feeling" (Blue 60). While the decimation of an entire town's population certainly seems to be unnecessary, the scene in Tull reminds readers of the importance of Roland's journey, or at least as he sees it.

By the same token, considering that perhaps the gunslinger's quest is as he reports, that, "'there's more than a world to win,'" some may view his deeds as forgivable when juxtaposed to the grand-scale purpose of seeking and storming the Dark Tower (King, *Drawing* 405). Tyson Blue offers a similar suggestion as it relates to the sacrifice of Jake as he says, "if, indeed, Roland's destiny is to repair the tear in the fabric of time, then Jake's life is a small price to pay for the restoration of Order in the universe" (65). And while it is easy to concede this point, the sacrifice of Jake is more than collateral damage. With the sacrifice of Jake being, "the second-most agonizing choice of his life," readers can only surmise as to what the gunslinger's most taxing decision actually is (King, *The Drawing of the Three* 2). One conclusion is that the sacrifice of Susan Delgado is Roland Deschain's most distressing choice, but he does not consciously choose her death as he learns of her fate only after she is burned alive. Then again, Roland does little to ensure her safety when he and Cuthbert and Alain leave to face Eldred Jonas and George Latigo. But, as Tyson Blue claims, "in every quest, there is an element of sacrifice, a price to be paid in order for a greater gain" (62). But what exactly is it that the gunslinger gains through the sacrifice of his lover, his friends, and even his followers? To Roland Deschain, everything is about his quest to the Dark Tower, and all is considered as expendable, with the exception of his guns. And readers are immediately informed of this mindset within the first few pages of *The Gunslinger*: "he still had the guns — his father's guns — and surely they were more important than horns ... or even friends. Weren't they?" (King 6).

With this latest textual reference to the gunslinger's character and psyche, one must wonder as to the fate of most anyone who crosses his path. As Jonathan Davis suggests, "at the close of the story, the reader can conclude that while Roland is indeed a lonely man, in light of the chaos arising from any contact with societal order, he is truly better off carrying out his quest without companions" (*Stephen King's America* 100). Additionally, another early view into the gunslinger as provided by the first three books in the series comes the claim that, "the gunslinger is a man without attachments; he is loved by no one, and there is no one for him to love. He lacks a sense of community or purpose beyond the incessant hunt for the man in black and [...] the Dark Tower" (Magistrale, *Second Decade* 143). As Roland perpetually seeks, and finds, solitude, even as he enters the Dark Tower in the last book alone, leaving his only remaining gun at the ghostwood door at the base of the Tower, his quest can be reduced to the sum of his actions. And the result is the gunslinger's continual penance through resumption, although change is promised if Roland can change himself and his ways. However, there is little in the *Dark Tower* that indicates Roland can or even will change for the better.

The gunslinger's growth as an individual, if one can claim with certainty that he does learn to love and to abhor the sacrifices he thinks are necessary for achieving his goal, sometimes seems to be without merit or importance, especially when the issue of determinism is brought up yet again under the moniker of *ka*. Robin Furth provides just one of many examples as to the sweeping reach of *ka* in *The Dark Tower* series as she proposes in the second volume of her *Concordance* that, "although this gunslinger believed that his only ambition was to climb to the top of the Tower to meet whatever being resided there, ka had greater plans for him" (408). However, as readers learn in the later books of the *Dark Tower* series, *ka* does not rule all and it can be challenged. But whether or not *ka* has decreed that the gunslinger perform various acts of evil, Roland remains as an evil character, not necessarily because he often chooses what appears to be evil to the reader but because he knows he is damned and does nothing to atone for his actions. He may shed tears, he may tell his new friends that he treasures their companionship and even loves them, but his continuous quest for the Dark Tower tells his peers, and readers of the tale, differently, that change is as unlikely as the gunslinger crying off his quest.

Randall Flagg: Sympathetic Villain

As Roland Deschain is primarily seen as an anti-hero, Randall Flagg is primarily seen as a villain, with little variation among the perceptions as to this label. Stephen King even says that, "Randall Flagg to me is everything that I know of in the last twenty years that's really bad" (Wolinsky and Davidson 29). Scholars have also aligned themselves with King and have perpetuated the view that Flagg is a purely evil character, perhaps more so than Roland Deschain. To this end, James Egan suggests that, "the Man in Black is not precisely Roland's alter ego, but rather the embodiment of what Roland might become, the sum of his negative capabilities. [Moreover,] Roland's 'double' warns him that searching for the Tower means risking his own soul" ("Gothic Western" 104). With Flagg being elevated above the gunslinger in terms of evil, and a capacity for evil, it is not surprising to see him cast in this light. When Heidi Strengell says that, "as an embodiment of the Dark Man, Flagg consciously chooses evil," she not only seeks to confirm thinking in that Flagg is a genuinely evil character, but she also places him within the realm of Stephen King's evil, that which chooses evil over any other alternative (145). And while Strengell has King's own words as support for her claim, Flagg is actually less evil than the gunslinger.

Despite envisioning much resistance to the claim that Flagg is more of a sympathetic character than a despicable one, there are indications in *The Dark Tower* that suggest Flagg is not exactly as some see him. Even when scholars like Tony Magistrale say that, "Flagg seeks to make trouble where none has been before — to wreck and destroy things just because they have been united and are flourishing. His evil is *disinterested*; he seeks power, but power is only a means to greater levels of destruction," most recollections of *The Stand* and *The Eyes of the Dragon* do little to offer rebuttals to such a view (*Second Decade* 137). Also, with others noting that Flagg fails at every turn — "Flagg is curiously inept, helplessly watching his well-laid plans go awry at every turn"— it seems as if King's treatment of this character, as one who is evil but never succeeds, suggests a particular view on evil as something that cannot win (Winter 61). This is certainly the case with Roland who is cursed to repeat his journey to the Dark Tower time and time again as a form of punishment for the various errors he makes along the way. And although Mary Pharr's views on Flagg do not differ from those already mentioned, as she says that, "Flagg is evil incarnate, but he is also folly incarnate [...] Flagg is a petty monster, his goal nothing more than dictatorship and his power merely that of limited magic, hypnotic skill and mechanical devices," such definitive and cold analyses of Flagg should not be readily accepted as wholly accurate (8). Of course, Flagg has tortured and even killed, but his brand of evil is not purely or wholly evil because he is a rape victim.

With a short paragraph devoted to Flagg's back-story in *The Dark Tower* just before this character dies, readers are given a key piece of information needed to better understand him and the possible rationale behind his devotion to chaos and destruction — that Flagg was raped as a young man: "he [Flagg] who had run away at thirteen, had been raped in the ass by another wanderer a year later and yet had somehow withstood the temptation to go crawling back home. Instead he had moved on toward his destiny" (King, *The Dark Tower* 184). Although several of King's characters have faced horrors in their fictional lives, perhaps Flagg's situation is the most sympathetic. Even though what brings Flagg joy usually brings sorrow to another, one scene, one minute piece of information — the recollection of his rape scene — allows readers to see him in an entirely new light. In knowing that Flagg was raped as a young man, it suggests that perhaps his brand of evil is that of retribution, which then seeks consideration of the psychological backdrop of his rape. First, it has been posited that, "male rape victims are more likely to deny aspects of their assault," which points towards questions of memory and even moving on from a sexual assault (Kaszniak, Nussbaum and Berren 103). Of course, Flagg's understandable sense of shame in being raped could easily account for the fact that he himself has never mentioned being raped to any one in any scene in King's canon. However, when it is noted that, "people often hold rape victims somewhat responsible for their fate," this points towards a constant remembering of rape for rape victims (Mitchell, Hirshman and Hall 369). While it is reasonable to hypothesize that rape victims tend to feel scarred, both physically and emotionally, reminders and even judgments from the outside world may lead towards a state of mind that seeks a way in which to erase or negate the violation that has occurred. Of course, conceptualizing retaliatory practices stemming from rape is speculation, but in suspending any disbelief in the possibility that reprisal is a reaction to rape, the life of Flagg becomes one that looks to strike a balance for the sexual crime committed against him. And although Flagg's possible search for justice and balance is that which becomes imbalanced and even prejudiced, the mitigating factor here is that Flagg is not an originator of evil — he is just caught up in its web as another wronged individual seeking justice. Also, with respect to Flagg and the atrocities for which he is responsible, if one were to take away the horror of the actions in and of themselves, or even consciously consider him in the role of a victim, all appears to be well if not understandable. Then again, with a character like Flagg the horror, and the evil, is always present.

In carefully tracing the Flagg's evolution, readers do not find the humorous overtones the character tends to overbearingly bestow upon the reader right away. In reading through *The Eyes of the Dragon*, all that is given, initially, is just a malicious and vindictive magician. Flagg's delight in slowly bringing down the kingdom of Delain is not entirely manifested through extreme outward professions of joy and happiness as encountered in *The Stand* and up until his last few living moments in *The Dark Tower*. First, all that is seen is that Flagg, "planned nothing more nor less than the complete overthrow of the monarchy — a bloody revolt that would plunge Delain into a thousand years of darkness and anarchy. Give or take a year or two, of course" (King, *Eyes* 64). But Flagg's sense of humor develops and becomes more prominent as he is later seen torturing a starving Lloyd Henried, with a mild bite of humor, in *The Stand*:

> "Jesus Christ, a rat isn't anything to eat! Why, do you know what I had for lunch? I had a nice rare roast beef sandwich on Vienna bread with a few onions and a lot of Gulden's Spicy Brown. Sound good? [...] Had some homefries, and chocolate milk to go with it, and then for dessert ... holy crow, I'm *torturing* you, ain't I? Someone ought to take a hosswhip to me, that's what they ought to do" [King 356].

But even before *The Stand*, Flagg expresses humor and finds joy in the death of King Roland from *The Eyes of the Dragon*: "'Yes, I brought him the wine ... and I *laughed* when his guts burned, and I laughed harder when you [Peter] were taken up the stairs to the top of the Needle'" (King 371). Within this speech it is discovered that Flagg, as disturbing as it may sound, does have a sense of humor. But still, the humor does not entirely temper the horror, especially the horror of being a rape victim.

It can be reasonably suggested that Flagg's sense of humor, as he is typically the one who instigates the laughter and inverts the victim-victimizer relationship he was faced with at the time of his own personal violation, is one means through which he exerts some form of control over others. He seems to revel in the laughter as long as he is the one laughing as it means that he is not the target of anyone's belittlement, and evidence of this is seen in *The Stand* when Flagg and Glen Bateman discuss the conditions of Glen's potential release after he has been incarcerated:

> "Of course I couldn't go without my friends."
> "Of course not. All you have to do is ask. Get down on your knees and ask me."
> Glen laughed heartily. He threw back his head and laughed long and hard. And as he laughed, the pain in his joints began to abate. He felt better, stronger, in control again.
> "Oh you're a card," he said. "I'll tell you what you do. Why don't you find a nice big sandpile, get yourself a hammer, and pound all that sand right up your ass?"
> Flagg's face grew dark. The smile slipped away [...] "Stop laughing."
> Glen laughed harder.
> *"Stop laughing at me!"*
> "You're *nothing!*" Glen said, wiping his steaming eyes and still chuckling. "Oh pardon me ... it's just that we were all so frightened ... we made such a *business* out of you.... I'm laughing as much at our own foolishness as at your regrettable lack of substance" [King 1055–6].

Here readers see Flagg become defensive at Glen's remarks and laughter, as well as a rare instance in which he seemingly has no power and lacks any sense of control; he is reduced to the butt of Glen's joke and once again placed in a position that he has desperately worked hard to avoid. In addition, readers also laugh with Glen at the ridiculousness of Flagg, and then push him into the realm of the weak victim who has previously managed to be the only one to laugh. Maybe Flagg is merely facing a situation he deserves, despite what is known about his past. Flagg is, after all, a purely evil character, right?

In light of what has been proposed thus far, there are those who view Flagg as a completely despicable character who meets a fitting end. Heidi Strengell offers the reminder that Flagg "has eagerly killed, raped, set towns on fire, and fed on human weakness, greed, and hate" (144). With such knowledge, most analyses of this character would result in a complete lack of empathy, especially with the knowledge of Flagg's own rape in conjunction with remembering that Flagg, too, has engaged in this very same act as the violator. While Flagg should not necessarily be forgiven for his deeds, an attempt to understand the catalyst that set him to commit such acts is needed. Consider another claim by Heidi Strengell: "neither the Walkin Dude nor King's other demonic villains suffer from a guilty conscience. Thus, the dark Man in King represents evil, cruelty, malice, deceit, and unpredictability" (140). Here Strengell assumes that the murderous, hate-filled Flagg actually has reason to feel guilty, and while Flagg's actions are not necessarily condonable, they are at least understandable if not also guilt-free, to a certain extent, which is certainly in contradiction to her claim which suggests that "the Dark Man archetype in the character of Flagg is genuinely evil" (144). Rather, a clearer and more accurate picture of Flagg is one that considers him as the individual that Douglass Winter depicts as he says that, "Randall Flagg is neither Satan nor his demonic spawn [...] he is a Miltonic superman" (60). Like many readers of *Paradise Lost* who find Satan to be a heroic character merely playing out the role he is destined to fulfill, perhaps Flagg, too, is a fallen angel who has a valid case supporting his devilry. Through all the masks and all the chaos sown through numerous lands, Randall Flagg/Walter O'Dim/Marten Broadcloak may be seen relishing in evil deeds at most every juncture, but no judgment can be passed without the full story, without the context explaining the origin of such hateful but somewhat comprehensible deeds.

Mordred Deschain: Destiny's Puppet? and the Crimson King: Impotent Malice

Aside from Randall Flagg, the gunslinger faces two other enemies of purportedly great stature, the Crimson King, and their shared son

Mordred Deschain. With little actually discussed regarding these characters until the last book in the *Dark Tower* series (although the graphic novels do provide some back-story for the Crimson King), these two characters are, like Flagg, almost instantly branded as evil characters. And while Heidi Strengell offers the claim that, "Roland encounters the Crimson King as an embodiment of evil," jumping to such a conclusion is certainly rash (153). Both characters, like Flagg, are nothing more than a continuation of blundering and inept villains that, not unsurprisingly, fall and fail in King's fiction. This is not to say that these characters do not perform evil, or that their respective impositions — prophecy and insanity — excuse the evil that they perform. Their particular brand of evil, inexcusable as such exercises of malignity are, is actually pathetic. Although Mordred and the Crimson King do act upon their particular whims and desires in the text of *The Dark Tower*, suggesting that they each choose to act in an evil manner, they each also have certain limitations to their evil — each is little more than a character that is coerced into performing evil by way of ancestry and ignorance.

When looking at the two primary reasons for explaining the evil found in Mordred and the Crimson King, ancestry and ignorance, these conduits of evil are not necessarily mitigating factors when analyzing the evil deeds that these characters carry out. However, when considering the lineage of these characters, as well as their respective mental impositions, their individual decisions to enact evil do not resemble the pure autonomy needed to do evil. Instead, these characters exhibit a sense of docility resulting in ignorance that represents evil stemming from a mindset that is not necessarily predetermined to choose evil but is generally steered towards evil. When faced with choices, one of which often includes a choice that is base and evil when compared to the alternative, these characters display a tendency to let their base instincts rule their thinking and push them towards choices that resemble evil. For example, when Mordred first sees his father Roland, he feels a pull to approach his father, a parent with which he belongs, and then ask to be included in his circle of love and respect along with the gunslinger's current ka-tet. And as Mordred realizes he has the option to avoid killing Roland and the others, to actually join their company, readers see him not necessarily choose to continue with his initial quest of killing the gunslinger but rather they see a young child ruled by pride as passed down from his other father: "suppose he went to them and was *not* killed? What if they were to welcome him in? Ridiculous idea, yes, but allow it for the sake of argument. Even then he would be expected to set Roland above him, accept Roland as dinh, and that he will never do" (King, *The Dark Tower* 170). In this passage, Mordred does choose to continue with the goal set out for him as outlined by his other father, the Crimson King, which resembles the autonomy needed to perform evil in King's fiction. But, Mordred's choice here comes mainly from instinct and an inner voice, one that is, at times, the actual voice of the Crimson King which does not necessarily demand that his son perform certain actions, but does suggestively persuade him as to the preference of certain actions that meet the ends sought by his red father.

Although it is prophesied that Mordred will kill his father — "he who ends the line of Eld shall conceive a child of incest with his sister or his daughter, and the child will be marked, by his red heel shall you know him. It is he who shall stop the breath of the last warrior"— he can be read as a character that is not dictated by destiny (King, *Song of Susannah* 252). For one, he fails to fulfill the prophecy that he would kill Roland, even though the gunslinger is not named in the prophecy, suggesting that Mordred may not be the one who is destined to end Roland's life. More to the point, Mordred is a character who is dominated, but not necessarily ruled, by thoughts and instincts that are founded in the Crimson King's feud with the gunslinger. And while Mordred chooses to continue with the imposed quest to kill Roland, of his own volition, his animalistic nature along with his genetic link to the Crimson King, suggests that Mordred's evil is that of a lesser degree than the gunslinger's evil which stems from choice and *training* instead of choice and *nature*. Roland certainly identifies his training as a source for his heartless and cruel actions, indicating that he is cognizant and conscious of his decisions. Mordred, on the other hand, seems to be less aware of the choices he makes, and although he is a tractable character, he shows enough flashes of introspection to suggest that he is not ruled by destiny and that he could have certainly exercised the control needed to avoid evil and oppose his impulses.

With respect to the Crimson King, he is a character that is purportedly a genuinely evil character with designs that are only devoted to chaos, destruction and death. When readers are given their first glimpse of the Crimson King in *Insomnia*, the visage that is portrayed certainly suggests his malevolence as he is described as being, "ancient and twisted and less human than the strangest creature to ever flop or hop its way along the Short-Time level of existence" (King 606). Moreover, when it is revealed that the death of Patrick Danville in *Insomnia* is largely orchestrated by the Crimson King—*"I intend that the boy your friends told you about should die in his mother's arms, and I want to see it happen. I've worked very hard here in Derry, and I don't feel that's too much to ask"*— it appears that he is a very intelligent being, one that does not even flinch at the prospect of killing (King 603). In addition to the *Dark Tower* texts and *Insomnia*, the Crimson King has also received some attention in the graphic novels, and through the first two series he is certainly portrayed as an evil character, one who is devoted to bringing the Dark Tower down. As further testament to the Crimson King's predilection towards evil, the graphic novels not only reveal that Marten/Walter/Flagg has been in league with the Crimson King since Roland's young years, but that their relationship is one indicating that the Crimson King is the pinnacle of evil as the murderous and hateful Flagg is simply his underling. But regardless of this hierarchy, the Crimson King is little more than a villain whose fearful image causes more directly observed discord than the Crimson King himself.

When Roland and ka-tet first see sign of the Crimson King in Topeka, Roland nonverbally denies knowledge of who the Crimson King is, but in acknowledging the name and the associated sigul, the open eye, the narrator notes that, "he looked troubled" (King, *Wizard and Glass* 91). Whether or not Roland actually knows who the Crimson King is, with the graphic novels indicating that he does while the books are more ambiguous in revealing this, further evidence of the fear linked to the Crimson King is seen when Eldred Jonas meets Walter. As Walter takes out a sigul bearing the open eye of the Crimson King as identification, he lays this totem on a table for Jonas to inspect, and when Jonas recognizes the object for what it is, he hesitates in acquiescing to Walter's request to touch the sigul and return it: "Jonas reached for it, but for once his normally steady hand had resembled his reedy, unstable voice. He watched his fingers tremble for a moment, then lowered his hand quickly to the table" (King, *Wizard and Glass* 407). Despite this display of fear by Jonas, and the fear of the Crimson King that Mia displays when she and Susannah first meet face to face in a todash version of Fedic — "'the King can fascinate even at a distance'" — the final confrontation between the gunslinger and the Crimson King is both an indication of the latter's frailty, even though accounts in *The Dark Tower* suggest that the Crimson King is insane by the time he faces Roland and Patrick Danville, and of his inability to be seen as a purely evil character (King, *Song of Susannah* 102).

Within the seventh book of the *Dark Tower* series, readers are finally given much information as to the nature and purpose of the Crimson King, who is ultimately presented as a weak character who has been crippled by insanity. Perhaps the mental frailty that he succumbs to is just another instance of the often frustrating work of the *deus ex machina* at work in the *Dark Tower* series, but past this potential complaint or explanation, the Crimson King is, simply put, a character that is a letdown in that he is supposed to be the ultimate villain of the *Dark Tower*. Even when it is discovered that the Crimson King has reached insanity yet displays a sense of wherewithal by making himself undead by swallowing a sharpened spoon and thereby fulfilling a certain prophecy, the character Feemalo notes that, "'it seems old King Red wasn't entirely mad, after all'" (King, *The Dark Tower* 608). By making himself undead, the Crimson King makes himself invulnerable to the gunslinger's guns, but this brief tangent of summary returns to the main critique of the Crimson King's designation as an evil character, that of evil tempered by feeblemindedness.

Although insanity is a rather disappointing source of the Crimson King's demise, it nonetheless serves as a means of examining and even understanding his approach to and use of evil. With insanity, and all the dispositions that result from dangerously faulty reasoning, evil becomes not so much of a choice to make but, as Heidi Strengell suggests, a mode of comfort, unless that insanity is identified: "virtually all of King's evil characters turn out to be insane and seemingly at the same time enjoy their mental state, unless they are reminded of it" (185). However, as the Crimson King slips deeper and deeper into his insanity, as accounted by various characters throughout *The Dark Tower*, this comfort also leads to complacency, stubbornness, and folly. As the Crimson King is Roland's sworn enemy, a man who is destined to die at Roland's hands if the gunslinger does not die first, he does little to ensure that the gunslinger will die and therefore fail to kill the him. Perhaps focused on another prophecy, the one concerning the birth of Mordred, the Crimson King actually avoids having the gunslinger killed by his minion Flagg—"'I could have killed him then,'" Flagg says of Roland when he slept in the golgotha at the end of *The Gunslinger*—which not only reflects the insanity of a villain devoted to the death of the gunslinger, but also reminds readers that the Crimson King may be evil, but he is certainly a foolish character (King, *The Dark Tower* 177). Indeed, the Crimson King is a malicious character whose evil is as impotent as it is unimpressive.

An Entire World Gone Mad?

From the beginning of the *Dark Tower* series to the very end, most every character that is introduced is shown to be drawn towards evil. From John Farson, Sylvia Pittston, Jack Mort, and Blaine the Mono, along with Eldred Jonas and Rhea of the Cöos, from the first four installments of the series to Cordelia Delgado, Ben Slightman, Andy the Messenger Robot, Mia, Richard Patrick Sayre, Paul "Pimli" Prentiss, and Joe Collins from the last three books, evil lurks around every corner in the *Dark Tower* universe. Evil surrounds Roland and Mid-World, with its degrees and gradations widen the spectrum of evil to be nearly all-inclusive and certainly almost present at all times and in all situations.

But one question that looms over the evil that purportedly permeates many of the people encountered in the *Dark Tower* stories is if they can be blamed for their madness or propensity for evil. It can be argued that neither Eldred Jonas nor Rhea of the Cöos from *Wizard and Glass* can be held fully accountable for their actions since it is learned in the graphic novels that these two were infected by Maerlyn's Laughing Mirror, a device which extols vice over virtue. Moreover, when King says that, "neither Eldred Jonas nor the crone on the hill had been of Marten's stature—nor even of Walter's—when it came to evil, but they had been evil enough," it seems that evil, regardless of its origin, is a blameworthy character trait, or flaw, that King places within most of his characters (*Wizard and Glass* 65). Regardless of the degree to which evil manifests itself, it seems as if criticisms of King see evil as a negative quality that almost immediately casts particular characters into the realm of the unforgivable and irredeemable: "no one can deny that characters like Randall Flagg [...] are purely concentrated evil; readers can easily dismiss any notion of moral redemption for these villains" (Davis, *Stephen King's America* 41). In this case, it looks as if King's fictional world is that which not only commonly witnesses evil at most every juncture, but sees evil as an inevitability in which little hope is offered.

In contrast to the views forwarded thus far which suggest evil is unavoidable in King's fiction, and that hope is scarce but present, many scholars forward the opinion that not only can evil be resisted, but it *should* be. As Jonathan Davis asserts his view on evil within the Stephen King canon, in which he says that, "those characters in King's fiction who do not behave morally and rather surrender the well-being of others for evil or selfish motives are those who are ultimately destroyed," he provides just one of many critical views that indicate evil is something that can and should be controlled (*Stephen King's America* 37). Also, this admonitory view coincides with Tony Magistrale's warning that evil sees few, if any, positive outcomes in King's fiction: "when a King character is mastered by evil, it destroys other people through him, but it also destroys him" (*Landscape of Fear* 65). With these views of evil in King's fiction implying a certain sense of hope in that evil can be destroyed, usually by its own machinations, one must wonder what actually draws King's characters to evil if cautionary sentiments are expressed through much of King's canon.

In answer as to why some characters in King's fiction do not choose what is best and do not always defy evil, Douglass Winter suggests that, "King tends to identify the internal element of evil with moral weakness," which indicates that although evil can and should be avoided in King's fiction, it is often embraced not because of destiny or determinism stemming from the authorial pen, but rather that such is simply human nature (80). Much like Mordred's instinctual move towards evil, the characters in King's stories all seem to act upon impulse and their own nature, but choices are still offered, and it is upon this noted autonomy that Tony Magistrale believes King's fiction rests:

> The stability of King's fictional universe is measured by moral choices: the men and women in his work struggle against the forces of evil, and from the encounter become less innocent. They are forced into decisions which make them better or worse, give their lives meaning or push them into

despair. Many of his characters are not directly responsible for the situations in which they suddenly find themselves, but all of them must eventually respond to their particular circumstances — and they are judged accordingly [*Landscape of Fear* 26].

Magistrale's assessment of evil and choice in King's fiction does suggest to the Constant Reader that hope is not entirely absent. When Magistrale also suggests that, "King tells us that evil can be resisted," the search for an individual who has been tempted by and resisted evil can be found in Donald Callahan (*Landscape of Fear* 65). For those who have only read *'Salem's Lot*, the priest has certainly not displayed any movement or action against evil as the novel closes and Callahan rides out of town. But, within the *Dark Tower* series, King gives this wanderer another chance: "given an opportunity for heroic deeds in the field of religion, Callahan readily takes the challenge, although he no longer possesses weapons against evil" (Strengell 200). Father Donald Callahan's presumed redemption as found in the opening chapter of *The Dark Tower* certainly recalls the sense of hope alluded to by scholars who see King's novels offering anything but an entirely bleak outlook. Moreover, if Callahan, a man once rejected by God, can find favor with his deity through various types of penance and redemptive actions, then perhaps the same can be assumed as available to King's more despicable characters. However, it must be recalled that Callahan's purported redemption comes with a mortal sin on his soul — suicide. While it seems that Callahan's release from his demons, both literal and metaphorical, is ironic in that his escape comes about by way of an action in direct opposition to his faith and belief, perhaps the father's death can be seen as just another instance in the Stephen King universe that even those who actively seek forgiveness will not find it.

Walking the road of the righteous and the good without straying into the path of the deceitful and evil is a line that few, if any, can walk with no deviations or missteps. But, when considering solutions to the desolation and despair in King's corpus, Jonathan Davis suggests that, "King's fiction serves to argue that society needs a collective good will" (*Stephen King's America* 39). Even through this sentiment is believable and valid, one must consider the practicality or applicability of such a world view. To see entire communities bond under a specific umbrella of goodness, joined together for a common cause, seems unlikely. And it is with this paradox that King's fiction serves as a powerful medium of not only social critique, but even that of damnation. Revealing the goals of the community while unveiling its hypocrisies and its call for impossible ends is certainly a clear marker of horror. But, even as the constant presence of evil in its various shapes and behind its multiple masks recalls horror, it also seems to recall King's perception of truth as reflected in the society surrounding him. King's choice to constantly take his characters outside of the good and into the realm of the evil is certainly a theme that speaks of limited hope, but it also speaks of a palpable reality. This is not to say that King believes people are necessarily damned. Rather, the difficult road of the good is depicted as nothing short of an impossibility, which suggests a reflection of the world in which King writes as well as a notable boldness to see that such a pessimistic yet accurate viewpoint is printed. The *Dark Tower* series may be fiction, but the sense of reality within the pages of this series, that which lacks hope and sees little redeeming quality in any individual, can easily be reduced to a writer simply calling things as he sees them, a blurring of the lines between good and evil that is not entirely founded in imagination.

Repetition, Integration, Immersion and Intertextuality: A Tale of *At Least* Two Stories

"'Good books don't give up all their secrets at once'"— Ted Brautigan, from *Hearts in Atlantis*

HAROLD BLOOM IS BY FAR one of the staunchest critics concerning Stephen King's writing, but he does provide a rather appropriate creed concerning the way in which a given reader approaches *any* text when he says that, "there is no single way to read well," which effectively captures the essence of the Stephen King canon (*How to Read* 19). With over fifty books and several hundred short stories to his name, King has displayed a large range of writing ability and style throughout his career, which certainly calls for various ways of reading and approaching his texts. However, in some cases, some ways of reading are indeed better than others. Fiction can be seen as a style of writing that is subject to the designs of the author, which is certainly a fair assessment as the author is responsible for the words which appear on any given page. However, authorial intentions aside, reading fiction as opposed to writing fiction is hardly a structured practice that is beholden to the desires of the author. Even as the author is generally seen as an individual who plans and plots his or her writing, Stephen King claims that the *Dark Tower* series escapes the classification of a planned story: "I had no idea of how things were going to turn out [...] To know, I have to write. I once had an outline, but I lost it along the way. (It probably wasn't worth a tin shit, anyway)" ("Introduction" xviii). The implication here is that King is more than a living filter for words whose meaning is determined by the reader, and, as Marnie O'Neill suggests, "the assumption that texts are neutral or inanimate objects from which the reader is free to make meanings seems untenable" (92). Additionally, on the subject of structure, O'Neill suggests that, "some texts, however, are constructed in such a way that avenues of meaning are progressively closed off, sometimes without the readers being aware that either is happening, or how it is happening" (90). But how does this apply to *The Dark Tower*? With King claiming that the composition of this series was anything but planned or staged, he suggests that his intentions as author are unimportant. As a negotiation between the questioned roles of the author as the provider of words and the reader as maker of meaning, the *Dark Tower* series can be read, and read well, through the art of re-reading.

Once a given reader knows the outcome of a particular tale, re-reading the text does not solely become an exercise in indulging oneself in a literary encore of reading for entertainment or mere repetition. Rather, re-readers scour texts for clues an author has written into the pages to reveal what will transpire, and the careful re-reader then reads beyond plot, character development and themes which are the foundations of most novels and the most prevalent aspects of many stories, yet which are also often limiting lenses of reading. For example, upon revisiting Stephen King's novel *Gerald's Game* knowing that Jesse Burlingame will free herself from being handcuffed to the bed, readers shed the burden of anticipation, undercut the purpose and excitement of her climatic and dramatic escape from Raymond Joubert, and begin to look at the story for different material and literary elements by means of newer or alternative reading approaches. Of course, this idea is not exactly revolutionary, but if one were to re-read the Stephen King canon while trying to piece together the larger tale King has woven through his *Dark Tower* series, especially as King's works, presumably, *all* come together to compose an epic tale told throughout King's stories which culminates in the gunslinger's quest, such becomes an endeavor to unmask the *entire* story behind King's fictional universe.

Stephen King's Constant Reader has undoubtedly seen King recycle characters, locations and references in his stories, all to the effect of somehow linking his tales together. More importantly, the additional information presented in separate volumes of his works that reference and rely on other texts within King's canon for complete meaning suggests that re-reading is an appropriate approach to his fiction. For example, King says in the foreword to *Dolores Claiborne* that this story is linked to *Gerald's Game* as, "both are tales of women in the path of the eclipse, and of how they emerge from the darkness," which indicates that a full reading of either novel cannot be completed until both are read (xvii). Also, with references to *ka* and the city of Lud in *Rose Madder* being of some consequence and context for the *Dark Tower* series, this text, "a real tank-job, at least in the sales sense," should ideally be read alongside the *Dark Tower*, or vice-versa (King, *Song of Susannah* 408). Or, as Michael Collings says, "each novel, each story he publishes is a self-contained entity that may share themes, settings, even characters from previous novels, but nonetheless moves readers in new and unexpected directions; King does not simply write sequels to bestselling novels to insure another bestseller" (*Scaring* 102). Although King does craft tales that are interconnected and inform one's reading of other texts within his canon, King also exerts an influence over his Constant Reader in that reading a single story by King demands reading at least one other *connected* story. This control of his Constant Reader can be seen as marketing, manipulation, or one of several other motives and methods. On the other hand, perhaps King is simply forcing his readers to consider their role and function in the reading process, as well as the writing process, in that they cannot be passive vessels into which words are delivered.

With the commentary of the *Dark Tower*'s author regarding his craft, alongside an examination of the series' content, it is revealed that the serial novel subverts the power of the reader while imbuing the author with a sense of power and control. However, the serial novel, especially within its contemporary framework of the *series*, i.e. Tolkien's *Lord of the Rings*, Lewis' *The Chronicles of Narnia*, Rice's *The Vampire Chronicles* or Rowling's popular culture phenomenon *Harry Potter*, employs the imagination of the author as well as the sustained interest of the reader to produce texts over a period of time. Still, in approaching Stephen King's fiction in its entirety, each tale unto itself is read in one of two ways: as an isolated, stand-alone story or as a connected piece to the *Dark Tower* series. Of course, any analysis of select novels from the Stephen King canon can unveil some of the lesser known connections among King's works, but while examining new readings of King's fiction as influenced by the *Dark Tower* series as a means of approaching King's ultimate role as author, it is discovered that King is an author who retains control over his creation by constantly re-working and essentially re-writing his entire oeuvre. Yet, when reading through the *Dark Tower* texts themselves, new information is acquired which becomes relevant to understanding and better interpreting King's other works, as well as understanding ambiguous references made early in the *Dark Tower* series which are unveiled as the story progresses. However, sometimes the information learned in King's fiction with respect to the connections made between his works, despite resulting in interesting discoveries and interpretations, is just that: *information.*

The "Serial" Novel and the Role of the Author

One of the primary assumptions at work here is that reading any story by King one time, and one time only, merely reveals *half* of the tale that King has composed. Moreover, King retains authorship over his creation by constantly re-writing his stories through intertextuality. By creating connections among his works and linking his various characters and realities to one another, the six-degrees of Stephen King create not only one large, singular tale that effectively becomes altered with each new addition to the King canon, but also ensures that the author does not fade into the background as simply a filter through which a given story is told. Nowhere else is the vital function of the author more apparent than in *The Dark Tower* as King becomes a character in his own book and further dictates the outcome of Roland Deschain's journey. And as King continues to exert his own creative mind and pen as means of control over his own writing, eliminating the sway of the reader as a potential source of discord and misinterpretation, he insists upon his role in sustaining the stories he writes by writing tales that, so far, have no true endings as he has yet to conclude his career.

At the same time that this idea is forwarded, Roland Barthes suggests exercising caution with such a view, one that leads to the problematic realm of the definitive or absolute reading and meaning of a text, as he says, "we know that a text is not a line of words releasing a single 'theological' meaning (the 'message' of the Author-God) but a multi-dimensional space in which a variety of writings, none of them original, blend and clash" ("Death" 1468). As Barthes indicates, writing is not necessarily something that results in a single meaning, especially one intended by the author. In addition to the intimation that writing and its meaning is dependent upon compositions that *precede* a particular work, King, while still allowing for varied interpretation of his writing even among his constant influence and presence, does invert the typical relationship found among intertextual works in that many of his writings become dependent upon stories that he creates *afterwards* instead of drawing on compositions which have come beforehand.

Consider the two versions of *The Gunslinger* that have been published. While many simply refer to the revised and expanded version published in 2003 as their frame of reference for the rest of the *Dark Tower* story, juxtaposing both versions in relation to what unfolds over the following six books forces readers to re-read these books and see what Roland has learned and how he has grown and changed in the new version. Assuming that King's first version of *The Gunslinger* initiates a journey to the Dark Tower and that the newer version is the beginning of another revolution on the wheel of destiny, or *ka* as it is called in the *Dark Tower* books, it appears that Roland has evolved ever so slightly as he, in the most recent version of *The Gunslinger* and not the original version published in 1982, has haunting memories of his lost love Susan Delgado who had been burned at the stake in which "*he could smell her burning hair*" (King, *The Gunslinger* 126). Also to consider is the foreboding vision of Jake Chambers' death in which the gunslinger, before Jake's actual death, envisions that, "*a spike had been driven through* [his] *forehead*," which is a clear premonition of death (King, *The Gunslinger* 126). These variations between the texts is more than simply added material in that these two characters whose deaths for which Roland is responsible, in conjunction with the new visions written into the updated version of *The Gunslinger*, provides readers a glimmer of hope in that perhaps Roland has evolved and grown, possibly attaining humility and feeling remorse in the latest renewal of his repetitive and circular quest.

In shifting to a specific focus on the serial novel, as the nature of writing in installments is at the heart of the *Dark Tower* series, it must be recalled that the common conception of the serial novel as appeared in 19th century serials has been modified here. This is not to say that there are no parallels between the 19th century serial and the modern fiction series. Much like King's manipulation of his *Dark Tower* series on the rest of his canon, the 19th century serial integrated other works into its story as, "the lengthy publication schedule of a major work allowed other publications to influence its reception, and each week or month before another issue of the periodical appeared, events in the real-world could affect response to the fictional worlds" (Lund 18). Additionally, the disruptions in the serial narrative are important to note in that, "the enforced pauses in serial publication also determined specific elements of meaning in many literary texts, for in that space between numbers readers reflected about the continuing stories, experienced more of their own lives, and read other literary and non-literary texts" (Lund 90). Of course, this implies that the reader of any serial novel has as much influence as the society in which the tale is written, especially when taking into account that, "one of the most important factors shaping periodical publication of fiction was the perceived existence of a known audience" (Lund 69). By the same token, an initial lack of readership for King's *The Dark Tower* series which saw the first installment of the series, *The Gunslinger*, being published in 1982 by the small and largely unknown Donald M. Grant Press, in addition to having little advertisement from King who had established himself as a best-seller by the early 80s, there was just enough audience interest in the text that called for the story to be continued. And concerning the gaps in publication, these can be attributed more to King's control over the texts instead of a purposeful pause for readers to become immersed in the tale and a subsequent demand for more story, albeit on the reader's terms. Still, while King has admitted that the interest on behalf of the reader had prompted him to continue writing the tale, this does not necessarily mean that the reader influenced the *content* of the tale.

Managing the gaps in publication of the serial novel, the temporal spaces in which various occurrences contribute to knowledge and growth in the reader that effectively influence any approach to any serial text, became an exercise for King to work his own craft and agenda rather than appease his reader. First, consider the breaks in publication among the first four novels: *The Gunslinger* (1982), *The Drawing of the Three* (1987), *The Waste Lands* (1991), and *Wizard and Glass* (1996). The temporal and creative space that separates each of these tales certainly allowed for both the reader and writer to exercise influence over the text, but the same cannot be said of the last three novels in the seven-book series which were all published within one calendar year — *Wolves of the Calla* (November 2003), *Song of Susannah* (June 2004), and *The Dark Tower* (September 2004) — which implies more authorial control than as found within the first four texts. More importantly, in recalling the pause in publication between the fourth and fifth volumes of this series, a space consisting of seven years saw one of the most memorable and tragic events of the 21st century: September 11, 2001. While it can only be speculated as to how this event affected readership and reading of texts published prior to this date, the effect 9/11 had on the novel can easily be imagined. And as it appears that a key problem of the serial novel is that gaps in publication only serve to bring about promised information, or resolutions alluded to as being necessary, King does not necessarily adhere to this general rule, nor does he display any worry in appropriating a major event like 9/11 into his writing despite the high probability for distaste among his readers. Yet, even as the serial novel takes into account happenings from the outside world and its readership during the lag in publication and often incorporates contemporary information and influences into the tale, there is an underlying sense of structure or planning involved. Additionally, within King's *Dark Tower* series is his own reaction to this event can be seen in the pages of *The Dark Tower* as specific references to 9/11 are made, contributing to the contemporary backdrop King often weaves into his fiction for a sense of timeliness and as a means of structuring the novel with known information.

Also to consider in terms of incorporating contemporary events and the subsequent structuring involved in *The Dark Tower* is the talisman of ultimate malice called Black Thirteen. Within the story itself, Jake Chambers and Father Callahan store it in a fictional long-term storage locker underneath the World Trade Center in the summer of 1999, believing that this item will be confined and restrained, "'until June of two thousand and two, unless someone breaks in and steals it'" (King, *Song of Susannah* 338). Then, as Jake ominously wonders what might happen if the twin towers were to fall in some way, Callahan, replies in an unknowingly ironic manner: "'Never happen. And if it did ... well, one glass ball under a hundred and ten stories of concrete and steel? Even a glass ball filled with deep magic? That'd be one way to take care of the nasty thing, I guess'" (King, *Song of Susannah* 338). With the volume containing the preceding text, the sixth installment of the series entitled *Song of Susannah*, which was published in June of 2004, readers know what will happen in this scene. And, as King mixes a blend of reality into his fiction, suggesting that 9/11 is a certainty to happen in his fictional world, he asserts another measure of control over his text in that he ensures the evil talisman will in fact be eliminated — no suspense, no questions, and no opportunity for the reader to exercise any sense of accurate speculation and interpretation other than the conclusion King himself has drawn.

In addition to 9/11 being a key occurrence that takes place in the publication gap of King's serial novel, King almost died after being struck by a mini-van in the summer of 1999. Of course, this brush with death delayed much of King's publishing as his recovery did not lend itself to writing, but aside from the calendar breaks in King's serial novel, the importance of King's own life as it happened outside of his texts holds as much importance, if not more, than September 11th. In *The Dark Tower*, King decides to write himself into his own story, a metafictional maneuver which, as King attempts to continue the semblance of reality in his fiction, necessitates the incorporation of his 1999 accident. Although King has revisited his near-death experience in several of his other novels and screenplays after this incident, to weave his own story into his fiction, a fiction that because of its serial nature has constantly undergone changes and alterations, is an inclusion that does not succumb to the pulls of the reader. While this decision may appear to be self-indulgent, King's use of his own life events further constrains the story. Moreover, it seems as if King is asking readers to assume a level of interest primarily because they do not have to act upon the text. This may reflect a sense of lazy reading with the reader neither being asked to provide input for the tale nor being given the opportunity to do so, but it would seem that despite Barthes proclamation that the author is dead, *The Dark Tower* series suggests that the author is alive and well.

When Roland Barthes claims that, "a text's unity lies not in its origin but its destination," noting that the destination of King's fictional universe, however, is yet to be determined reminds readers of King's power as an author to consistently hold the destination of his writing in his own hands ("Death" 1469). Even when King puts the pen away and stops writing, the repetitive tale of *The Dark Tower* negates the idea of genuine destination in that any linear attributes placed upon the novel can be dismissed. Intertextuality in the Stephen King canon creates a large, singular tale that is purposely interwoven rather than connected by mere happenstance or even generic classification as is the case between King's connections to authors like Poe or Lovecraft. All in all, it is with this planned, complex and intricate network of fiction that King reminds readers that not even the death or removal of the author would allow for readers to take over their own readership of King's fiction because the pulls and designs of Stephen King as an author are ubiquitous and anything but negligible. To be sure, King's constant control over and redirection of his fiction keep the reader reading. However, T. S. Eliot claims that, "no poet, no artist of any art, has his complete meaning alone" (1093). Yet, when considering the conscious construction of meaning within King's canon at the expense of disempowering the disdained reader, his writing may insist upon his isolation, which, while inaccurate, is nonetheless an indication and allusion to the overarching sense of power King exercises in his craft while avoiding reader alienation but also dismissing the influence and pull of the audience.

The involvement of the reader in not only reading a text but influencing meaning and interpretation is at the heart of post-structuralist thought, especially that of Roland Barthes and his cornerstone writing "The Death of the Author": "to give a text an Author is to impose a limit on that text, to furnish it with a final signified, to close the writing" (1469). Agreement with Barthes is found with David Miall who suggests that a one-sided relationship is not possible with writing: "a text is not a self-sufficient autonomous entity: it requires realisation, a conscious input from the reader" (10). Annette Lavers also suggests that structuralism and the role of the author can be reduced down to, in essence, "a denial of the possibility of choice" (16). Aside from the theoretical bent of this statement, one must wonder as to whether or not choice is important regarding a text, especially when a variety of readings and interpretations based on choice can easily fall within the category of mere opinion instead of informed critique or analysis. Also, Roland Barthes' discussion of the myth of Jason and the Argonauts, specifically their ship the Argo, lends a useful metaphor regarding the dynamics of the serial novel. Of the Argo, Barthes comments on the nature of this vessel which required constant repair and notes that with, "each piece of which the Argonauts gradually replaced, [...] they ended with an entirely new ship, without having to alter either its name or its form" (*Roland Barthes* 46). The serial novel, too, functions in this manner because the original title under which a serial novel is composed never changes, yet the content is effectively altered with each installment. The gaps in publication also affect the tale in that social occurrences influence readership, both as it relates to the early parts of the serial novel as well as the subsequent additions. Yet, Barthes indicates that despite the constant alteration to the ship, the image of the Argo is an, "allegory of an eminently structural object," that which despite the changes, alterations and decisions by the crew to fix the ship, it remains as an object of design rather than flexibility (*Roland Barthes* 46). This seems to be at the heart of the discussion here in that the Argo, an image of the serial novel, functions more as a construction than that of a fluid nature.

The paradox of Stephen King's serial novel is that texts which both precede and come after the *Dark Tower* series become subject to re-contextualization and acquire new meanings via the plot and content written into *The Dark Tower*. The connections between King's works, and not those limited to his *Dark Tower* series, however, are not constructed as a series of stories, tales that purposely and directly link to one another to create a single and *seamless* tale. King's overarching story, which is composed through all of his stories with the *Dark Tower* series functioning as the axle through which the other tales, or spokes, are linked, may have its holes, but this missing information instigates curious reading in that hopes for more story prompts readership and gives King numerous canvases on which he can craft his story as well as new tales.

The Dark Tower and the Stephen King Universe

Merely noting connections and links among King's work may be interesting, but such observations take readers towards literal and figurative dead-ends. In noting that there are evil wolf characters in *Cycle of the Werewolf* and good wolves in *The Talisman* or even finding a link between *The Dark Half* and *Hearts in Atlantis* as Ted Brautigan comments on a straight-razor (George Stark's weapon of choice) he and Bobby Garfield see in a store window, saying that, "'when people buy razors like that, they don't shave with them,'" is simply finding delicate bridges among King's fiction as opposed to some startling discovery that unveils a deeper meaning in the text or reveals a new layer of reading and plot that cannot be understood without the context or information found in another book (King, "Low Men in Yellow Coats" 151).

Old, tired interpretations are inevitable with any field of literary study, and the same holds for King. There can be only so much said about Jack Torrance's alcoholism and abuse, or Carrie White's traumatic high-school experiences, or the function of the family in *Pet Sematary*. However, King's *The Dark Tower* series functions as the nexus of his corpus, and it is through this tale that all of King's other writings gain their full meaning and story. Careful readings of King's canon reveal that all of his works are in some way interconnected, whether by means of geo-graphical similarity or even singular cultural references to brand-name products. Moreover, the abundance of psychic phenomena and haunted places imbued with dark spirits such as The Overlook, The Agincourt, Rose Red, Black House, Sara Laughs and the Dutch Hill Mansion, all reflect a sense of constant thematic, or mimicry, in King's fiction, which can be viewed as either a tired writer simply recycling old ideas or a writer attempting to somehow unify his writing through the similari-ties. Either way, the journey for the reader of *The Dark Tower* is certainly not easy.

With the various genres blending and combating one another, along with the consistent mystery weaved into a tale that takes place in a world that is largely unexplored by both the author and the reader, the *Dark Tower* series is, without doubt, a difficult read. One means of easing the reading burden is to contextualize the story, which can be done by way of re-reading the *Dark Tower* stories as well as re-reading each and every text that King has written. While it may become difficult, if not trying and tiring, to find connections among King's corpus to aid with under-standing the *Dark Tower* series, it has been noted that a fictional uni-verse is exactly what King has created with the gunslinger's tale:

The Dark Tower is nothing if not ambitious: it seeks to blend disparate styles of popular narrative, from Arthurian legend to Sergio Leone western to apocalyptic science fiction. More than that, it tries to knit the bulk of King's fiction together into a single universe (or a set of interlocking universes), and on some level even to accommodate *all stories* known and unknown, into a master narrative that encompasses the whole of creation [O'Hehir B11].

Attributing success to this endeavor is not easy for anyone say, but general observation suggests that merely reading the entire Stephen King canon is not necessarily a figurative key that easily unlocks the mysteries of his writing. Since the completion of the *Dark Tower* series, readers have found themselves wrapped up in a quandary: if Roland's world is circular, then what would re-reading the series accomplish? If readers have been there before, what is the point in going back over the thousands of pages to only end up back at the beginning? As the last sentence of the seventh book in the *Dark Tower* series is read, readers are transported back to the very beginning of the tale, accompanying Roland once again on his quest for the elusive Dark Tower. Yet, even though Roland has the Horn of Eld at the end of the series, which *implies* a new story will unfold, why would anyone re-read the text? There is only a hint towards hope, and there is certainly not a different tale with a new resolution awaiting readers. There may be the possibility within the mind of the imaginative reader that there is something new to be found in re-reading the *Dark Tower* series, but the books have been written, and are permanent, with the words set on paper and unwavering in their presentation. In short, it is easy to conclude that *The Dark Tower* books do not promise anything new or different for a second reading, but drawing such a conclusion too quickly is a mistake.

One of the best examples as to how re-reading affects and alters the tale of the gunslinger is found in the last section of *The Gunslinger* where Roland receives the most critical clue concerning the nature of his quest. Consider the original scene between Roland and Walter O'Dim at the golgotha when they begin to palaver. After Roland is shown the universe in the first version of *The Gunslinger*, a failed attempt by Walter to force Roland to cry off from his quest, Roland later discovers the identity of the Man in Black and then says, "'I ought to kill you now'" (King 213). Walter's original response in this first version of *The Gunslinger* is, "'That would hardly be fair. After all, it was I who delivered Marten into your hands'" (King 213). At first, Roland's desire to kill Walter, and the Man in Black's subsequent response, appear to be of little consequence to Roland's journey. However, in the revised version of *The Gunslinger*, Walter's new response, in reference to the guns that Roland is about to fire, is, "'those do not open doors, gunslinger; those only close them forever'" (King 227). What is important about Walter's words, especially now that readers know Roland has been to the Tower before, is that Walter intimates that Roland's means of entry to the Tower, his sandalwood guns, do not necessarily open the door that Roland wants. While the guns do allow Roland access to the Tower, this door does not remain open for Roland. If Roland were to forego entering the Tower, as entering the Tower may not be necessary, he just may find the answer to his dilemma of resumption and repetition; if Roland decides against entering the Tower, he may be saved. If Roland does not use his gun to open the door at the base of the Tower, consequently closing the door at the top of the Tower, then perhaps the gunslinger may truly fulfill his destiny and duty. Consider that the gun that Roland lays at the door to the Tower does not just represent Roland's seeming worthiness to enter the navel of Gan as Roland is a descendant of Arthur Eld. Rather, the guns, by this point in Roland's adventure, come to symbolize all that Roland needlessly sacrifices to merely satisfy his curiosity: knowledge of who or what resides at the top of the Tower. Yet, even though such knowledge is not relevant to Roland's primary duty as a protector of the Dark Tower, this information is certainly pertinent to the careful (re)reader of Stephen King's fiction.

All things considered, re-reading the *Dark Tower* series is a useful approach to fully understanding the content and context of these books. But rather than visiting every single tale that King has written from his early days as a writer in the late 60s all the way to the fiction that has been composed in the first decade of the 21st century, a careful selection of novels and writings are to be brought forth into the light of intertextuality. This is not to say that each and every tale that King has written is either drastically altered by way of its relation to the *Dark Tower* series, or vice-versa. Rather, the connections found among many of the stories are often simply information, or context, that is surely helpful to have in mind when approaching Roland's tale. But, in some instances, the links that are forged between King's works prompt alternative views and readings of particular stories that could not be seen without the presence and influence of another story within King's corpus. Yet, even when there are noted connections among King's works, sometimes the only result is that of two tales being brought together as related fictions that simply add more characters and references to the growing story of *The Dark Tower*, which is the most common form of intertextuality in Stephen King's fictional universe.

"The Little Sisters of Eluria"

"The Little Sisters of Eluria" is the only story connected to *The Dark Tower* series, aside from the graphic novels, solely based upon the original tale. Featuring Roland Deschain as the main character, this story gives some back-story for the gunslinger and even some additional context to the *Dark Tower* series, much like how *The Stand* and *The Eyes of the Dragon* provide a detailed back-story of Randall Flagg. But, in determining its place and influence on the larger story of the gunslinger, "The Little Sisters of Eluria" functions much in the same manner as the graphic novels — despite King's sole control and reign over the story itself, including the characters, plot, and references that situate this story alongside and even within the *Dark Tower* story, it does very little to prompt any new readings or views into Roland and his quest. Upon reading this piece, readers discover that the action takes place while the gunslinger is searching for the Man in Black, and aside from the geographical link that is created between this story and *Desperation* in that "The Little Sisters of Eluria" takes place in the Desatoya Mountains, there is not much else to be discovered in these pages.

"The Little Sisters of Eluria" situates Mid-World as a land that is somehow connected to that of Earth with religious references to Jesus as well as, "Baal, Asmodeus, and a hundred others," as well as seemingly placing this land in the same world as Delain, the kingdom from *The Eyes of the Dragon* (King 171). Even so, such connections and references seem to be the limit of this story's influence The Little Sisters themselves are only an obstacle for the gunslinger to overcome, and although Roland once again finds someone who ends up as a willing sacrifice — Sister

Jenna, she who dies and is rewarded with but a simple kiss from the gun-slinger—the Little Sisters themselves become little more than a some-what obscure reference alluded to in *Black House*:

> "What is this place?" he asks.
> She smiles. "To some, a hospital."
> "Oh?" He looks up and once more takes note of the cross. Maroon now, but undoubtedly once red. *A red cross, stupid*, he thinks. "Oh! But isn't it a little ... well ... odd?"
> [...] "Yes, Jack. *Very* old. Once there were a dozen or more of these tents in the Territories, On-World, and Mid-World; now there are only a few. Mayhap just this one. Today it's here. Tomorrow...."
> [...] "Doesn't exactly look sterile."
> [...] "Yet if you were a patient, you would think it beautiful out of all measure. And you would think your nurses, the Little Sisters, the most beautiful any poor patient ever had."
> Jack looks around. "Where are they?"
> "The Little Sisters don't come out when the sun shines" [King 391].

Even as this passage suggests that a full understanding of *Black House* cannot be arrived at unless one has read "The Little Sisters of Eluria," this is an instance in which King has connected one story to another by way of common characters instead of a geographic location, like Derry or Castle Rock. The point, though, is to say that as King connects his stories together by whichever means or links he chooses, there are instances in which all he has accomplished is uniting his writings together under one common story. And while it has been indicated that such a fusion of stories implies a need to re-read and recontextualize King's fiction, the relationships that some stories share in the Stephen King canon are not always revealing or indicative on much more than a joining of two or more stories. And this is the case with "The Little Sisters of Eluria" in that it does little more than add information to the larger story, some of which is hardly germane to the plot of *The Dark Tower*.

"The Little Sisters of Eluria" may provide the reader with new locations within Mid-World like Tejuas, Kambero and Lexingworth, along with a brief and vague introduction to the *sigul* called the Dark Bells, as well as the first introduction to the doctor bugs, the *can tam*, that show up again in the last book of the *Dark Tower* series, and which bear a strange similarity in nomenclature to the *can tah* of *Desperation*, but these pieces of information that the story provides do not necessarily help any reader to better understand *The Dark Tower* series. The story itself is certainly enjoyable and able to stand alone, despite many ambiguous and dropped references that only those familiar with the *Dark Tower* would be able to recognize, but it is simply a story that has become attached to *The Dark Tower*, giving the original story a bit more girth and information that does enrich and enliven the words found in the seven books of the primary series. Above all else, this tale is mostly a teasing glimpse into the history of the gunslinger that actually reveals very little.

Directly Connected Stories: *Insomnia, The Eyes of the Dragon, The Stand* and *'Salem's Lot*

Insomnia is the one of the few novels by King that receives direct mention in *The Dark Tower*, one which is depicted and presented as the cornerstone work for unveiling the mysteries of Roland Deschain's quest. Yet, like much of King's recent novels, *Insomnia* has received little, if any, critical or scholarly attention. Regardless of any plausible explanations for the wandering critical eye concerning this story, King attempts to forge a connection between this book and the *Dark Tower* series, primarily through the characters of Patrick Danville and the Crimson King. With the former character, King suggests in *Insomnia* that his life is not only a danger to the Crimson King, who has taken a vested and personal interest in the life, and hoped for death, of this budding artist. And as knowledge of the *Dark Tower* series undoubtedly helps to unravel the references made to this series in *Insomnia*, including Patrick's apparent awareness as to who the gunslinger is—"*Him's name is Roland, Mama. I dream about him, sometimes*"— this book is one that functions much in the same way as "The Little Sisters of Eluria" as an add-on story that gives more content to the *Dark Tower* series instead of context (King 615). Although reading the *Dark Tower* books certainly provides much needed context for understanding *Insomnia*, the book itself is problematic in the larger scope of the Stephen King universe. Or, as the gunslinger says in the last book of the *Dark Tower* series, "'it feels tricksy to me'" (King 524).

For all the attention and explanation provided in *Insomnia* regarding the four constants of existence — Life, Death, Random and Purpose — their presence in *The Dark Tower* is absent, suggesting that these themes in particular do not necessarily aid in understanding the tale of the gunslinger. Additionally, with no reference to these constants in *The Dark Tower*, the context that this series provides for *Insomnia* is minimal. Knowledge as to who Roland and the Crimson King are is quite helpful for any reader, but providing information that has previously been hidden or denied does not necessarily lead to the recontextualization envisioned and described earlier in this chapter. Moreover, the plot discussed in *Insomnia* regarding Patrick Danville's role in the *Dark Tower* books is misleading and inaccurate: "*Eighteen years from now, just before his death, the boy is going to save the lives of two men who would otherwise die ... and one of those men must not die, if the balance between the Random and the Purpose is to be maintained*" (King, *Insomnia* 620). In *The Dark Tower*, Patrick Danville, the artist, does save two lives — his own and Roland's — but the implication is that he would save two lives other than his own. Such a reading, or even a misreading, is not uncommon when it comes to fiction as particular word combinations can be vague and deceptive, but with this critique of erroneous writing, much like that which is found in the *Dark Tower* graphic novels, King does have a rationale for this and any other mistakes that have been made in the process of crafting the *Dark Tower*. As Marian Carver gives the gunslinger a copy of *Insomnia* in *The Dark Tower*, she discusses with Roland that King has been referencing *The Dark Tower* in several books outside of this series for years, but that, "'King's references to the Dark Tower are almost always masked, and sometimes mean nothing at all'" (King 514). With this declaration pushing readers to disregard connections to the *Dark Tower* series as discovered in King's other texts, this does not negate the existence of King's attempts to weave a fictional tapestry to include all the works of his creation. But, sometimes the information that King gives in one tale which references another is simply information which can be easily dismissed if it is discovered that said information is false or incongruous.

The Eyes of the Dragon has already been mentioned as text that simply provides *information* in relation to the *Dark Tower* series by way of giving Randall Flagg a back-story that adds to what is discovered in *The*

Stand. And while it has been argued that some of Flagg's back-story is rather pertinent information when discussing his character, neither *The Eyes of the Dragon* nor *The Stand* gives readers any substantial content or context to carefully consider and recall when reading *The Dark Tower*. When Roland and his *ka-tet* arrive in Topeka, Kansas in *Wizard and Glass*, knowing that this land has seen the superflu from *The Stand* simply tells readers that the gunslinger and his companions are in a place that holds certain significance within another Stephen King story, and little else. For that matter, Robin Furth, in the second volume of her Dark Tower *Concordance*, offers several suggestions and questions as to the nature of *The Eyes of the Dragon* as being directly linked to Mid World, including a rather detailed and critical analysis of the fictional geography of King's imagination:

> For example, both Delain and Gilead are referred to as In-World baronies, yet how can this be so if Roland Deschain seems unaware of the places so frequently mentioned in *The Eyes of the Dragon*— The Sea of Tomorrow, the Far Forests, the Northern, Eastern, Western and Southern Baronies? Wouldn't they have appeared on the map Roland saw as a boy, the one which depicted the Greater Kingdoms of the Western Earth? Any why is the Delain that we learn about in "The Little Sisters of Eluria" closer to Eluria — an Out-World town — than to Gilead? [431].

While Furth does posit some keen questions and observations regarding the placement of *The Eyes of the Dragon* in the *Dark Tower* universe, or specifically within the *Dark Tower*'s own Mid-World, a simple explanation is offered by King within the pages of *The Dark Tower*: the land is constantly moving. This inconsistency seen with the points of a compass in Mid-World and other geographical paradoxes, such as the declaration in *Song of Susannah* that Roland's grandfather, Alaric, once "'went to Garlan,'" a land situated within both *The Dark Tower* and *The Eyes of the Dragon*, is yet another example of King offering some sort of explanation or rationalization of the inconsistencies that are noticed in careful readings of his novels (King 197). However, the mystery and debate that King creates with geography is found to be of interest to several scholars, including Douglass Winter who proposes that, "*The Eyes of the Dragon* is set in the Territories, the parallel world of *The Talisman*— that mythical, medieval land of kings and queens, two-headed parrots, and magic — although it occurs in a different time and place than Jack Sawyer's quest" (155). Additionally, even as Tony Magistrale also asserts that, "*Eyes* is set entirely in the Territories, the parallel universe Jack Sawyer discovers in *The Talisman*," such statements can hardly be read as definitive interpretations of the story (*Second Decade* 135). But, more importantly, there is doubt as to whether or not such avenues of discussion open up this or any of King's tales in any meaningful way. As is the case with *Dolores Claiborne* and *Gerald's Game* in which the female protagonists both witness the total eclipse of the sun on July 20, 1963, between 5:41–5:45 P.M., such a link is merely a connection, and knowing the story of both Dolores and Jesse Burlingame, like knowing the story of Flagg in *The Eyes of the Dragon* and *The Stand* (as well as within *The Dark Tower*), is neither extraordinary nor revealing of anything beyond a link forged between two texts.

The Stand functions much like *The Eyes of the Dragon* in that besides providing a reference point for the superflu which finds a place in *The Dark Tower* and providing a few details as to Randall Flagg's history, there is little in this tale that calls for careful scrutiny in the hope of discovering a key piece of King's fictional puzzle. Of course, there are elements of this story that parallel those found in *The Dark Tower*, such as the convenience of *deus ex machina*. But, when considering *'Salem's Lot* within the discussion of intertextuality, this text falls under the same critiques. Donald Callahan, as readers are well aware, leaves his home in Jerusalem's Lot and eventually wanders into the tale of *The Dark Tower*, and as much of his history is recollected within the pages of *Wolves of the Calla*, *'Salem's Lot* then becomes a negligible reading in that most of what readers need to know about Callahan is told in a separate text. The information about vampires like Barlow and the few other pieces of information presented, like how dogs with cross-like patches of fur are feared by vampiric individuals (just like in "The Little Sisters of Eluria"), is interesting, but not enlightening. This is not to say that knowledge of either Flagg's history or Callahan's story is moot. Yet there does seem to be something lacking in these tales concerning their connection to *The Dark Tower*, which might be explained by the publication dates of their stories, which extends no later than 1987, a year that had only seen two of the *Dark Tower* novels published by this time.

Many of the novels outside of the *Dark Tower* published after *Wizard and Glass* have the benefit of hindsight, in that the connections King has created among his works are more noticeable, prevalent, and even clearer in some of the later novels, such as *Hearts in Atlantis* and *Everything's Eventual*, which both feature characters who are brought into Mid-World, like Randall Flagg and Donald Callahan. However, unlike the villain and the priest, Ted Brautigan and Dinky Earnshaw are created as characters whose destinies were planned to coincide with the gunslinger's quest, whereas the prior pairing had uncertain futures when King originally finished their tales. But even though King discovered how to incorporate these characters into the *Dark Tower* story, their connection to the gunslinger is inconsequential. In short, "Everything's Eventual" merely recounts Earnshaw's work under the mysterious Mr. Sharpton. Presumably, with no knowledge of the *Dark Tower* series, or even the suspicion that mentally-gifted individuals like Earnshaw would become essential to the *Dark Tower* plotline, "Everything's Eventual" is then presented as just another story about an odd individual with peculiar abilities, which is not uncommon in King's fiction. Of course, re-reading "Everything's Eventual" after reading *The Dark Tower* undoubtedly makes for an interesting read, filling in the gaps of information that can be resolved by bringing these two texts together which begins to complete the puzzle of King's fiction. Again, by reading all of King's writings, the entire story behind his career can be seen, but merely finding and seeing all the pieces of this fictional picture is the first step in not just re-reading the Stephen King canon, but re-*contextualizing* it, that is if certain connections and links among King's stories do reveal more than just information.

In moving from Dinky Earnshaw's tale to Ted Brautigan's, "Low Men in Yellow Coats" is almost as problematic as "Everything's Eventual" concerning its designation as just another story devoted to character history. However, the mysteries and ambiguities included in "Low Men in Yellow Coats" does suggest that there is more than just information to be found in this story and by reading it alongside *The Dark Tower*. When most Constant Readers first read *Hearts in Atlantis* and discover at the end of the book that Brautigan was supposedly once again free from the Low Men — "There was no letter, no note, no writing of any kind. When Bobby tilted the envelope, what showered down on the surface of his desk were rose petals of the deepest, darkest red he had ever seen"— they most likely wonder exactly how he escaped, and, of course, the answer is not given until *The Dark Tower* (King, "Low Men in Yellow Coats" 321). More importantly, readers who read "Low Men in Yellow Coats" for the first time are probably a little mystified as to the origin and nature of the low men as they had not been thoroughly discussed in any other book written by King, although their relation to *The Dark Tower* can be surmised when Brautigan first mentions the word *gunslinger* in a dialogue with the low men who have finally caught up to him:

> "There is a gunslinger [...] he and his friends have reached the borderland of End-World.... If I give you what you want instead of forcing you to take it, I may be able to speed things up by fifty years or more. As you say, I'm a Breaker, made for it and born to it. There aren't many of us. You need every one, and most of all you need me. Because I'm the best" [King, "Low Men in Yellow Coats" 285].

Beyond Brautigan's brief reference to the story of Roland Deschain, information about the low men remains veiled, at least as they relate to the gunslinger's story, which pushes readers to read the *Dark Tower* series for more information and context. And once *The Dark Tower* is read, revisiting Brautigan's tale undoubtedly makes more sense, which supports the call for re-reading as it invariably opens up doors to King's canon that had previously been closed. Moreover, while *Hearts in Atlantis* has been made into a motion picture, suggesting at least some attention given to King's more recent work, any Constant Reader familiar with the text as well as *The Dark Tower* notices that most all references to *The Dark Tower* woven into the novel *Hearts in Atlantis* are lost in the film. But, returning to the text, Brautigan's tale, seems to reflect just another example of the false leads that King's writes into his stories outside of *The Dark Tower*, like when Brautigan tells of his escape: "'There are others like me. And there are people whose job it is to catch us, keep us, and use us for ... well, use us, leave it at that. I and two others escaped. One was caught, one was killed. Only I remain free'" (King, "Low Men in Yellow Coats" 239). While readers come to learn of Ted's eventual return to Algul Siento, as well as his initial departure with the help of Sheemie Ruiz, there is nothing to be learned of the others who reportedly escaped with him, which reiterates that intertexuality in King's fiction is, at times, tenuous. Yet King does somewhat rectify this issue with the composition of *Black House*, and to a lesser degree *The Talisman*.

The tales of *The Talisman* and *Black House* have a rather distinguished separation despite being linked together. *The Talisman*, as is the case with most stories followed by a sequel, only gathers its entire meaning and context by reading the second story, *Black House*, and vice-versa. However, *Black House* is positioned in an awkward place as its own context and completion does not necessarily come from its predecessor, *The Talisman*, but rather *The Dark Tower* series. Even though *The Dark Tower* was three years away from completion when *Black House* was published, this book primarily rested upon knowledge and familiarity with *The Dark Tower*. The eventual focus on and discussion of the Crimson King, for example, in *Black House* is difficult enough considering that this character has very little introduction or treatment in the story, and as the same can be said of the *Dark Tower* circa 2001, dismissing, of course, the Crimson King's brief mentioning in *Wizard and Glass* and rather vague presentation in *Insomnia*. But, it is certainly appreciated when King does examine the Crimson King and his plans in *Black House*, finally revealing that this being is attempting to topple the Dark Tower, and that he is supposedly imprisoned at the top of the structure. Of course, when Jack Sawyer asks Parkus of the apparent idiocy of the Crimson's King's plans to topple the Dark Tower, and likely killing himself in the process, Parkus replies, "'just the opposite: he'll set it free to wander what will then be chaos ... *din-tah* ... the furnace. Some parts of Mid-World have fallen into that furnace already,'" which, again, is rather, if not misleading, information and muddled context for the *Dark Tower* story (King, *Black House* 400). The implicit dialogue between *Black House* and *The Dark Tower* is noteworthy in that the plot of the former text essentially collapses in upon itself without the influence of the latter. And, of course, the same can be said of *The Dark Tower* even though the series itself possesses more self-sufficiency than King's other tales. This does not mean that *The Talisman* is relegated to nothingness and emptiness without knowledge of *The Dark Tower*; but it does suggest that in order for the links in the literary chain that King creates to fully function and hold together, *The Talisman* does need *Black House* as much as *Black House* needs *The Dark Tower*.

As *The Talisman* looks for re-contextualization and even re-reading with the publication of a sequel in 2001, the addition of more *Dark Tower*-related story as is found in *Black House* actually brings two supplemental tales into the overarching storyline of the gunslinger, unifying and completing these stories. In noting that, "the landscape of *The Talisman*, particularly that part of the Territories traversed by the railroad and inhabited by strange creatures, strongly resembles the dying, desert lands the Gunslinger travels through," Jack Sawyer's story becomes positioned as one that inherently has ties to *The Dark Tower* due to its own content (Collings and Engebreston 102). Additionally, when it is observed in *The Talisman* that, "throughout the novel, every event of any consequence that occurs in the United States is purported to produce some sort of parallel reaction within the mythical Territories," another link between this book and *The Dark Tower* is formed in that the overlapping nature of the worlds in the gunslinger's story, namely the influence of Sombra and North Central Positronics in Mid-World and Earth, is brought forth as yet another way to join King's fictional worlds (Magistrale, *Moral* 40).

In short, any sense of completeness and unity within King's canon relies upon knowledge of all of his works, but simply gathering information does not always lead to new readings or even any sense of definitive story. Moreover, completeness may imply a sense of resolution and clarity in terms of this fictional relationship, but one would do well to exercise caution in attributing any sense of finality to King's writing; the links among *The Talisman*, *Black House*, and *The Dark Tower* are not necessarily linear or finite but perhaps, much like the gunslinger's quest, circular and open, therefore denying any sense of full understanding through established boundaries or limits to the tale.

Other Connected Tales

With the rest of Stephen King's canon, much of the links and connections to be found in his tales in relation to *The Dark Tower* fall under the same umbrella of criticism previously outlined in that these tales are, generally speaking, nothing more than sources of information. With various *Dark Tower* references and allusions, including the foregrounding of the Turtle as an important cosmic figure in *IT* to the exploration of The Shop in *Firestarter* as a potential branch of the infamous Sombra Corporation or even North Central Positronics, other tales such as *Bag of Bones, Dreamcatcher, The Mist, From a Buick 8, Rose Madder, Desperation*, and all of the Bachman books certainly can be seen as tales that somehow are aligned with Mid-World and Roland Deschain's voyage. With *Desperation* and *The Regulators*, for instance, Stephen King's alter ego, Richard Bachman, is finally revealed to be a key element in the overarching tale, which is also seen with the reference of Raymond Garraty from *The Long Walk* in *Bag of Bones*. Still, these stories only bring into the light a few minor but interesting elements that help one's reading of *The Dark Tower* become a bit clearer. With the mention and brief explanation of the *can-toi*, or the little gods, along with the choice in geography that King uses in *Desperation*, the Desatoya Mountains, these novels join with *Rose Madder*'s inclusion of various Mid-World notions and references — "'I've seen wars come n go like waves on a beach that roll in n rub out the footprints and wash away the castles in the sand. I've seen bodies on fire and heads by the hundreds poked onto poles along the streets in the City of Lud'" — as more instances of information that is connected to *The Dark Tower* (King, *Rose Madder* 270–1). Still, even though some of these references are not only easily observed by even a cursory reading of these books, such information hardly proves to be anything pertinent to the *Dark Tower* story.

In addition to King's fiction, his ventures into film also have become a focal point within his fictional universe as they are often patterned after King's writing to include references that bring his stories together. The reference to The Shop in *Golden Years* certainly creates a link to *Firestarter* and the placement of Nozz-A-La Cola in *Kingdom Hospital* establishes some sort of connection between this television series and *The Dark Tower*. But these references, along with other connections observed such as the ability to make oneself *dim* in *Sleepwalkers*, are often little more than inside references that King writes into his creations, just as the nature of the living house in *Rose Red* appears to be crafted and even contrived as a purposely linked reality to *The Dark Tower*. Although the constantly changing floor plans of Rose Red recall the slippage and constant transformation seen in Black House, as well as *The Dark Tower* as the points of the compass in Mid-World are not trusted as reading true, all that can really be said about these connections is that they foreground similarities among King's novels that are certainly not uncanny or indicative of anything of real importance.

4. Repetition, Integration, Immersion, and Intertextuality

More to the point, with the release of *Wolves of the Calla* in 2003, King brought forth to his Constant Reader a supposedly definitive list of all the books in his corpus that were related to the *Dark Tower* series in one way or another. Of course this list included texts already mentioned like *The Stand* and *'Salem's Lot*, but among the surprise inclusions were *From a Buick 8* and *Skeleton Crew*. Regarding *From a Buick 8*, this story is only connected to the *Dark Tower* stories in that the Buick Roadmaster discussed in this tale likely came from the gunslinger's world and is a living car that the low men use, a vehicle not entirely unlike the Plymouth Fury found in *Christine* but does not bear any real importance in better understanding *The Dark Tower* series. Also, concerning *Skeleton Crew*, it has been surmised that the primary tale in this collection, *The Mist*, is presumed to be an extension of the *Dark Tower* tale with its horrifying creatures from assumed alternate dimensions mirroring the mutated animal atrocities witnessed from inside Blaine the Mono in the waste lands outside of Lud. Yet, confirmation of this link was not wholly revealed until *The Mist* was adapted into a film and presents in the opening scene the main character, David Drayton, painting a familiar figure donning western garb and appearing before a dark, rising spire, as well as confirmation from one of the military men trapped in the supermarket that the Arrowhead Project was designed to create windows into other dimensions instead of the doorways that resulted in the assault by the horrific creatures that are, unsurprisingly, not the worst monsters in the story. Even as Douglass Winter notes that, "this short novel is a paradigm of the complicated metaphors of Faustian experimentation and technological horror consistently woven into the fiction of Stephen King," reminding readers of the consistent use of particular themes in King's writing, little is revealed or shown to be overly useful in observing repetition in terms of content, genre, theme, character, or locale (86).

Although it may seem counter-productive and even repetitive to spend a great deal of time lamenting the connections King has drawn among his fictional works, the purpose is to highlight and underscore the clear meaning of intertextuality set forth in the early pages of this chapter. With intertextuality, merely linking one text to another may result in a dialogue of sorts between two works, but the intertextual relationship forged in an instance such as this, is one in which little is learned of one book or the other beyond *information*. However, this is not the case with all of King's stories. While the case of learning relevant or significant information to be used in re-reading and then re-contextualizing a story can be made for the novels and stories discussed between "The Little Sisters of Eluria" and *The Mist*, a better example of King's use of immersing one tale into another and creating a *useful* intertextual link is better seen within his older and more popular works.

The Art of Re-reading: *The Shining, Carrie, The Dead Zone* and *Pet Sematary*

In what has seemed to be a move to undercut the main thesis of this chapter, that re-reading the Stephen King canon in the search of context and information pertinent to better understanding his works is not always productive, there are certainly examples of how re-reading and carefully considering particular pieces of information as more than just information does open up King's fiction in a manner generally unseen. To start, most readings of *The Shining* focus on questions of addiction and the contemporary American family unit, which is certainly the central focus of this novel. But, one wonders when or if such attention has its limits, or if analysis along this line will ever be exhausted. On the other hand, with the Overlook being just one of many horrific locales in King's fiction, one that shares similar characteristic to other haunted dwellings like Rose Red, Sara Laughs, the Dutch Hill Mansion, the Agincourt and Black House, the function of the evil dwelling, too, has been observed. As Douglass Winter says that, "the Overlook Hotel has become, in the public mind, a premier archetype of the *genius loci* or 'Bad Place,'" he iterates a common view of this building, one that is common to the point that is of little use in further examining this aspect of the Overlook (45). However, when Winter also says that, "the destruction of the Overlook Hotel is not a triumph over evil," he implies that the hotel is much more than a malignant structure (52). The evil of the Overlook, then, stems from an entity that is both a part of the hotel and is also separate from it. With the Overlook burnt to the ground in the explosion from the untended boiler, it cannot be said that the evil force residing therein has been defeated or eliminated as only the structure of the hotel has been destroyed while the animating spirit lives on.

By becoming aware of new insights and events in the larger story behind the *Dark Tower*, and that structures which prove to be more than wood, concrete and plaster are not uncommon in King's fiction, new ideas and opinions are seen which suggest that a reduction of the Overlook to a malicious hotel is a limited look that fails to consider its overall purpose in King's universe. With a look at the Overlook as not solely an evil entity, one which carries an, "authority [that] extends beyond the hotel itself," the hotel becomes situated in a larger picture of evil created and to work for the ends of chaos and destruction in allegiance to the villain of *The Dark Tower* series, the Crimson King (Magistrale, *Moral* 20). For example, in *The Shining* when the voices in Jack Torrance's head mention that his son Danny is an exceptional child — "'your son has a very great talent, one that the manager could use to even further improve the Overlook, to further ... enrich it, shall we say?'" — one might read this as an allusion to the Breakers from *The Dark Tower* series who were known as a collection of mentally gifted and talented individuals who had been recruited, in a manner of speaking, to use their skills. Of course, speculating that the Overlook is an agent of the Crimson King is not an overwhelming speculation or discovery, depending on one's view, but conceiving of ways in which King's fiction not only folds into the gunslinger's story but also become new tales that are related to the *Dark Tower*, aside from simple connections like shared characters, which suggests that, again, re-reading the Stephen King canon is almost an exercise of necessity in gathering meaning, as is the case with King's first novel, *Carrie*.

Within King's first published book, the title character's telekinetic abilities position her as a prime candidate for what is called a Breaker in the Dark Tower universe, as is suggested of Danny Torrance and even Charlie McGee from *Firestarter*. But rather than attempting to re-write Carrie's story, a more appropriate means of looking at this tale would be to reconsider its content as being incomplete in that there are significant elements of this tale that are not found within its pages but are found in other fictions by King. One cannot dismiss the basics of the tale in that Carrie, "is the archetypal teenager, grappling with the weight of misunderstanding and feelings of impotence and paranoia, needing ever so badly the cathartic release from adolescence" (Winter 32). Of course, forgetting Carrie's background and suffering would lead to poor readings of this story, but more beneficial and productive is incorporating new information and context as provided in King's later tales, especially considering that people like Carrie White are thought to be threats which may have a place in King's other writings: "What happens if there are others like her? What happens to the world?" (King, *Carrie* 214).

The development of Carrie's abilities becomes important within the framework of re-reading. Her mother, a devoutly religious woman, has a child out of a moment of weakness and bliss, which pushes Ms. White to reaffirm her faith by way of sheltering and even abusing her offspring. Through the tool of religion, and ironic persecution, Carrie's predisposition for keen mental abilities is heightened by her mother's religious fervor. What is striking about this scenario is that it is eerily similar to that of Sylvia Pittston, the bride of the Red King, from Tull. Her pregnancy by Walter is welcomed as she believes that she is carrying a savior and works to protect her child, primarily through her religion and her sway over the townsfolk of Tull. Each mother seems to be specifically chosen to carry each child, and the Crimson King's experiments with childbirth for the sake of creating his own offspring and for creating Breakers, helps to transform *Carrie*'s story in a way that answers the question posed at the end of the book, that more people like Carrie, at least within the *Dark Tower* story, are at the root of the end of the universe.

On the other hand, with respect to *Carrie* and the primary focus on the role and function of extraordinary skills, Ben P. Indick suggests that, "they are a curse to the characters, who must try to control the powers, and to understand that they can never be a magic carpet of escape" (160–1). In addition, another character from King's body of fiction with extraordinary psychic abilities, Ted Brautigan from *Hearts in Atlantis* and *The Dark Tower*, asserts that, "'the only thing that talent wants is to be used,'" which seems to recall Indick's sentiments about talent being denoted as a curse as Brautigan's statement reveals that control over one's abilities is nearly impossible (King, *The Dark Tower* 290). However, with this idea of unwieldy talent simply yearning to be used and therefore denying any impediments, one could assume that the eventual vengeance that Carrie enacts upon her small town was that of inevitability rather than a manifested curse or that of rage initiated by victimization. This is not to say that Carrie's position as a victim of Chris Hargensen's cruel prank with the infamous pig's blood is mitigated by the context provided regarding Carrie's telekinetic abilities and the suggestion that her rampage was just waiting to happen. Yet, this does serve as a means of re-reading her tale as one that, upon reading King's other texts, becomes not so much a tale of a sympathetic and awkward teenager but one of eventual and seemingly necessary destruction as Carrie's particular abilities, according to Ted Brautigan, would have been used no matter what the circumstances. And it is with this notion of inevitability, or the idea that many actions and choices in King's fiction are, at times, inconsequential, that *The Dead Zone* can be read as a tale that offers more than just Johnny Smith's personal sacrifice.

In looking at *The Dead Zone* as a tale that can be illuminated by outside context and re-reading, the Constant Reader can begin to look at the life and deeds of Johnny Smith as more than just the attempt of a humanist to ensure the safety of the world. Recall what is learned of Greg Stillson's future through the eyes of Johnny Smith: if Stillson were to become president, he would eventually initiate a nuclear war that could potentially destroy the world. Johnny Smith does agonize over the affect his actions could have, whether or not taking Stillson out of the picture would have any positive outcomes. Surely, it seems that Johnny's actions ultimately lead to the downfall of Stillson's run at the American presidency and ensure a sense safety and security for future generation. But what if Stillson needed to become president? What if the nuclear war that would undoubtedly surface was a necessary event of history? In other words, viewing *The Dead Zone* as a tale in which destruction has a purpose is not unwarranted when looking past this text in and of itself.

Considering the apparent need for discord in conjunction with the desire to avoid such is brought up when Smith wonders, "*If you could jump into a time machine and go back to 1932, would you kill Hitler?*" (King, *The Dead Zone* 327). A similar question is posed to Ralph Roberts in *Insomnia* by Clotho and Lachesis as these characters explain to him that Hitler's life, and the subsequent extermination of millions of people due to the war and the concentration camps, was in line with the Purpose, the overarching universal influence that attempts to create balance and reason even through actions, deeds and people that seem to be less than reasonable. Yes, the actions and deaths which resulted from Hitler's life came the unfolding of the world which Ralph Roberts knew, but, were Hitler to die (or any other historical figure, whether noble or despicable), the entire span of human history would be drastically altered, at least within King's fictional universe. Although Hitler himself stunningly altered the course of history, the content of *Insomnia* suggests that his existence is needed:

> *Every now and then a man or woman comes along whose life will affect not just those about him or her, or even all those who live in the Short-Time world, but those on many levels above and below the Short-Time world. These people are the Great Ones, and their lives always serve the Purpose. If they are taken too soon, everything changes. The scales cease to balance. Can you imagine, for instance, how different the world might be today if Hitler had drowned in the bathtub as a child? You may believe that the world would be better for that, but I can tell you that the world would not exist at all if it had happened* [King, *Insomnia* 576].

Several characters in *The Dead Zone*, like Hector Markstone and Chuck Chatsworth, would go back and kill Hitler if the opportunity arose. But more important to consider is that, supposedly, the nuclear war that Stillson's presidency promised did eventually come to pass. With even a passing glance at the gunslinger's world, a world that appears as a futuristic projection of what King would dub the *keystone* world, it seems that the fallout that Johnny Smith aimed to prevent did occur (his actions only *presumably* halted the fallout from Stillson's projected lunacy). It is certainly believable that the cause of the desecration seen outside of Lud in *The Waste Lands* is of a nuclear origin, and this suggests, albeit speculatively, that Johnny Smith's actions were to no avail in that, "by stopping Stillson's election, he *may* have averted a global catastrophe" (Collings, *Facets* 53, emphasis added). And if this is true, then the general feel good ending of *The Dead Zone* (disregarding Smith's death, that is) undergoes a transformation in that readers may come to consider the non-existent Stillson presidency is merely a delay of the inevitable.

Whereas the three prior examples of re-contextualizing works within the Stephen King canon primarily consider speculative connections that somewhat forcibly alter the texts to become aligned with *The Dark Tower* series, *Pet Sematary* is a novel that provides the best and clearest example of a story in which a second reading while considering outside sources reveals more than conjecture. When reading in *Insomnia* that the agent of Death and the Random, Atropos, possesses a sneaker once worn by Gage Creed from *Pet Sematary*, readers discover not only a direct connection between the two books but also find that it is very possible that Atropos was a key player in King's earlier novel. In order to collect Gage's sneaker, Atropos had to have been present at Gage's death, and considering that he only takes trophies from those whose lives he takes, he can and should be held responsible for Gage's premature demise. Also, considering Atropos' predilection for senseless violence and death, as such is his nature, it is certainly possible that as Jud Crandall's wife passes from his grip with a natural, or purposeful death, he then positions himself to take his share of life the Creed and Crandall families as he orchestrates the devastation that unfolds in the last pages of *Pet Sematary* by some sort of allegiance with the Wendigo.

To clarify the influence of *Insomnia* on *Pet Sematary*, when Tony Magistrale asserts that, "King's Wendigo, the wrathful Indian spirit that animates the unholy Micmac burial ground beyond the Pet Sematary and deadfall, exploits human weakness and vulnerability," the implication is that the influence of the Wendigo extends past resurrecting the dead ("Hawthorne's Woods" 129). While the Wendigo actively seeks to destroy human life by possessing the dead with its spirit and then directing their actions, it does not just passively wait for the dead to be buried. Considering that the Wendigo is just a spirit, lacking corporeal form and unable to physically arrange any deaths necessary for possession, and also considering that the it only promises to bring the dead back to life through its disembodied influence. What this means is that the Wendigo is unable to first manipulate death and then resurrect anyone who is interred at the Micmac burial ground. Therefore, the Wendigo would need some outside means of ensuring the original death of those who venture into the its circle of power and then under the dirt of the burial ground. Enter Atropos, one with a proclivity towards death, chaos and destruction, one who appears to work in conjunction with the Wendigo that needs dead people to fully enact its own evil designs, as manipulating Louis Creed with the promise of dominion over life and death is only a part of the Wendigo's performance.

By placing the Wendigo alongside Atropos, the claim to be made is that the Wendigo and its highlighted influence in *Pet Sematary* is not the whole story for any reader to consider. As the connection between *Pet Sematary* and *Insomnia* may be merely another example of King simply tying his tales together, the unwritten importance of Atropos' presence is that which undercuts the power of the Wendigo, which does not necessarily erase Louis Creed's defilement of nature in an, "inward-looking narrative, focused upon the question of moral responsibility for interference with the natural order," but it does suggest that Creed had more than the Wendigo to contend with (Winter 134). Of course, in reference to Creed and his exercise and abuse of the power offered to him to bring his son back from death, Tony Magistrale notes that, "there are certain mysteries man must simply learn to accept, certain secrets he has no business attempting to discover, and certain ethical barriers that he only transcends at the expense of his soul," indicating that Creed ultimately must take blame upon himself for the events that transpire in the later pages of *Pet Sematary* ("Hawthorne's Woods" 133). Also, Magistrale also says that the Wendigo's power is that which, "exploits human weakness and vulnerability; it thrives on the doctor's inability to discipline his curiosity and to recognize the distinction between saving lives and playing god," it must be remembered that the Wendigo is not the only force at work in *Pet Sematary*, which does mitigate some of Creed's questionable decisions ("Hawthorne's Woods" 129). At the same time, the inclusion of new and relevant information for reading *Pet Sematary* and re-reading Louis Creed as well as the Wendigo may not always result in the alternative readings suggested here, or even by King. But, re-reading King's fiction, whether by way of self-directed re-reading or under the influence of King's suggested direction by way of considering outside references and information, does warrant the *consideration* of King's canon as being a singular tale and consideration of the effects that this distinction holds for his readers.

The Longest Story Ever Written? (Questions Concerning Readership)

The preceding examination of the Stephen King canon is certainly neither exhaustive nor all-inclusive. Readers and scholars have noted connections among King's works for quite some time, but the exclusions made here should not be seen as forgetfulness. The use of the *White* as a power which negates Leland Gaunt's evil in *Needful Things* and which is referenced as the force of good in *The Dark Tower* is just one example of the omissions that can be noted easily within this examination, but the task of this chapter is not to comb through all of King's texts and reveal to the Constant Reader much of what is already known, but rather to take this information and discuss the implications beyond just noting the links between the stories. And one of the largest issues at the heart of King's attempt to unify his writing is the consideration of his audience. Of course, in acknowledging that, "Stephen King has indeed expressed his fears, frustrations, and angers over his audience for a very long time," the implication is that King is a writer who falls into his category of the *serious* writer who writes for himself (Lant 145). The conclusion to be drawn is that the audience is forgettable and that King's one and only desire is to construct the tale which he wants to see written, which is not an unreasonable thought, but also gives the wrong impression when examining the role of intertextuality in King's fiction.

Even though King may acknowledge his role in providing his readers the text—"having built the Dark Tower in the collective imagination of a million readers, I [had] a responsibility to make it safe for as long as people wanted to read about it"—he does not necessarily suggest that he has a responsibility to provide the readers what *they* want ("Introduction" xvii). To the contrary, when challenged with displeased readers who question King's designs, he responds by saying, boldly and bluntly, that, "if you tell me I fell down on the job and didn't tell all of [the] story there was to tell, I say you're all wrong. On that I *am* sure" (King, *The Colorado Kid* 184). With this said, it is not startling to see King anticipate displeasure and lamentation regarding the conclusion of the *Dark Tower*: "I wasn't exactly crazy about the ending, either, if you want to know the truth, but it's the *right* ending. The *only* ending, in fact" (*The Dark Tower* 844). King's anger at some readers who seek clear-cut solutions comes as no surprise in that while the text of King's works suggest particular outcomes are likely when the climax in question is not written down, readers nonetheless wish to be directed to a conclusive outcome, often leaving little to the imagination. One conclusion to consider is that when deliberating this strange relationship between an author and his audience is that perhaps King properly sets the audience aside when composing his novels. Perhaps the function of intertextuality is one that depends on the absence of the audience to create a tale that may not fulfill the needs or desires of the reader, which some may consider as arrogant or even self-serving. But, the initial distance King creates between his and his Constant Reader does result in a reading experience that is, on the whole, pleasurable, even if the author remains as the ultimate determining presence regarding reading. King's *Dark Tower* may have its gaps, for which he is responsible, but this missing information instigates curious reading in that hopes for more story prompts readership and gives King numerous canvases on which he can craft his story, albeit not entirely from scratch as the pre-existing story contained in his other works necessitates consideration and even incorporation, thus ensuring that none of his fictions are entirely or truly stand-alone.

Invoking Jacques Derrida and his theories on deconstruction, Tom Moylan notes that, "no literary text can be read as to achieve a full understanding of its unique place in the world, for the web of relations and forces in which text and reader are situated is complex and shifting and prevents a final and complete reduction" (196). Of course, while any given text is necessarily positioned among a wide range of other texts, whether by design or not, King's novels do seem to bend towards the definitive in that he has displayed an exceptional sense of control over his creation, producing texts which must be referenced for full meaning rather than leaving his compositions to be situated among other outside works by other authors. This is not to say that King's fiction has no place among established, classical, or popular novels by which and through which additional meanings and interpretations are found; rather, King's authorial control over his own writing has rendered the outside text as secondary to his own writings as a means of understanding the full range of meaning and implication found in his oeuvre. In short, before one seeks King's literary ancestors, perhaps along the lines of Poe and Lovecraft, one must begin with King himself as the initial and primary source for information and interpretation.

Critics may suggest that wading through the pages of *The Dark Tower* is more of a chore than anything else, a tale that provides an overbearing feeling of length and writing that is drawn out and dragged on.

4. Repetition, Integration, Immersion, and Intertextuality

However, the range and scope of this series reminds readers that Stephen King's fiction is certainly a collection that depends on each and every novel written for any semblance of understanding and as a basis for even somewhat accurate interpretation. Immersion and intertextuality in the Stephen King canon creates a large, singular tale that is purposely interwoven rather than connected by mere happenstance or even generic classification (horror and Gothicism) as is the case between King's connections to authors like Edgar Allen Poe or H. P. Lovecraft. To wit, it is with this planned, complex and intricate network of fiction that King reminds readers that not even the death or removal of the author would allow for readers to take over their own readership of King's fiction because the pulls and designs of Stephen King as an author are ubiquitous and anything but negligible. More than anything, King's constant control over and redirection of his fiction keep the reader *reading* instead of interpreting or imposing meaning, which certainly suggests a particular pleasure within such a text despite the reader's loss of sway and influence over the words contained therein.

Conclusion

"Time is a face on the water": or Will *The Dark Tower* Endure?

THE QUESTION AS TO WHETHER or not the *Dark Tower* series will endure as fiction that is constantly read and appreciated by readers and perhaps scholars is difficult to answer. More to the point, speculating as to how well Stephen King will remain as an author with not only booming sales but also sustained readership is a question that cannot be answered at this time. However, looking at the trends in fiction and then anticipating the course King's fiction will take is not exactly an endeavor grounded in futility. When considering the reception and attention given to King's more classical works, such as *The Shining*, *Carrie*, and *The Stand*, all indications suggest that King will not likely be forgotten ten, twenty or even one-hundred years down the road. Of course, only time will tell if King is remembered for contributing to the growing body of American fiction, or if he is, rather, remembered as one that served as more of a detriment to readership than anything else.

Attempting to laud King for good writing is as subjective as criticism that excludes him from the literary establishment based on the purported inferiority of the popular novel. Any move to attribute particular markers of adeptness, mastery, or other measures of worth and merit are rather flimsy and highly debatable. However, the composition of this book assumes a certain level of good and meaningful writing held within the pages of King's fictional universe, especially that of the *Dark Tower* series. But, as is the case with criticism on King that surfaced in the 80s and 90s, contemporary studies on King's fiction all face the certainty that interpretive scholarship bears the stress of becoming forgettable or outright false. This is not to denigrate literary interpretation or to bring up arguments against the mercurial nature of such writing; instead, this is a nod towards King and his writing. With each and every novel King writes, he adds to his fictional universe, and as is the case with celestial bodies, any alteration to the configuration or alignment results in noticeable and even drastic change. Case in point, the graphic novels based on the *Dark Tower* that have been produced enter and alter the dialogue created within the original texts, constantly pushing for re-reading of the original texts as well as attempting to accommodate new information into old interpretations. But does this exercise in constant and conscious alteration of one's own canon guarantee some sort of place and position in the world of fiction as the years go by? Assuredly, it can certainly be speculated that *The Dark Tower* will grow into a series that stands tall and alongside some of the more noted series of the last fifty years, namely those of *The Lord of the Rings* and even *Harry Potter*.

When Tony Magistrale says that, "we live in a post-literate society; nobody reads any more," he paints a rather bleak picture regarding the future of fiction and the novel, suggesting that King's fiction may find trouble in sustaining readership (Davis, "Interview with Tony Magistrale" 122). On an optimistic yet cautious note, King believes that his work will, "still be in the libraries [...] I'm not sure it'll be in bookstores, the paperback racks. The real test of how good a writer is, particularly a popular writer, is whether or not their work can outlast their deaths by five, ten, fifteen years. That remains to be seen" (Robertson 237). In generalizing a few points of explanation for the stamina certain texts have seen over the years, it is fair to say that the content of masterful and even canonical works includes that which holds the reader in awe, and that which delivers a memorable message. Affecting a reader through the written word can be a daunting task, but one way in which King attempts to connect with his audience and therefore create tales that function as more than brief escapes from reality is the use of honesty in his craft: "I like to think that I have told the truth, as best as I've been able to manage it, about the human beings that the books are mostly about" (King, "Typhoid Stevie" 15). Of course, the fiction which surrounds the reality that King tries to bring into his stories often clouds and muddles not only reception of a given tale as well as the truth behind the lies, visiting scenes that are easily found within the American landscape — abuse, alcoholism, disease, deceit, madness, vengeance — resonate with a sense of veracity that cannot be ignored and should not be overshadowed by the paranormal. And the *Dark Tower*, for all of its complexities and ventures into numerous genres and arenas of the inexplicable, certainly has its share of resounding reality.

Before attempting to posit an argument that lends credence to the view that the *Dark Tower* will secure some sort of place among readers and possibly academics, it is necessary to discuss much of what is going against this series. For starters, not all pieces of the puzzle that is the story-line fit together snugly. Inconsistencies run rampant in the *Dark Tower* series, and sharp readers have most certainly taken note. More to the point, one review of the *Dark Tower* stories suggests that King's name is the only item of importance when looking at these texts as he wonders, "would anyone read these things if they weren't by Stephen King?" (Agger B14). Still, despite the influence of name recognition and marketing alongside the errors and incompatibilities, both within the fiction and the scholarship that desperately tries to keep up with King's pen and imagination, research forges on. And even though criticism and analysis can only go so far with the full context yet to be revealed, as King has a few more stories to tell, a foundation can be set, as is the attempt in this volume.

With the academic pushing forward with interpretation and analysis, the other side of the scholastic coin is that of King's labeling as a genre writer who does not deserve attention within institutions of higher learning. For these arguments against the horror novel and their authors ("hacks" they are sometimes called), Marlene Barr denotes elitism shown towards fiction that does not necessarily aim to be literary as *textism*. And while King's position on the bookshelves or perhaps even in the canon is a debate that has yet to resolve itself, Barr is somewhat pessimistic concerning matters of literature in the mold of King's as she believes that, "the hoped-for defeat of textism is a future utopian goal" (Barr 430). Signs and trends certainly support Barr's speculation as to the standing of fiction, largely that which is classified under genres that are not typically considered to be literary. But the issue, or struggle, concerning King's endurance cannot be limited to academic circles, even though their influence and perception is dominant. Of course, it is encouraging to see King able to shrug off the critiques that academics have poured onto him as, "criticism, King concludes, is 'their business, not mine. I just write stories'" (Collings, *Scaring* 79). King's own distancing from the literary elite and the academic realm may not be all that is needed to undercut the harsh views and critical opinions regarding his writing, but to remind readers that he is a storyteller, above all else, is a move in an promising direction.

Although literary critics do not control the reading world beyond academia, or even within academia at times, their criticisms of King nonetheless are a key element for consideration when speculating as to King's endurance as a writer. As Greg Smith bluntly notes that, "guardians of taste and guardians of morals do not like him, but his readers do not seem to care," he reminds academics that the ultimate resting place of King's writing is ultimately determined by the readers (344). Such empowerment and responsibility certainly seems like a large task, especially when King has been less than cordial with his audience from time to time. Consider what King says directly to his reader in the first pages of the last chapter in *The Dark Tower* in which he, essentially, chides readers who have approached the series as a tale in which the ending is all that matters. He says that the ending is less important than the story itself, that the reader should be content with having followed the gunslinger *to* the Dark Tower instead of *inside* the Dark Tower, and he then says to his reader:

> Some of you who have provided the ears without which no tale can survive a single day are likely not so willing. You are the grim, goal-oriented ones who will not believe that the joy is in the journey rather than the destination no matter how many times it has been proven to you. [...] You are the cruel ones who deny the Grey Havens, where tired characters go to rest. You say you want to know how it all comes out. [...] I hope most of you know better. *Want better.* I hope you came to hear the tale, and not just munch your way through the pages to the ending [*The Dark Tower* 817].

As King attempts to not only argue against reading solely focused on climax but also prepare readers for an ending that might not be well-received, he anticipates reluctance on behalf of his reader to be enamored more with the story instead of the climax. And King utilizes a similar mode of scolding his reader in the afterword of *The Colorado Kid*:

> Mystery is my subject here, and I am aware that many readers will feel cheated, even angry, by my failure to provide a solution to the one posed. Is it because I had no solution to give? The answer is no. [...] I'm not really interested in the solution but in the mystery. Because it is the mystery that kept bringing me back to the story, day after day [182].

Conclusion

Even with such criticisms of his Constant Reader, King has found continued reception and acceptance among the masses, and with a career spanning over thirty years with few signs of a substantial drop in readership, one would be hard-pressed to consider King as a writer who will whither and fade into the literary background. But while the readership may sustain King in one way, the literary critic still has a role to perform concerning King's endurance, at least within academic circles.

On the subject of King's endurance, he has faced battles in securing a place among the ever-critical academic. On one hand, Tony Magistrale asserts that the academic elite, "is confident that he [King] will never be more than a hack writer preying upon the tasteless sensibilities of a popular audience that equates a meal at McDonalds with dining at a gourmet restaurant" (*Landscape of Fear* 1). Aside from this bleak view of King's aesthetic appeal, the author himself provides a glimmer of hope for his standing as his former teacher Burton Hatlen recalls that, "once he [King] said to me that one of the things about the contemporary period is that there is no dominant major novelist who is going to be regarded historically as the major novelist of our moment" (Davis, "Interview with Burton Hatlen" 157). Although King's popularity is certainly immense, and as his name is without question a household one, he does find himself in a large mix of current authors who all have their moments of attention and focus, but seldom, if ever, sustain a position that is foregrounded or perhaps even exalted for any lengthy period of time. Like the phases of the moon, it looks as if the contemporary novelist waxes and wanes in popularity and readership, and even though some writers rarely leave the public spotlight, regardless of the intensity of any such gaze, King looks to be correct in his assessment that no single writer has emerged as the summation of contemporary literature. But, as hinted at, this does not necessarily eliminate a fiction's endurance.

Despite any sentiments to the contrary, there are scholars and readers who believe in King's craft and writing as fiction that has a chance at being considered as not only literature, but good literature. Of course, for those who laud King's novels and stories there is always oppositional criticism lurking around the corner, including Linda Badley's rather scathing view of King and his audience: "readers lose themselves in King's novels because Kingstyle seems to be no style. King takes a hack's pride in having no affectations or aesthetic purposes (outside of liking to scare people) and his own inner compulsion" (116). Unsurprisingly, criticism extends beyond the subjective analysis of King's artistry and into questions of gender and feminism with Chelsea Quinn Yarbro leading the charge against King's reportedly male-dominated and even misogynistic writing: "it is disheartening when a writer with so much talent and strength and vision is not able to develop a believable woman character between the ages of seventeen and sixty" (49). King's attempts to address this concern with *Dolores Claiborne*, *Rose Madder*, and *Gerald's Game* has certainly seen mixed results as these books are less-mentioned and less-publicized than King's other works which limits their exposure to the reader. And while his move to write strong female characters to show his range and even appease his female readership has not entirely resulted in dwindling criticisms or growing acceptance of King's writing and portrayal of women, the variety of concerns facing his writing do not deter some scholars, like Gary Hoppenstand, from suggesting that he is not as repulsive or tasteless as some may think:

> Great literature does three crucial things. It, first, effectively deals with, or reveals, some significant aspect of the human condition. It, second, allows its reader to be emotionally or intellectually uplifted, to learn something new of life, to become thoroughly involved with characters or with a story that subsequently has some important meaning for the reader. And it, finally, must survive the "test of time." It must not be overly topical in its appeal. King, I think, has fulfilled the first two requirements for great literature, and only time will tell if he accomplishes the third [Davis, "Interview with Gary Hoppenstand" 174].

The "test of time" that Hoppenstand refers to is undoubtedly a major factor to consider when analyzing King's writing, but a clear prediction cannot be given and is purposely avoided. However, Hoppenstand does imply that because of all that King has working in his favor, endurance certainly seems likely. But while King is foreseen to be a writer who is read and appreciated by future generations, his endurance as a writer does not necessarily secure endurance for all of his works, especially *The Dark Tower*.

King's fiction, specifically *The Dark Tower*, resonates with a range of writing that shows a willingness to experiment and escape classification, despite the constant barrage of labeling, which reflects a sense of perseverance that he and his writing needs in order to survive the next several decades. True, King is a frightening writer whose books cause lights to be kept on while one sleeps, but the scares come in more shapes and forms than phantasms, monsters, or cunningly cued music to create startled moviegoers, as is suggested by Michael Collings:

> His monsters represent the modern world as it impinges upon the individual; as a result, they are frequently constructs of that modern world. In spite of the presence of vampires, werewolves, and ghosts in some of his fictions, most of King's truest (and most effective) horror lies in the evocations of the unknown within the known [*Scaring* 26].

Pushing aside concerns of King already noted, Collings' view of King's writing as a serious reflection of the world he knows, suggesting that his imagination is hardly overactive or an impediment to discussing very real issues. Moreover, Tony Magistrale also says that King's writing has an element of significance and honesty: "King must be viewed as a serious social critic whose work reflects some of the core concerns treated throughout the American literary tradition" (*Second Decade* 157). Of course, merely linking King to canonical writers and those bound within the accepted "American literary tradition" that Magistrale mentions does not result in either an automatic acceptance of King as a serious writer or a consideration of his writing as at least equal to established literary works because they share certain elements. However, recognizing particular traits within King's writing that are noted as present in works that have earned him certain fame and reputation, or even a canonical standing, does not hurt his case when it comes to the question of endurance.

For any foibles that can be detected within King's body of fiction, one of which is the claim that he is, "not the most prolific of wordsmiths," he is nonetheless a writer who has accomplished much as an author (Roberts 31). King has given the horror genre a face, one that has revitalized the Gothic, which is important to consider as, "literary content is often separated only by its varying surfaces; the concerns beneath are universally the same" (Davis, *Stephen King's America* 110). With King composing tales that examine the very same issues as serious literature, albeit from a different angle and through a genre which has not exactly been a boon to King's reception in some instances, his stories have nonetheless initiated serious speculation as to whether or not he will survive as a historical literary figure, especially considering that his immense popularity can hardly be foreseen to be forgotten. The name King itself, as well as the characters, the places, and the mass acquaintance with the public by means of the cinema, suggests a lasting impression on the American reading public, academic and otherwise. But popularity, of course, does not necessarily translate into sustained readership.

When considering the reviews of the *Dark Tower* books that appeared in the *New York Times* as each tale was released, the general consensus was that these stories were not King's best writing. Although one critic begrudgingly says that, "the longer you stick with this lumbering, likable epic, the more its everything-but-the-kitchen-sink enthusiasm and its hypnotic blend of suspense and sentimentality begin to work on you," agreement is not easily found with other reviewers (O'Hehir B12). Ben Sisaro's review of *Song of Susannah* says that, "the story has become dauntingly overstuffed and complex," which suggests that King had lost control over his creation (16). And while *The Dark Tower* does have a few frayed ends that King would do well to mend upon, perhaps, a revision of the entire series, *The Dark Tower* should not be dismissed because of one critique which suggests it is the result of an expansive imagination turned loose. Yet, with the incorporation of somewhat overly creative elements, Michael Agger's review of *The Dark Tower* implies that the imagination involved is a detriment to the series, which he views as, "a double-black-diamond ski run for fantasy nerds" (B14). Adding to this barrage, Agger observes the links King has forged between these books and the rest of his oeuvre, and critically comments that, "at times, the series feels like a dumping ground for his wackier notions (a talking monorail that likes riddles) and for the further explication of ideas from his previous books (the superflu from *The Stand*)" (B14). And when Agger also says of the *Dark Tower* that, "you can see the puppet strings, and the suspense sinks to the level of a B horror film," it would seem that despite any ground King has covered as a writer, his *Dark Tower* series might function as more of an anchor than anything else (B14). But, when Gary Hoppenstand provides the generous reminder that, "no author is divine. No author is perfect," one can only hope his words foreshadow a sustained acceptance and celebration of *The Dark Tower* as a bold, innovative and ground-breaking fiction not only within King's canon, but outside of it as well (Davis, "Interview with Gary Hoppenstand" 164).

Conclusion

On one hand, the *Dark Tower* series may be too inventive to continue as a respected and read section of the Stephen King canon. Fantasy is certainly a difficult genre to write, although the *Dark Tower* tends to bury the fantasy elements in favor of several other genres, often meshing and combating each other throughout the duration of the story but resulting in an exceptional fiction. Indeed, as is the case with the rest of King's fiction, a generous step away from reservations about genre and arbitrary standards of taste and value help position the *Dark Tower* as a story that is much more than a murderous cowboy on a quest. Within this tale of death and destruction, damnation and redemption, and caution and speculation is a story that need not be reduced to an author indulging himself in a concocted tale that he has the means to write and publish. Rather, *The Dark Tower*, like King's other novels, is a story that not only calls for subsequent reading, but also a story that can be simply enjoyed. King himself admits that his writing is often a pleasurable experience for him, one which carries acute messages behind the horror or the laughter: "one thing that most reviewers and scholars have missed so far is that I have tried to have some fun in these novels and that I've tried to poke some fun along the way. I guess that if people have missed one glaring point, it is that fantasy and horror can be wonderful tools of satire" (Magistrale, "Writer Defines Himself" 16). Regardless of King's intentions and pleasures when it comes to his writing, specifically that of the *Dark Tower* series, the books continue to await new readers while seeking to return engagements from familiar readers. And as far as King is concerned, "I've told my tale all the way to the end, and am satisfied" (*The Dark Tower* 817).

Whether or not King's readers are as satisfied as he is remains to be seen, especially when considering that King is perhaps not as pleased with the final product of *The Dark Tower* as he claims in that he has pressed on with the graphic novels and has allowed a movie to be optioned on these books. Perhaps these additional ventures into other mediums will help sustain readership of *The Dark Tower*. Perhaps not. Whether or not these texts will gain more readers over the next few years and decades is yet to be seen. But, on the account of the relationship readers, scholars and critics will have with King, it is not unreasonable to believe that he will be a name that will not be forgotten. Even with the sales, the popularity, the notoriety, and the status as the world's best-selling novelist,

Conclusion

King still wonders if he will continue to be a fixture on the bookshelves and nightstands of his Constant Reader, and one can see this sentiment implied when he says that, "I'd just like to be remembered" (Landa 249). On this account, at least, King has nothing to worry about.

As for the *Dark Tower* series?

For the time being, the door to the Tower is open and readers are walking through it. King is certainly doing all he can to keep the path to the Dark Tower cleared for his readers, but even an author with such popularity and control over his creation cannot ensure that the *Dark Tower* will live on. Mayhap it will, mayhap it will not. Still, the tale of the gunslinger is being read, and that is certainly a promising start.

Works Cited

Agger, Michael. "Pulp Metafiction." Rev. of *The Dark Tower*, by Stephen King. *New York Times* 17 Oct. 2004: B14.

Ash, Brian. *Faces of the Future — The Lessons of Science-Fiction*. New York: Taplonger, 1975.

Badley, Linda. "The Sin Eater: Orality, Postliteracy, and the Early Stephen King." *Bloom's Modern Critical Views: Stephen King* (Updated Edition). Ed. Harold Bloom. Philadelphia: Chelsea House, 2007. 95–123.

Barr, Marleen S. "Textism — An Emancipation Proclamation." *PMLA* 119.3 (2004): 429–441.

Barthes, Roland. "The Death of the Author." *The Norton Anthology of Theory and Criticism*. Ed. Vincent B. Leitch, et al. New York: Norton: 2001. 1466–1470.

_____. *Roland Barthes*. 1975. Trans. Richard Howard. New York: Hill and Wang, 1977.

Bayer-Berenbaun, Linda. *The Gothic Imagination: Expansion in Gothic Literature and Art*. Cranbury, NJ: Associated UP, 1982.

Bloom, Harold. "Afterthought." *Bloom's Modern Critical Views: Stephen King* (Updated Edition). Ed. Harold Bloom. New York: Chelsea House, 2007. 207–208.

_____. *How to Read and Why*. New York: Scribner, 2000.

_____. "Introduction." *Bloom's Modern Critical Views: Stephen King* (Updated Edition). Ed. Harold Bloom. New York: Chelsea House, 2007. 1–3.

Blue, Tyson. *The Unseen King*. Mercer Island, WA: Starmont House, 1989.

Browning, Robert. "Childe Roland to the Dark Tower Came." *Robert Browning's Poetry*. Ed. James F. Loucks. New York: Norton, 1979. 134–139.

Card, Orson Scott. "The Problem of Evil in Fiction." *Ethics, Literature, & Theory: An Introductory Reader*. 2nd ed. Ed. Stephen K. George. Lanham, MD: Rowan & Littlefield, 2005. 225–230.

Carrier, David. *The Aesthetics of Comics*. University Park, PA: The Pennsylvania State UP, 2000.

Colatrella, Carol. "Science Fiction in the Information Age." *American Literary History* 11.3 (Autumn 1999): 554–65.

Works Cited

Collings, Michael R. *The Films of Stephen King*. 1986. San Bernardino, CA: Borgo, 1988.

_____. *The Many Facets of Stephen King*. 1985. San Bernardino, CA: Borgo, 1988.

_____. *Scaring Us to Death: The Impact of Stephen King on Popular Culture*. 2nd ed. San Bernardino, CA: Borgo, 1997.

_____, and David A. Engebreston. *The Shorter Works of Stephen King*. 1985. San Bernardino, CA: Borgo, 1988.

David, Peter, Robin Furth, Jae Lee, and Richard Isanove. *The Gunslinger Born* #1–7. New York: Marvel, 2007.

_____, _____, _____, and _____. "Comments from Peter David." *The Long Road Home*. #5. New York: Marvel, 2008. 39–40.

_____, _____, _____, and _____. The Long Road Home #1–5. New York: Marvel, 2008.

Davis, Jonathan. "Interview with Burton Hatlen." *Stephen King's America*. By Jonathan Davis. Bowling Green, OH: Bowling Green State U Popular P, 1994. 141–160.

_____. "Interview with Gary Hoppenstand." *Stephen King's America*. By Jonathan Davis. Bowling Green, OH: Bowling Green State U Popular P, 1994. 161–176.

_____. "Interview with Tony Magistrale." *Stephen King's America*. By Jonathan Davis. Bowling Green, OH: Bowling Green State U Popular P, 1994. 119–130.

_____. *Stephen King's America*. Bowling Green, OH: Bowling Green State U Popular P, 1994.

Egan, James. "*The Dark Tower*: Stephen King's Gothic Western." *The Gothic World of Stephen King: Landscape of Nightmares*. Eds. Gary Hoppenstand and Ray B. Browne. Bowling Green, OH: Bowling Green State U Popular P, 1987. 95–106.

_____. "Technohorror: The Dystopian Vision of Stephen King." *Bloom's Modern Critical Views: Stephen King*. Ed. Harold Bloom. Philadelphia: Chelsea House, 1998. 47–58.

Eisner, Will. *Comics and Sequential Art*. Tamarac, FL: Poorhouse P, 1985.

Eliot, T. S. "Tradition and the Individual Talent." *The Norton Anthology of Theory and Criticism*. Ed. Vincent B. Leitch, et al. New York: Norton, 2001. 1092–1098.

Freedman, Carl. *Critical Theory and Science Fiction*. Hanover, NH: Wesleyan UP, 2000.

Frye, Northrop. *Anatomy of Criticism: Four Essays*. Princeton, NJ: Princeton UP, 1957.

Fuller, Richard. Rev. of *The Gunslinger*, by Stephen King. *New York Times* 8 Jan. 1989: BR22.

Furth, Robin. "The Laughing Mirror, Part 1." *The Gunslinger Born*. #4. New York: Marvel, 2007. 31–37.

_____. "The Laughing Mirror, Part 2." *The Gunslinger Born.* #5. New York: Marvel, 2007. 25–30.

_____. "Maerlyn's Rainbow." *The Gunslinger Born.* #2. New York: Marvel, 2007. 29–35.

_____. "The Sacred Geography of Mid-World." *The Gunslinger Born.* #1. New York: Marvel, 2007. 40–45.

_____. *Stephen King's* The Dark Tower: *A Concordance.* Volume 1. New York: Scribner, 2003.

_____. *Stephen King's* The Dark Tower: *A Concordance.* Volume 2. New York: Scribner, 2005.

Gagne, Paul R. "Interview with Stephen King." *Feast of Fear: Conversations with Stephen King.* Eds. Tim Underwood and Chuck Miller. New York: Carroll & Graf, 1989. 90–108.

Gravett, Paul. *Graphic Novels: Everything You Need to Know.* New York: Collins Design, 2005.

Greene, Thomas. "The Norms of Epic." *Comparative Literature.* 13.3 (Summer 1961): 193–207.

Gunn, James. "Toward a Definition of Science Fiction." *Speculation on Speculation.* Eds. James Gunn and Matthew Candelaria. Lanham, MD: Scarecrow P, 2005. 5–12.

Heldreth, Leonard G. "The Ultimate Horror: The Dead Child in Stephen King's Stories and Novels." *Discovering Stephen King.* Ed. Darrel Schweitzer. San Bernardino, CA: Borgo, 1987. 141–152.

Hoppenstand, Gary. "Country Club Literature and the Thriller." Editorial. *The Journal of Popular Culture* 38:5 (August 2005): 793–795.

_____. "Series(ous) SF Concerns." Editorial. *The Journal of Popular Culture* 38:4 (May 2005): 603–604.

Indick, Ben P. "King and the Literary Tradition of Horror and the Supernatural." *Fear Itself: The Horror Fiction of Stephen King.* Eds. Tim Underwood and Chuck Miller. San Francisco: Underwood-Miller, 1982. 153–167.

Jones, Daryl. *The Dime Novel Western.* Bowling Green, OH: Bowling Green State U Popular P, 1978.

Kaszniak, Alfred W., Paul D. Nussbaum, Michael R. Berren, and Jose Santiago. "Amnesia as a Consequence of Male Rape: A Case Report." *Journal of Abnormal Psychology* 97.1 (1988): 100–104.

King, Stephen. *Carrie.* 1974. New York: Pocket Books, 1999.

_____. *The Colorado Kid.* New York: Dorchester, 2005.

_____. *The Dark Tower.* Hampton Falls, NH: Donald M. Grant, 2004.

_____. *The Dead Zone.* 1979. New York: Signet, 1980.

_____. Foreword. *Dolores Claiborne.* New York: Signet, 1993.

_____. *The Drawing of the Three.* 1987. New York: Plume, 2003.

_____. *The Eyes of the Dragon.* 1987. New York: Signet, 1988.

Works Cited

_____. Foreword. "On Becoming a Brand Name." *Fear Itself: The Horror Fiction of Stephen King.* Eds. Tim Underwood and Chuck Miller. San Francisco: Underwood-Miller, 1982. 15–42.

_____. *The Gunslinger.* 1982. New York: Plume, 1988.

_____. *The Gunslinger* (Revised Edition). New York: Plume, 2003.

_____. "I Want to be Typhoid Stevie." *Reading Stephen King: Issues of Censorship, Student Choice, and Popular Literature.* Eds. Brenda Miller Power, Jeffrey D. Wilhelm, and Kelly Chandler. Urbana, IL: National Council of Teachers of English, 1997. 13–21.

_____. *Insomnia.* 1994. New York: Signet, 1995.

_____. "Introduction." *The Gunslinger* (Revised Edition). New York: Plume, 2003. xi–xviii.

_____. *IT.* 1986. New York: Signet, 1987.

_____. "The Little Sisters of Eluria." *Everything's Eventual.* 2002. New York: Pocket Books, 2003.

_____. "Low Men in Yellow Coats." *Hearts in Atlantis.* 1999. New York: Pocket Books, 2000. 1–323.

_____. "An Open Letter from Stephen King." *The Gunslinger Born.* #2. New York: Marvel, 2007: 44–5.

_____. "A Preface in Two Parts." *The Stand: The Complete & Uncut Edition.* 1990. New York: Signet, 1991. xi–xv.

_____. *Rose Madder.* 1995. New York: Signet, 1996.

_____. *The Shining.* 1977. New York: Pocket Books, 2001.

_____. *Song of Susannah.* Hampton Falls, NH: Donald M. Grant, 2004.

_____. *The Stand: The Complete & Uncut Edition.* 1990. New York: Signet, 1991.

_____. *The Waste Lands.* 1991. New York: Plume, 2003.

_____. *Wizard and Glass.* 1997. New York: Plume, 2003.

_____. *Wolves of the Calla.* 2003. New York: Scribner, 2004.

_____, and Peter Straub. *Black House.* New York: Random House, 2001.

Koehn, Daryl. *The Nature of Evil.* New York: Palgrave Macmillan, 2005.

Landa, Elaine. "I Am a Hick, and This Is Where I Feel at Home." *Feast of Fear: Conversations with Stephen King.* Eds. Tim Underwood and Chuck Miller. New York: Carroll & Graf, 1989. 249–258.

Lant, Kathleen. "The Rape of the Constant Reader: Stephen King's Construction of the Female Reader and Violation of the Female Body in *Misery*." *Bloom's Modern Critical Views: Stephen King* (Updated Edition). Ed. Harold Bloom. Philadelphia: Chelsea House, 2007. 141–166.

Lavers, Annette. *Roland Barthes: Structuralism and After.* Cambridge, MA: Harvard UP, 1982.

Lewis, R.W.B. *Trials of the Word: Essays in American Literature and the Humanistic Tradition.* New Haven, CT: Yale UP, 1965.

Works Cited

Lund, Michael. *America's Continuing Story: An Introduction to Serial Fiction, 1850–1900.* Detroit: Wayne State UP, 1993.

Magistrale, Tony. *Hollywood's Stephen King.* New York: Palgrave Macmillan, 2003.

_____. *Landscape of Fear: Stephen King's American Gothic.* Bowling Green, OH: Bowling Green State U Popular P, 1988.

_____. *The Moral Voyages of Stephen King.* San Bernardino, CA: Borgo, 1989.

_____. *Stephen King: The Second Decade,* Danse Macabre *to* The Dark Half. New York: Twayne, 1992.

_____. "Stephen King's *Pet Sematary*: Hawthorne's Woods Revisited." *The Gothic World of Stephen King: Landscape of Nightmares.* Eds. Gary Hoppenstand and Ray B. Brown. Bowling Green, OH: Bowling Green State U Popular P, 1987. 126–34.

_____. "The Writer Defines Himself: An Interview with Stephen King." *Stephen King: The Second Decade,* Danse Macabre *to* The Dark Half. Ed. Tony Magistrale. New York: Twayne, 1992. 1–19.

May, John R. *Toward a New Earth: Apocalypse in the American Novel.* Notre Dame, IN: U of Notre Dame P, 1972.

Miall, David. "Text and Affect: A Model of Story Understanding." *Re-Reading the Short Story.* Ed. Clare Hanson. New York: St. Martins, 1989. 10–21.

Miller, David A. *The Epic Hero.* Baltimore: The Johns Hopkins UP, 2002.

Mitchell, Damon, Richard Hirshman, and Gordon C. Nagayama Hall. "Attributions of Victim Responsibility, Pleasure, and Trauma in Male Rape." *The Journal of Sex Research* 36.4 (November 1999): 369–373.

Moylan, Tom. *Demand the Impossible: Science Fiction and the Utopian Imagination.* New York: Methuen, 1986.

Nicholls, Richard. "Avaunt Thee, Recreant Cyborg!" Rev. of *The Waste Lands*, by Stephen King. *New York Times* 29 Sept. 1991: BR14.

Notkin, Deborah L. "Stephen King: Horror and Humanity for Our Time." *Fear Itself: The Horror Fiction of Stephen King.* Eds. Tim Underwood and Chuck Miller. San Francisco: Underwood-Miller, 1982. 131–142.

O'Hehir, Andrew. "The Quest for North Central Positronics." Rev. of *Wolves of the Calla*, by Stephen King. *New York Times* 4 Jan., 2004: B11–B12.

O'Neill, Dennis. *The DC Comics Guide to Writing Comics.* New York: Watson-Guptil, 2001.

O'Neill, Marnie. "Molesting the Text: Promoting Resistant Readings." *Reading and Response.* Eds. Michael Hayhoe and Stephen Parker. Milton Keynes, U.K.: Open UP, 1990. 84–93.

Pearsall, Derek. *Arthurian Romance: A Short Introduction.* Malden, MA: Blackwell, 2003.

Perakos, Peter. "Stephen King on *Carrie, The Shining*, etc." *Feast of Fear: Conversations with Stephen King.* Eds. Tim Underwood and Chuck Miller. New York: Carroll & Graf, 1989. 63–70.

Works Cited

Pharr, Mary. "'Almost Better': Surviving the Plague in Stephen King's *The Stand*." *A Casebook on* The Stand. Ed. Tony Magistrale. San Bernardino, CA: Borgo, 1992. 1–19.

Punter, David, and Glennis Byron. *The Gothic*. Malden, MA: Blackwell, 2004.

Roberts, Garyn G. "Of Mad Dogs and Firestarters — The Incomparable Stephen King." *The Gothic World of Stephen King: Landscape of Nightmares*. Eds. Gary Hoppenstand and Ray B. Browne. Bowling Green, OH. Bowling Green State U Popular P, 1987. 31–36.

Robertson, William. "Reality Too Frightening, Horror King Says." *Feast of Fear: Conversations with Stephen King*. Eds. Tim Underwood and Chuck Miller. New York: Carroll & Graf, 1989. 231–238.

Schweitzer, Darrel. "Introduction." *Discovering Stephen King*. Ed. Darrel Schweitzer. San Bernardino, CA: Borgo, 1987. 5–7.

Shattuck, Roger. *Forbidden Knowledge: From Prometheus to Pornography*. New York: St. Martin's Press, 1996.

Sisario, Ben. Rev. of *Song of Susannah*, by Stephen King. *New York Times* 20 June 2004: 16.

Smith, Greg. "The Literary Equivalent of a Big Mac and Fries? Academics, Moralists, and the Stephen King Phenomenon." *Midwest Quarterly* 43.4 (Summer 2002): 329–345.

Stableford, Brian. "How Should a Science Fiction Story End?" *The New York Review of Science Fiction* 7.6 (Feb 1995): 1, 8–15.

Strengell, Heidi. *Dissecting Stephen King: From the Gothic to Literary Naturalism*. Madison, WI: U of Wisconsin P/Popular P, 2005.

Summers, Montague. *The Gothic Quest: A History of the Gothic Novel*. London: Fortune, 1938.

Westbrook, Max. "The Themes of Western Fiction." *Critical Essays on the Western American Novel*. Ed. William T. Pilkington. Boston: G.K. Hall, 1980. 34–40.

Winter, Douglass. *Stephen King: The Art of Darkness*. New York: New American Library, 1984.

Wolinsky, Richard, and Lawrence Davidson. "Interview with Stephen King." *Feast of Fear: Conversations with Stephen King*. Eds. Tim Underwood and Chuck Miller. New York: Carroll & Graf, 1989. 22–31.

Yarbro, Chelsea Quinn. "Cinderella's Revenge: Twists on Fairy Tale and Mythic Themes in the Work of Stephen King." *Fear Itself: The Horror Fiction of Stephen King*. Eds. Tim Underwood and Chuck Miller. San Francisco: Underwood-Miller, 1982. 45–55.

Index

Index

Index

191

Index